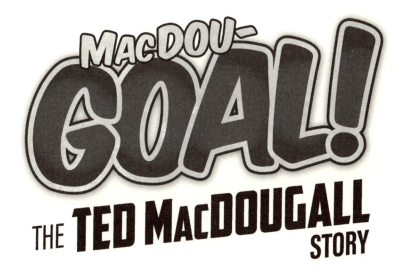

MacDou-GOAL!

THE TED MacDOUGALL STORY

Neil Vacher
& Ted MacDougall

First published by Pitch Publishing, 2016

Pitch Publishing
A2 Yeoman Gate
Yeoman Way
Worthing
Sussex
BN13 3QZ

www.pitchpublishing.co.uk
info@pitchpublishing.co.uk

ISBN 978-1-78531-201-4

Typesetting and origination by Pitch Publishing

Printed by TJ International

Contents

Foreword

by Lawrie McMenemy MBE LLD MBA

LOOKING back on a fairly long career in football, certain events, games and players stand out. Ted MacDougall falls into that category.

Southampton had just won an extremely hard League Cup tie, the crowd were delighted, the dressing room was buzzing – suddenly a boot flew across the room and missed a young player's head by inches.

It was thrown by Ted, who followed it up with a lecture to the youngster, telling the lad how he should have passed to him in the 70th minute instead of trying a shot himself.

Ted had an in-built determination to do well and win, probably to show those who had turned him down earlier in his career, similar to other legends such as Kevin Keegan and Alan Ball. All three climbed the ladder to the top level for club and country.

In this book, Ted talks about his highly successful on-field partnership with Phil Boyer at four different clubs. We also hear how he became one of the first British players to help launch top-level soccer in Canada and the USA and how he continued to be involved there when he finally hung up his boots.

He still shows the same determination, work rate and skill which took him to the top. Fascinating.

Acknowledgements

I WOULD like to thank everyone who has helped and encouraged me in the preparation of this book, and especially the following: Ted MacDougall, for taking me seriously and sticking with me! Lawrie McMenemy, for providing the foreword.

The *Bournemouth Daily Echo* and the *Southern Daily Echo* for providing many of the illustrations.

Louise John; Ian, Paul and Jacqui Vacher; Neil Wyatt; John Harriss; Max Fitzgerald and Matt Payne at AFC Bournemouth; Neil Perrott at the *Bournemouth Daily Echo*; Simon Carter and Jez Gale at the *Southern Daily Echo*.

Paul and Jane Camillin at Pitch Publishing – thank you for showing faith in a first-time author, and Duncan Olner at Olner Design for his patience!

And last but not least, my late Mum and Dad for instilling in me the joys of following the Cherries.

Neil Vacher

1

Finding His Feet

EDWARD John MacDougall was born in Inverness, Scotland on 8 January 1947, the only child of Alexander and Kathleen MacDougall. Sometimes referred to as the Capital of the Highlands and with a population of around 28,000 at the time, Inverness lay close to where Bonnie Prince Charlie fought the final confrontation of the Jacobite Rising in 1746, and in more peaceful times, had established itself as a mecca for bagpipe enthusiasts. When young Edward was making his first appearance in life, it was also home to three Highland League football clubs, as Ted himself recalls, 'We lived just across the road from Grant Street Park, the ground of Inverness Clachnacuddin, for whom my father played as a goalkeeper. My mother used to say that I had football boots on from about three years of age, so I certainly developed a love for the game very early on in my life! Later on, I remember my father making me practise wearing a slipper on my right foot to encourage me to use my left. That's why I was always quite useful with my left foot!'

Ted's father, a slater and tiler by profession and known to his friends as 'Eck', was in fact a goalkeeper of some distinction locally, says Ted, 'The "Lillywhites", as Clachnacuddin were known because of their white strip, were semi-professional and as a young boy I used to go with my Dad to watch them train twice a week, and then go to their match on the Saturday. I enjoyed watching my Dad play but I never thought of becoming a goalkeeper myself. The other teams in Inverness at that time were Caledonian and Inverness Thistle. Of course they eventually amalgamated to become Inverness Caledonian Thistle in 1994 and have gone on to reach the Scottish Premier League.

'I attended Merkinch Junior School and played my first matches for the school side there before I went on to Inverness High School, where I became centre-half and captain. We played on Saturday mornings but that wasn't enough for me, so in the afternoon I played on the right-wing for the local Boys' Brigade! I remember once travelling with the school team to play a match in Inverary, which is near Aberdeen, and we had to go by bus which was a really big deal at the time! Inverness was a beautiful place to grow up in but it was quite isolated in those days, the road network was very poor and to get from Inverness to Glasgow for example would have taken around five hours.

'The first time I hit the ball into the net as a lad I thought it was fantastic, a different feeling altogether to scoring without one and of course we didn't have to go and fetch the ball! It was great when I first played under lights as well instead of a lamp post!

'Apart from following the local sides, I also became fanatical about Manchester United and once, as a treat, Mum and Dad took me to watch a game at Old Trafford. If going to Inverary was quite something then you can imagine how I felt about this! It was about a 1,000-mile round trip to Manchester and back, and for a young lad coming from a small town like Inverness as it was then, I thought the place was phenomenal, just out of this world!

'However, a big change in my life occurred when I was 12 years old. My Dad had worked on the railways for many years, but as more and more of them were being closed down things were becoming increasingly difficult for him. He managed to find work in Widnes, Cheshire which was an industrial town on the northern bank of the River Mersey, so Mum and I moved down there with him. Chemical plants dominated the town and you smelt Widnes before you saw it. It was quite a contrast to the clean air that we had been used to in Scotland but my parents knew that moving there would also give me a better chance of having a football career.'

Unfortunately for Ted however, the major sporting interest in Widnes centred almost exclusively around the town's rugby league club, 'I attended Fairfield High School, which, no surprises, was of course a rugby playing school! It was all about rugby, the only lads who played football apart from me were those that were not very athletic types, or wore glasses or had one of those pink NHS eyepatches! We had the traditional house system and when it came to the inter-house football competition I represented York house and one year scored something like 45 goals in three games! My schoolmates gave me the nickname "Jock" – a lot of thought must have gone into that – and I became a bit of a celebrity, not because I was particularly good but because I was one of the few boys who played football rather than rugby league.

'Funnily enough a lot of the bigger guys used to look after me at school whenever there was any trouble. They seemed to like me because there was something strange about me, as I preferred football to rugby and I was Scottish!'

Despite the prevalence of rugby league locally, MacDougall's feelings towards the sport did not change, 'Widnes RLFC, or the "Chemics" as they were nicknamed, played on Friday nights and I used to go along and watch but I never fancied playing much. No, thank you!

'When I was 15 I left school on the Friday and the following week I went for an interview at the Swale Press in Widnes, who printed the *Runcorn, Widnes and Liverpool Weekly News*. My mother was a strong character so she came with me and the foreman, who was very polite and respectful, seemed to like the idea that I was the only kid who came for an interview with his Mum! He thought that was fantastic and I started work there the following Monday.

'I was a trainee compositor earning the equivalent of £3.50 a week, and in those days you used to have to set every letter individually into the print case which took a heck of a long time, so there was quite a large number of staff employed at the works. It wasn't just newspapers we printed, in fact the company used to offer a design service for all kinds of printed items, so I attended a Print and Design course at Liverpool College of Art three nights a week, the same college that John Lennon went to.

'Unfortunately I never met John but I did see the Beatles perform, as they used to play in Widnes every Monday night at this time. It used to cost half a crown to go and see them! I was given a photograph signed by all four of the Beatles and many years later my Dad sold it for £500! I didn't visit The Cavern but I loved the music coming from the Liverpool area. We also printed the weekly *Merseybeat* newspaper, so we got the first details of what was happening in the music scene.

At the time, if you came from Liverpool people really thought you were somebody.'

Meanwhile, Ted had progressed into adult local league football, 'I had been playing men's football in the local leagues since I was about 15 for teams like ICI and Everite, who were big chemical companies. They were the sort of leagues where most players used to smoke cigarettes in the dressing room before they went out for the game. Anyway, I'd done well, scored a lot of goals and was making headlines in my own newspaper! Of course I made sure those headlines were a little bit bigger and bolder than they might have been otherwise! I was always a better player than I really was!'

2

Learning the Trade

MACDOUGALL'S reputation in Merseyside football continued to grow and he scored goals at such a rate that as a 17-year-old in 1964, he was handed the opportunity to have a trial for Liverpool. It came through his foreman at the printing works, 'He knew somebody at Liverpool and asked if he got me a trial, would I go? I said yes, of course, so I went over to Melwood on a Tuesday night and there were lots of young lads present from all over the country, and Scotland as well. The first person I was introduced to was a guy called Tom Bush. He was an elderly gent, a former scout who used to always have a small cigarette fixed in the corner of his mouth and wore a flasher raincoat! Joe Fagan, who would of course later go on to manage Liverpool for a couple of seasons in the 1980s, was also there as he was then the reserve team trainer, together with a wonderful character called Reuben Bennett whom I grew to love dearly. Joe and Reuben were also part of manager Bill Shankly's famous boot room staff, which guided the club so successfully for many, many years.

'Anyway, I did okay and I was invited to come back on the Thursday, when I was asked if I would like to sign amateur forms. I grabbed the opportunity and played in the "C" team the following Saturday. I scored a few goals and gradually progressed through to the "B" team, then to the "A" team. I managed to keep scoring and eventually I displaced some young professionals and got into the reserve side. I actually scored probably the worst goal of my career playing for Liverpool reserves –

although I must confess I didn't know much about it at the time! The opposing team's goalie had the ball and I turned my back as he was set to boot it upfield, but the ball struck me on the back of the neck and just flew into the open net. I don't know who was more embarrassed – him or me!'

For 18 months Ted played as an amateur, but after scoring twice in only his second reserve game at Bolton, the day after his 19th birthday in January 1966, he was offered the chance to turn professional, 'I was summoned from training and was told to go and see "The Boss", the great Bill Shankly. I began shaking like a leaf because I had never met him before and had to pinch myself to believe that Bill Shankly actually wanted to see me! But Bill was marvellous, he sat me down and told me I'd done great, and said he would like to offer me a professional contract at Anfield with a basic wage of around £16–£18 a week, I can't remember the exact figure but it was twice as much as I was earning at the time! Typically, Bill said I should go away and talk to my parents before I decided whether or not to accept.'

The chance to sign as a professional arrived at a time when MacDougall had spent four years in the printing industry and still had another two years ahead of him to complete his apprenticeship, 'It was a six-year course and in a day and age when everybody told you to get a trade to guarantee you'd be made for life. I reckon 95 per cent of parents would have insisted their son should see it through however, my parents had brought me down from Scotland hoping just such a chance might arise. When Dad asked me if I thought I could make it as a pro, I told him "yes". What youngster wouldn't? But what the hell did I really know?

'Imagine how elated I felt when both Mum and Dad replied that if that was the way I felt, then I should go for it! My parents were so influential in changing the course of my whole life. You hear of many other guys less fortunate than I was, who reach 30 years of age and are still left wondering whether or not they could have made it in the game, and wished they had taken a chance. Well my parents gifted me the opportunity and I loved them until the day they died because they changed my life.'

When Shankly finally called time on his own distinguished playing career in 1949, he immediately began his managerial apprenticeship at Carlisle United. Spells in charge of Grimsby Town, Workington and Huddersfield Town followed before he took charge at Anfield in December 1959. Liverpool were then a mid-table Second Division side but gradually, together with his backroom staff, Shankly turned things around. Promotion in 1961/62 was followed by the First Division championship two years later and he now presided over a very strong side that had added the FA Cup to their list of honours in 1965, and established itself as one of the major forces in the English game. MacDougall was just one of a number of young players hoping for a chance to break into the side, 'There were guys like Geoff Strong, Phil Chisnall, Alf Arrowsmith, Peter Wall, Bobby Graham, Doug Livermore and Ian Ross all fighting for a place in the senior side. Doug and Ian started their careers at the same time as me and the three of us became great mates. However, opportunities were very limited as Liverpool were on their way to winning the Football League championship in 1966 and did so using just 14 players. Not like the rotational system used by clubs today – what a load of crap that is by the way!'

Nonetheless, Ted has fond memories of his formative years in the professional game, under the guidance of the legendary Shankly, 'We used to report to Anfield and get changed there for training. Shankly would always change with the reserves and afterwards we would all get into the big bath together. The training ground at Melwood was about three or four miles down the road and we travelled there by bus. Training with Shankly was all about the five-a-sides at the end of the session. If you were in his team you had to win and he would also act as referee, so if you weren't winning, he would award you a crazy penalty or something right near the end!

'Shankly's house overlooked the Everton training ground at Bellefield and he would look out the window and watch them train. Long before psychology was even thought of, while we were all in the bath he would say things like, "I just watched them train – big fat arses, their shorts don't fit, they cannae play!" We used to dote on every word he said of course. He was special and I loved him.

'The first Christmas I was at Liverpool we had the traditional party and as it was my first one, like all new players, I had to sing a song in front of everyone! So I chose "You'll Never Walk Alone". I thought I was on to a winner there and sure enough everyone soon joined in!

'When I eventually became a member of the first-team squad I would regularly be training with players like Roger Hunt, Tommy Smith, Ian St John, Ron Yeats and Willie Stevenson, and I loved that and I believe they liked me! These players were on about £30 a week, twice as much as me and they also got £1 for every 1,000 spectators who turned up for home matches over 28,000. We regularly had gates of around 48,000, so that meant they would also be getting some good bonuses!'

Unfortunately though, the nearest MacDougall got to First Division football with Liverpool was being named as substitute for a game at Aston Villa in March 1966. He was not called into action as two goals from Roger Hunt and another from Ian Callaghan ensured that the Reds came away from Villa Park 3-0 winners. Ted now treasures a picture of him in the Liverpool team group that day, 'I didn't realise that my Mum and Dad had this picture, but in fact my Mum had it on her wall the day she died. That was the first time I saw it.'

The Reds went on to claim their seventh league title at the end of 1965/66 and also reached the final of the European Cup Winners' Cup, where they suffered defeat against Borussia Dortmund. In October 1966, MacDougall was again a substitute for the European Cup first round second leg encounter against Romanian champions Petrolul Ploiesti. Defending a 2-0 lead from the first leg at Anfield, the Reds went down 3-1. Away goals did not count double in those days so a play-off match was hastily arranged at the Heysel Stadium in Brussels which Liverpool again won 2-0, with Ted watching on from the bench once more. Liverpool's interest in the competition ended at the next stage however, where they suffered a comprehensive 7-3 aggregate defeat against Ajax, 'Unfortunately I got into trouble while we were in Belgium. I was rooming with Ian Ross but I was out all night following the match, although I wasn't drinking because I didn't drink then. What used to happen was that the English guys in the Liverpool squad used to go off in one direction and the Scottish lads in another. Anyway I was supposed to be looking after Willie Stevenson, who was a top player and he was having a drink! When I eventually got back, Ian told me Bill Shankly had come into the room during the night looking for me. Anyway when I reported back to the ground the following week, Bob Paisley, who was a trainer at this time, called me over and gave me a big dressing down, calling me a "Billy Big Bollocks" who thought he could stay out all night and swan around with the first-team players! I explained what I was doing but even so my behaviour was frowned upon as I was still considered a young kid.'

MacDougall was a regular in Liverpool's reserve team throughout the first half of the 1966/67 season before falling prey to an unusual illness which hampered his progression, 'We were getting crowds of up to 10,000 for reserve games at Anfield which was just amazing. Then unfortunately I got this illness and nobody really understood what it was at the time, but it was mononucleosis. Lots of young people used to get it, it was also known as the "kissing disease". It debilitated me for about six months and made me feel permanently tired and lethargic. They couldn't diagnose it but that's what I had and I went down and down, and eventually found myself back in the "A" team. Bill Shankly was terrific though, always trying to help me get through it and I had so much respect for him.'

Ted now admits that at times he found his days at Anfield unnerving. Despite deep ambitions, he clearly found it difficult to imagine himself one day on equal terms with the stars around him, 'Looking back I can see I was too much in awe of the other Liverpool players at the time. I virtually hero-worshipped them and I suppose in a way it gave me an inferiority complex. I became very introverted and it was a big mistake.

'Ronnie Moran, who later became another of the "boot room" team at Liverpool, was still playing in the reserves when I was there. I remember we had a game against Aston Villa and I missed some chances during the match. We were having a "pee" alongside each other afterwards and Ronnie made a very unpleasant remark to me, so I told him to "piss off". Of course, that was exactly the response he wanted because I wasn't coming out and expressing myself vocally.

'I learned later in my career that confidence is vital in football. You must always think and believe you're better than the next man – and of course the opposition.'

Unable to retain their title, Liverpool finished the season in a somewhat disappointing fifth position. Soon after, MacDougall and many of the playing squad headed off to Majorca, although not for the same reason. The first team flew out for an end-of-season tour while Ted travelled for a working holiday of his own choosing. However, as he enjoyed his break in the sunshine, the youngster soon faced a big decision regarding his immediate future in the game, 'I took myself off to Majorca on my own for six weeks, and Ian St John fixed me up with a job in a bar. Quite a few players used to do this sort of work during the close season in those days. While I was there the Liverpool side came over and stayed in a nearby hotel, I would go and see them, and they would give me food and look after me because, to them, I was still only a kid!

'I was lying on the beach in Majorca one day when my career suddenly took a change. I had been working out there for about six weeks and was with the Chelsea lads John Hollins and Joe Fascione, when we met up with some of the Liverpool boys. They showed me a paper from home and there it was, "Ted MacDougall signs for York". I thought no, they can't do that? Then I got a telegram from my father telling me I needed to come home and sort things out. I was still under contract at Liverpool and of course they couldn't do anything without my agreement, but I was young and naïve and I didn't realise that.

'When I got back Bill Shankly called me in to his office and told me I didn't have to go and that he did not really want me to go, but it was up to me. He was fantastic about it but Mum, Dad and I went and met York's representatives and they took us to a nice hotel, ordered us a slap-up dinner, then offered me £21 a week rising to £24 during the season. I thought this was good, what nice people, so I signed!

'I felt I needed to establish myself somewhere, and needed to play regular first-team football. Even so, I didn't fully appreciate what I was doing leaving a First Division club like Liverpool to go to York, it was the worst decision ever really. I was silly but when you're just 20 years old you get carried away when someone comes along with a better offer than what you are getting. I was very naïve, I nearly got into the First Division and Europe with Liverpool.'

Shankly later confirmed that he would have been happy to let MacDougall stay at Anfield but after spending so much time in the reserves, the manager fully understood why he decided to leave.

Some years later, Shankly recalled that although Ted had an awkward style about him at the time, he had always shown a fair measure of promise, and believed him to be a genuine lad with real character who could be relied upon to give everything he had for 90 minutes. It should be remembered that during MacDougall's days at Anfield, he was competing for a place with international class forwards like Hunt and St John, together with the emerging Bobby Graham.

Nobody could knock Shankly for letting Ted go at the time, although the legendary Liverpool scout Tom Saunders later admitted it was a decision he and his fellow boot room colleagues lived to regret.'I left Liverpool on the best of terms and that's how it always remained,' said Ted 'Later in my career when I was at Norwich, if we were playing up north on a Saturday, I would stay a while afterwards with my Mum and Dad, and I would ring Joe Fagan to ask if I could train with Liverpool at Melwood on the following Monday morning. I was always welcomed back and of course I would end up playing in the five-a-sides again! I would be doing my usual trick of not tracking back and staying up front scoring all the goals, then from about three fields away I would hear Joe or someone else shout out, "Hey MacDougall – you gotta get back!" It was wonderful of Joe to let me train with them and so typical of everyone at the club.

'Years later, when I was player-coach at Blackpool I was scouting with Alan Ball when I saw Shankly at an Everton reserve match, and he repeated exactly what he had said to me before I left Liverpool. I thought that was phenomenal, it was one thing a 20-year-old kid remembering what he had said to me, but I thought for Bill to remember what he had said to that kid was amazing. He also mentioned that I turned out to be a thorn in his side because when I was playing for other teams, I always seemed to score against Liverpool!

'I think starting off my career at Anfield gave me a good understanding of a high level of football, and an opportunity to see how top players handled themselves and how they reacted with the public. When I left it soon made me appreciate that I had dropped down to a lower level and that I had to make my way up again. I have never lost my love for Liverpool. I still love the club and I loved the way I was brought up there.'

3

Johnny on the Spot

SIXTY-ONE-YEAR-OLD Tommy Lockie had already experienced the highs and lows of football management when he brought Ted MacDougall to York City for a fee of £5,000 in July 1967. A Scotsman by birth, Lockie had been a commanding centre-half and after starting his career with Glasgow Rangers, he went on to play for Leith Athletic and Barnsley before spending a season at Bootham Crescent in 1933. After subsequent spells at Accrington Stanley and Mansfield Town he returned to City as reserve team trainer three years later. He was soon given responsibilities with the senior side as the Minstermen reached the FA Cup quarter-finals in 1938. Then, when manager Jimmy McCormick left the club in 1954, he and club secretary Bill Sherrington took temporary charge and went one better, guiding the team to an FA Cup semi-final the following year. Sam Bartram eventually took over permanently but when he departed in July 1960, the Fourth Division club turned again to Lockie.

Having just missed out on promotion in each of his first two seasons in charge, a couple of poor seasons followed and as a result the club had to apply for re-election to the Football League in 1964. Granted a stay of execution, City were remarkably promoted to the Third Division at the end of the 1964/65 season. Sadly though, they spent just the one season at the higher level and having suffered relegation, were then forced to again apply for re-election at the end of 1966/67. So after 18 months in the Anfield shadows, MacDougall quickly became immersed in the harsh realities of life at York City. The transfer fee involved was reported to be £5,000 although Ted remains quite sure that the actual figure was £5,500, 'Tommy Lockie was a nice gent although I didn't really get to know him well. His outlook on things reflected a person of his age or even perhaps someone older. I think he had probably done his tenure and the game was beginning to pass him by. It didn't take me long once I joined York to wonder just what had I let myself in for!

'It was a bit of a joke at times, for example, you would bring all your training kit and underwear in with you then take it home to wash, because you didn't dare leave it at the ground in case somebody else took it! I remember seeing a players' car park at the ground but I wasn't sure why it was there as most of us could only afford pushbikes!

'There were a number of players at York who were never really good enough to ever make it any further. When I first joined I told them I was on £21 a week in the summer and £24 during the season and one of the other players immediately went in to ask for a rise. The manager offered him £24 during the season and £18 during the summer, so he enquired why I was therefore getting £21? The manager told him it was because I was a better player than him. "Not during the fucking summer he isn't!" was the player's reply!'

MacDougall made his Football League debut wearing the number ten shirt for York City at Bootham Crescent on 19 August 1967, the opening day of the 1967/68 season, and scored City's goal in a 1-1 draw against Workington. Playing alongside him was ex-Southampton forward Tommy Spencer, who had top-scored for City with 23 goals in all competitions the previous season and Tommy Ross, another newcomer making his debut for City after having been signed from Peterborough United during the summer, 'Tommy Ross hailed from Dingwall in the north of Scotland and originally came down to England from Ross County. He immediately became "top man" because he had a car, well a mini-van actually. We quickly became friends, roomed together and used to travel around together in the van. In fact all the players soon became pretty close because none of us had much money. Fortunately the rent for my digs was only a pound a week at the time so I was probably the best off of all of them!'

The York City team line-up that day was Fallon, Joy, Turner, Collinson, Jackson, Burrows, Alderson, Ross, Spencer, MacDougall and Provan.

A League Cup first round exit at Darlington was then followed by a disastrous run of results which saw City plummet to rock bottom of the Fourth Division, having failed to gain a victory in any of their first 13 league games and thus creating an unenviable club record with the worst start to a season in City's history. Ted had remained ever-present during this period and had added to his opening day strike with goals in a 3-1 defeat at Luton and a 1-1 draw at Swansea Town, as they were then known.

Lockie became the first manager in York's history to be sacked when he was dismissed in mid-October. The team then produced two successive home wins against Swansea (2-1) and Notts County (4-2) before former Sheffield United centre-half Joe Shaw was appointed as the new City manager in November. It was Shaw's first managerial appointment after a 20-year playing career at Bramall Lane, which encompassed 629 Football League appearances, and at 39 years of age he was able to bring more modern techniques to the manager's role.

MacDougall was again on target in a 4-1 home win against Chester early in November, a game that also saw Tommy Ross score his first two goals for City and attracted 5,226 spectators to Bootham Crescent, the highest attendance since the opening day of the season. The following month, Shaw signed versatile forward Billy Hodgson from Rotherham as player-coach. They had previously enjoyed a long playing spell together at Bramall Lane before Hodgson left for Leicester, Derby and Rotherham.

Nonetheless only two more victories followed before the turn of the year, both at home, 4-0 against Exeter and 4-1 against Rochdale. Ted contributed a goal in the first of these and another two in the second and having missed just one game in the first half of the season, he had by then brought his personal goal tally to nine in all.

City's league performances away from home had yielded just four draws in 14 games before they gained their first away victory at Lincoln at the end of January 1968. Despite Ted being absent from the side through injury, a goal from Ross then secured a home draw against league leaders Luton before further victories followed at Southend and at home to Wrexham, as City began to climb the table. After a two-goal defeat at home to Chesterfield in late February, they went through the month of March unbeaten. It was a significant period for both the club and MacDougall.

A goalless draw at fellow strugglers Bradford Park Avenue was followed by a single-goal victory at home to Lincoln, then successive 1-1 draws against Crewe at Bootham Crescent and away at Notts County. When Bradford visited City for the return fixture on 25 March they found themselves on the end of a six-goal mauling, with both Ted and Tommy Ross scoring two goals each alongside a goal apiece from wingers Andy Provan and Rowland Horrey. The following Saturday Port Vale were the visitors and they too were duly despatched in a 5-1 defeat that saw MacDougall score the first hat-trick of his senior career, 'I honestly cannot remember that first hat-trick, which is unusual for me, but I do remember that things improved after Joe Shaw was appointed manager. He was a really good guy, I liked him a lot and also his assistant Billy Hodgson, who was a tricky Scottish midfielder, sort of a "Billy Bremner" type of player.'

Having climbed up to 14th, City then suffered six defeats in their last nine games to plunge back into the re-election places at the foot of the Fourth Division. Only one more goal was to follow for MacDougall, in a 2-2 draw at Aldershot in early May, although injury meant that he missed a further three games. The goal at the Recreation Ground meant Ted finished the season as York's leading goalscorer with 15 goals in 38 appearances, one more than his friend Ross and two ahead of Provan. Nonetheless, York finished 21st and had to apply for re-election for the second successive season. This they successfully did, with 46 votes out of a possible 48 in their favour, 'After we had to apply for re-election at the end of my first season the manager got rid of a lot of the other players – in fact I think we only had 11 left. Joe then brought in some different lads either cheaply or on free transfers. I felt I had established myself as a league player, although I was still a kid really and very naïve. I didn't understand much about what was going on at the club. Joe helped me a bit but nobody else did much to give me any direction. I was scoring goals but I didn't really know how or why. I was just "Johnny on the Spot".'

While living in Widnes prior to his move to York, Ted had met a local young lady called Joan Moffat and their friendship had blossomed, so much so that during his first season at Bootham Crescent, she moved from Lancashire to be closer to him, 'I met Joan when I was about 19 or 20 and she was just 18. When I moved to York I rented a house from the club in Shelley Grove, at £1 a week, so when Joan came down we had to make a big fuss about her leaving the house each night and going round the corner, to make sure the club would not think that she was living with me and charge me extra rent! It was just out of convenience we lived together really because of the considerable distance involved when going to see each other. It could take as long as four or five hours to get from York to Widnes over the top of the Pennines in those days. This carried on until we eventually decided to get married in April 1969, mind you I still couldn't afford to pay for a honeymoon – not on £21 a week.

'Tommy Ross was my best man and, ironically, Joan's father was a scout for Stan Cullis at Wolves and he had come to see me play when I was 15 years old and turned me down for a trial. My mother never let him forget that in all the time Joan and I were together! Then of course Bill McGarry wanted to sign me for Wolves in 1971 when Derek Dougan and all that lot were there. It would have been ironic if I had joined them after originally having been turned down by my father-in-law. What a twist of fate that would have been. My success elsewhere made it awkward for Joan's father for about ten years!'

During the summer of 1968, York City's board of directors decided to scrap the club's reserve team and maintain only a pool of 16 players. Shaw did his best to strengthen the side with the resources available to him and one of his signings was 26-year-old goalkeeper Bob Widdowson from Sheffield United, who had been understudy to former England international Alan Hodgkinson while at Bramall Lane.

Another signing was half-back Graham Carr, who joined City from Northampton, 'Graham was a real character and a great laugh. He had been part of that ugly midfield at Northampton along with John Kurila. They had kicked everything that moved as they made their way up to the First Division in the early 1960s, then did the same as they fell back down to the Third in successive seasons. Graham went on to have a good career as a scout and manager though and of course his son is the television presenter Alan Carr.'

However, Shaw's most significant new signing turned out to be a lively and strong-running young forward called Philip Boyer. The 19-year-old Nottingham-born Boyer was an exciting player with a sharp mind and good ball skills. He was allowed to leave Derby County by manager Brian Clough for £3,000 without having made a league appearance for the club, 'That's right, Cloughie got shot of him!'

MacDougall and Boyer were both in the starting line-up at Chester on the opening day of the 1968/69 season, a match which City lost 2-0.

Ted struck his first goals of the season with two at home to Barnsley in the League Cup, but could not prevent City losing the tie by the odd goal in seven. Then on the eve of their first home fixture of the new league campaign, Shaw surprisingly resigned for personal reasons, 'I had a lot of time for Joe. I think he left because he wanted to continue living in Sheffield and the directors wanted him closer by.'

Indeed, Shaw's wife had a wool and baby clothes shop in Sheffield which they were having trouble selling and this had prevented them from purchasing a property in the York area. The matter had been causing him considerable worry and he found the constant travelling between the two cities a strain.

Before a new manager was appointed, Wales under-23 international goalkeeper Mike Walker moved to Third Division Watford for a fee of £5,000. Walker's last game saw City gain their first league victory of the season at home to Peterborough in late August, a match which saw Boyer score his first goal in York colours. By the end of October though, as the search for a new manager continued, City had mustered just three victories from 16 league fixtures, while having suffered heavy defeats at both Brentford (5-1) and Bradford City (5-0) along the way, and were again struggling near the foot of the league table, 'Mike was a good lad, always immaculately dressed – the "Beau Brummell" of Bootham Crescent. I nicknamed him "Percy" because he just looked like a "Percy". Always so elegant! I had a lot of time for Mike and I was pleased that he subsequently went on to do well in the game both as a player and then a manager.'

Finally the board turned to the 49-year-old former Rotherham, Grimsby and Huddersfield Town manager, Tom Johnston. An outside-left during his playing days, Johnston had scored over a hundred goals during spells at the two Nottingham clubs, first Forest and then County. A fully qualified FA coach, the Scotsman's first professional management appointment came at Rotherham in 1958, where he built a side that challenged for promotion to the First Division and also reached the League Cup Final against Aston Villa in 1961. He had little luck at Grimsby but took Huddersfield to a League Cup semi-final in 1967/68 before leaving Leeds Road at the end of that season. He arrived with the reputation of a shrewd strategist and a strong disciplinarian who ruled his clubs with a rod of iron.

Johnston's first game at the helm was greeted by an attendance of just 2,462 at Bootham Crescent, but those who came saw him record his first victory as City beat Aldershot thanks to two goals from Tommy Ross. Defeat at Grimsby was then followed by a potentially tricky FA Cup first round trip to Northern Premier League side South Shields. However, the Minstermen proved too strong for their non-league opponents and with MacDougall adding two goals of his own to a Ross hat-trick and a penalty from full-back Gerry Baker, they ran out comfortable 6-0 victors. Successive league draws at Notts County and at home to Darlington and Lincoln were wrapped around further progress in the FA Cup, where Ted struck both goals in a 2-0 home victory over Morecambe, then also a non-league side, in front of a far more healthy crowd of 5,071, 'Tom Johnston came in as manager and at training he would wear a baggy tracksuit with string tied around the bottom of each leg like bicycle clips, with shoes not training shoes, and he just used to stare at you while puffing away on his pipe! I found him a nightmare to deal with, he was always trying to take the mick out of players and was very sarcastic.

'Training involved running and lapping – there was no warm-up or cool-down, no psychologists or sports scientists. We never bothered doing much ball work, the club used to wash the match ball after each game and use it for the next match. This went on until the ball was ruined and they would have to replace it, which meant we could use the old one for training! I always remember Fridays when it was Scotland v England, we played behind the stand. It was five-a-side and we would knock the crap out of each other. It was the hardest game of the week – on a Friday, the day before a match!

'I can tell you a true story about Ron Spence, our trainer at the time and a former City player. In those days the trainer washed the kit, rubbed down the players – in fact he did the lot. Ron's stock item was a jar of Vicks, the well-known vapour rub associated with the treatment of colds and flu. He used it on everything and would rub you down with it without fail. I didn't see how this helped with muscle tightness or soreness so I once asked him why he always used the stuff? He said, "I don't know but you never catch a cold!"

'In those days you couldn't get a lump of ice for your drink let alone have an ice bath. I got a knee injury once and all the towels were filthy but I had to wrap one of these towels around my knee and lean it over a sink. Ron would turn both taps on and put my knee under hot and cold alternately for about 45 minutes. That was my treatment, there was no physiotherapist around!'

A shock victory at promotion-chasing Southend just prior to Christmas was notable as the first occasion that MacDougall and Boyer had each contributed goals in the same game. The latter's speed of thought and movement, together with his willingness to act as a supplier had begun to combine well with Ted's ability to stick the ball in the back of the net, and although City's performances in the New Year were woefully inconsistent, both players began to attract attention from scouts of other clubs. Boyer would later describe their partnership as a kind of telepathy and already the pair seemed to revel in each other's company, 'Phil, or "Charlie" as we called him after the French actor Charles Boyer, started as a right-winger at York, he didn't play off me or anything to begin with. But he was a clever lad and he began to do everything I didn't like to do! He was always making himself available to receive the ball anywhere on the pitch and was able to link the play which I wasn't good at. I wanted to make sure I got on the end of anything coming into the box, so after a while we complemented each other quite well.'

York had reached the third round of the FA Cup for the first time since 1960/61 and the club's highest crowd for nearly three years, 11,129, turned up early in the new year for the visit of First Division Stoke City. Unfortunately, despite a spirited performance on the day, City's run ended with a 2-0 defeat. Apparently undeterred by their cup exit, another goal apiece from MacDougall and Boyer contributed to an excellent 4-0 league victory a fortnight later at high-riding Halifax. Unfortunately though, the two points gained that day turned out to be the last City would gain on the road that season, despite the goals continuing to flow steadily for Ted. Five more came in the next eight games, including City's consolation goal in a 2-1 defeat at league leaders Doncaster in front of a crowd of over 12,000 at Belle Vue.

A clear trend had now begun to appear in York's results – they would win, often convincingly, at home and lose, sometimes badly, away. From late February until their last two home games in early May, City won all eight home games while losing all ten on their travels. Boyer grabbed his first two-goal haul in a 2-0 home win against Colchester in late March and this was followed by a notable 3-1 victory over Port Vale, in which MacDougall briefly followed in his father's footsteps by taking over in goal, 'Bob Widdowson got injured and he couldn't play on. Of course we didn't have substitute goalkeepers on the bench in those days, just the one outfield player. I didn't realise the manager had asked everyone else if they would go in goal before he asked me, but when he did so I said, "Okay, I'll give it a go." It was probably the most frightening thing I have ever done in my life on a football pitch!

'We were winning 1-0 and the first thing that happened was they got a corner. I went to punch the ball clear and it flew off my fist and just missed the top corner of the goal! The second thing was I couldn't kick the ball outside the penalty area from a goal kick. My mouth started to dry up, I completely lost my bearings and had no idea where my goal was or where I was come to that! Port Vale had a big centre-forward with a broken nose and cauliflower ears called Roy Chapman, and this big guy comes running through and I had to dive at his feet! I thought to myself, "This is not good!" But I prevented him from scoring! Thankfully we won the game, but as far as I was concerned, the end couldn't come quickly enough!'

Unfortunately City's results were not good enough to avoid the club having to make a third successive application for re-election to the Football League at the end of the season, after their campaign had come to a tragic end when, during a goalless draw in the final home game against promoted Halifax, referee Roy Harper collapsed and died, 'The referee just keeled over on the pitch. I think one of the players blew the whistle to stop the game, but by the time they could get the referee into the ambulance he was dead. Very, very sad.'

MacDougall again ended the season as the club's leading goalscorer and in a division of 24 clubs, it was something for him to be one of only seven players to have topped their club's scoring lists in successive seasons. The others to do so in the Fourth Division that season were Jack Howarth (Aldershot), Kevin Randall (Chesterfield), Alick Jeffrey (Doncaster), Les Massie (Halifax), Roy Chapman (Port Vale) and Ray Smith (Wrexham). However Ted, who had not missed a match during the season, went one better than all of these, as only he alone had improved on his 1967/68 haul of 15 league goals by scoring 19. Having proved himself as a goalscorer at this level, the time was now right for him to take a step back up the football ladder.

4

The Beautiful South

YORK City retained their Football League status during the summer of 1969 thanks to the support of their fellow league members, but the prospect of another season of struggle at Bootham Crescent prompted MacDougall to ask for a transfer, 'I just told the manager that I wasn't happy. I wanted to play for a club that was doing something, or at least looked like it could.'

While he and manager Tom Johnston had rarely seen eye to eye, Johnston knew his side would miss Ted's goalscoring ability and his increasing knack of being in the right place at the right time. He had however been critical of MacDougall's work rate and performance outside the penalty box, 'I was a bit introverted at the time, I had an edge to me and I was very single-minded to be successful as a goalscorer. I admit that I could be selfish and demanding but goalscorers play inside the box. Tom had been quite successful at Huddersfield and he went on to do well for York, but he was no help to me on or off the pitch. In fact he was about as useful to me as tits on a bull!

'I had been the leading scorer for each of the last two seasons and his first response was to ask me to take a pay cut for the following year. It wasn't really all about money, but he was so tight that when York were promoted together with Bournemouth in 1971, their players joined in our celebrations that evening because he hadn't laid on anything for them.

'I didn't know about any definite offers but I found out Bournemouth were interested, so in July I drove down for a few days, together with Joan and our dog, a crazy border collie called Sam, and we set off to meet manager Freddie Cox. We slept overnight in the car on the way down but when we got there the club put us up at the East Anglia Hotel, and once we settled in we took a walk down to the beach. The weather was so nice, it was like being in Spain or the south of France compared to where we had come from.'

Freddie Cox was in his second spell as manager at Bournemouth, where together with his wife Eileen and son Barry, he also ran a local newsagents shop. Born in Reading, the 48-year-old Cox began his distinguished playing career on the Spurs ground staff, then later played for Arsenal and appeared at outside-right for the Gunners in their 1950 FA Cup-winning team. He also collected a runners-up medal against Newcastle two years later, before beginning his managerial career as assistant manager at West Bromwich Albion in 1955. He was first appointed manager of Bournemouth in 1956 and during his initial season at the helm, he oversaw the club's famous FA Cup run when they defeated First Division Wolves and Spurs, before narrowly being beaten by Manchester United in the quarter-finals.

Cox then had spells in charge at Portsmouth and Gillingham, steering the latter to promotion from the Fourth Division in 1963/64, before returning to Dean Court in January 1966. He was given a five-year contract at the start of the 1968/69 season and having gone on to finish fourth in the old Third Division, Bournemouth, or 'Boscombe' as they remain affectionately known locally to this day, were expected to push for promotion the following year. Cox had followed MacDougall's progress during his brief professional career having spotted that even as a schoolboy, he had been a goalscorer.

Although Ted was not particularly tall at 5ft 10in, the Cherries manager had been impressed by his timing and accuracy when going for the ball in the air, together with his more than useful ability to accept chances in the penalty area. He believed MacDougall would provide the goal power that the Cherries had been missing the previous season, 'The first time I met Freddie he turned up in his white MGB GT, wearing a smart mohair suit and looked like the dog's bollocks! I thought he was a nice guy and he offered me a wage of £28 per week, plus an extra £7 for each appearance and finally a set of curtains as a signing-on fee. Well, it was a done deal. Looking back though, I should have asked for an extra £500 instead of settling for the curtains!'

Although Fulham had also shown an interest in signing him, MacDougall joined Bournemouth for £9,500 and signing him was probably the best coup Cox ever made. In addition to the curtains, the club also paid his removal expenses and gave him a signing-on fee of £500. As well as the usual match bonuses and incentives, a further bonus of £800 was included for each year's service with the club. It was perhaps not a lucrative deal but for a Third Division club at the time, it was at the least a very fair one. Ted wasted no time in signing and the man the town would later embrace as its very own 'Supermac' had arrived.

Having been a permanent fixture in the Third Division since the club first entered the Football League in 1923/24, Bournemouth were certainly overdue a promotion and supporters believed that Cox now had the nucleus of a side capable of achieving it. He had spent a further £10,000 in signing West Ham winger Trevor Hartley and the early signs were good, 'All went well during pre-season and I certainly believed we had the ability in the squad to do well. I began to really enjoy training, we worked hard and sometimes we would go on a run to Hengistbury Head, about five miles away. Often when we got there it would be so hot, we would just lie down and sunbathe. Remember, I had come from the frozen north so this was quite something. From the first time we trained on the beach I more or less fell in love with the place.'

Ted's first league game for Bournemouth, on the opening day of the season, was unfortunately neither glamorous nor memorable, and ended in a 1-0 defeat at Barnsley, 'Before the game, Freddie told me to close my eyes and pretend I was playing at Wembley but it didn't work!'

The Cherries team line-up at Oakwell was Jones, Gulliver, Foote, J. White, Stocks, Bumstead, Hartley, Hold, MacDougall, East and Meredith.

Undeterred, MacDougall got off the mark with two goals in the next match, a three-goal League Cup victory at home to Bristol Rovers. His first league goal for the club was a late equaliser against Brighton at Dean Court two weeks later, when he side-footed the ball home from ten yards to earn the Cherries their first point of the season.

Prior to the game, the club paid its respects to former centre-forward Ron Eyre, who had passed away at the age of 68. Eyre had set the club record of 40 goals in a season in 1928/29 and was acknowledged as the greatest goalscorer in the history of the club, having accumulated 259 goals in 367 first-team appearances between 1925 and 1933. It is probably fair to say that not too many Bournemouth supporters would have expected the first of those records to be beaten not once, but twice by their latest goal-getter in the following three seasons.

At the end of August Ted and Joan moved into a new house approximately ten miles to the west of the town at West Moors. Director Harold Walker, a local solicitor who also had business interests in property, encouraged players to purchase their own homes in the area and John Meredith, another close-season signing from Gillingham, had already bought a property in the vicinity. Soon after, Trevor Hartley and his new wife Julie also moved in nearby, 'Our home was in Heathfield Road, John and Trevor were both good lads and we all helped each other to quickly settle in. They were good players too.'

September began well for the Cherries, with a battling performance in the League Cup against First Division Sheffield Wednesday at Hillsborough, which saw them return from Yorkshire with a 1-1 draw. This was followed by a 5-1 away win at Tranmere, and then a replay victory over the Owls, with 21-year-old John Hold scoring the only goal of the game. Cox had never been afraid to give an opportunity to the club's younger players and had taken great satisfaction in his youth side's progression to the semi-final of the FA Youth Cup the previous season. Now, with injuries to a number of his experienced players, Cox had fielded as many as four 18-year-olds in the senior team – forward Eddie Rowles, midfielder Dennis Longhorn and two defenders, Chris Foote and Allan Summerhill. Indeed on a number of occasions the average age of the senior side was only 21.

Despite the excitement of the League Cup victory over Wednesday, early results in the league had been generally disappointing and there were soon signs of unrest among the club's supporters. Cox's omission of the popular Hartley after the first few games drew the most criticism, but some was also directed towards MacDougall, and a section of the crowd began to give him the bird, picking up on deficiencies in his overall play despite him having scored five goals in his first 12 appearances for the Cherries. Cox sprang to his player's defence in the local press insisting supporters allowed Ted a chance to settle in, while reminding them that at just 22 years of age, he needed time to adapt to his new surroundings.

MacDougall dropped to the substitutes' bench when another First Division side, Leicester City, were the next cup visitors to Dean Court, the experienced Keith East being recalled in his place. City ran out comfortable 2-0 winners but crowds of almost 15,000 for each of the last two cup ties served to show that the public would support a successful team in Bournemouth.

An embarrassing three-goal home defeat against Rochdale was followed by a similar reverse at Southport which meant, that after 12 league games, Bournemouth were just four places from the foot of the Third Division. In fact, the team went six matches and a total of 563 minutes without a goal before Ted ended the drought against Fulham in mid-October at Dean Court. Having now been reinstated to the starting 11, he gratefully accepted a flick-on from Hold to head the ball home. Cox had pushed Hold and Rowles forward with MacDougall to form a much livelier three-pronged attack but unfortunately, despite leading twice during the game, the Cherries still had to settle for a draw.

Cox remained certain that Ted would come into his element as the season progressed and grounds got heavier, and a fortnight later at home to Bristol Rovers, MacDougall displayed the opportunism in front of goal which had prompted Cox to bring him south. First, after just ten minutes, he thumped home a volley from a Mel Simmonds corner, before stabbing in the rebound after Simmonds' shot had been blocked a minute before the interval. His second two-goal haul of the season against Rovers gave him a total of eight in all competitions, but once again poor defending by Bournemouth allowed the visitors to go home with a point.

With injuries also beginning to take their toll, the supporters' thoughts were turning to the likelihood of a long, hard winter ahead. Their disappointment was soon conveyed to the players, who had difficulty in coping with the fans' initial expectations. The squad that had started off full of optimism, had been cruelly hit by injuries which had forced Cox to continually make changes to the side. Key men like Hartley, together with defenders Tommy Naylor, Ralph Miller and Chris Foote had all suffered enforced spells on the sidelines, 'On occasions, the crowd were at least hostile, even before the game had started! Injuries meant our defence had remained unsettled all season and our problems stemmed from the fact we simply conceded too many goals as a result. Freddie did everything he could to patch up the side and was very supportive of the players. We couldn't have asked anything more of him.'

England under-23 international goalkeeper Roger Jones became the next player to fall victim to the injury curse, when he sustained a broken bone in his left hand during training and as a result was forced to miss five games during November. In the first of these his deputy, Kieron Baker, endured a difficult afternoon as the team went down 3-0 at Leyton Orient, but then remarkably, the team remained unbeaten in the league for the rest of the month, picking up four consecutive victories along the way.

MacDougall struck a match-winning penalty against Gillingham at Dean Court and was on the scoresheet again four days later, when he hit the third goal in a convincing 3-1 home victory against Doncaster as well as combining with East to set up a goal for skipper Jimmy White, normally a defender, but who was forced to play up front in place of the injured Hold. The Cherries' purple patch also brought their first away win in 12 weeks, with left-winger Meredith grabbing the all-important goal at Plymouth. Importantly, some stability appeared to have been restored and with the gradual easing of the injury problems, Cox had been able to field a more settled team.

There was no joy for Bournemouth in the FA Cup though, as they went out of the competition in a first round replay at Third Division leaders Luton in mid-November. Included in the Hatters side in both cup matches was Ted's future rival for the title of 'Supermac', Malcolm Macdonald. Ted recalls, 'There was never any rivalry between us – it was a press thing and nothing to do with us. We became friends and I appeared on his television show in Newcastle when I stayed up there one weekend while I was with Norwich. Malcolm actually started as a full-back at Luton. He was a different type of player to me, he was quick and he scored different types of goals to me, we were two different animals. He was a bit over the top at times but he was a great character and did very, very well, and I respect him for that. I respect anyone who can score goals because it's not that easy.'

Despite another goal from MacDougall, the Cherries' winning sequence in the league came to a halt at high-flying Torquay, although they held on for a creditable 2-2 draw, which left them 18th in the table. Interestingly, the Torquay side that day included five players who would later become Ted's team-mates at Bournemouth under the management of John Bond, another former Gulls favourite, namely

John Benson, Bill Kitchener, Tony Scott, Micky Cave and Tommy Mitchinson

After going seven games without defeat, the Cherries ended 1969 with a three-goal loss at Rotherham, and unfortunately the New Year did not start well. It was not only on the pitch that Bournemouth were finding it hard going. Having failed to pay their way through the turnstiles for the past 30 years, the club's overheads were getting bigger all the time and they were now suffering something of a cash-crisis. Reportedly losing around £1,000 a week and with average attendances lower than expected, any reasonable bid for almost any player was likely to be accepted.

The club's most valuable playing asset was goalkeeper Jones and he made his last appearance for the Cherries in a 2-1 defeat at Reading before being sold to Blackburn for £30,000 the following week. Although the club was undoubtedly strapped for cash, it seemed a ludicrously low fee at the time for a player of such potential. Cox was heartbroken having discovered and developed Jones to now have to sell him, but he was at pains to point out to supporters that sheer economics left the club with little choice.

The sale brought further criticism from supporters and the timing of Jones's departure subsequently proved to have disastrous consequences. Having accepted Northampton Town's £5,000 offer for reserve goalkeeper Kim Book earlier in the season, it left the club without adequate cover for a key position at a crucial stage of the season and with third choice Baker injured, 17-year-old England youth international Ron Tilsed stepped into the breach at Halifax but he could do little to prevent a 4-1 defeat. Worse was to follow in the next game against Bradford City, where Bournemouth crashed to their heaviest defeat for 12 years as they were thrashed 8-1 at Valley Parade. Tilsed had been injured in a collision with City striker Bobby Ham as the sixth goal was scored just before half-time and was unable to continue after the break, leaving defender David Stocks to take over in goal. Ted remembers, 'Roger Jones was a top goalkeeper and when he left there just wasn't proper cover. Ron Tilsed was only a kid, but nonetheless he blamed everyone else for all the goals he conceded! I remember Bobby Ham got four goals that day. That game scarred me, I couldn't believe it.'

Despite the debacle at Bradford, the team immediately bounced back to winning ways with two successive victories, the first against mid-table Rochdale at Spotland, coming just two days later. Both matches were decided by single goals from MacDougall while Baker, fit again, could claim credit for two clean sheets. The second victory, at home to promotion-chasing Southport, saw Ted rise high at the far post to head a perfect cross from right-back Terry Gulliver firmly into the visitors' net. It was his 16th goal of the season in all competitions.

Now playing regularly up front with East, the latter having turned down a move to Colchester, MacDougall was showing the consistency and opportunism Cox had expected and having settled in, he was proving to be a marksman of menace. In the next match against Fulham, the pair were joined in attack by the hard-running 23-year-old former Reading and Spurs forward John Sainty.

A long-term target of Cox, the club somehow managed to raise the £4,000 fee needed to bring Sainty to Dean Court. The match at Craven Cottage saw Ted score possibly his best goal of the season and gain the Cherries a valuable point from a 1-1 draw. Climbing early to meet Meredith's corner, he rose high above the Fulham defence and made perfect contact with the ball to send it powerfully into the back of the net.

The second hat-trick of MacDougall's career came in the next match at home to Barnsley, in which Bournemouth ran out 3-1 winners. It took his season's tally of league goals to 18, exactly half of those scored by the team in total, and in the process completed his half-century of Football League goals in less than three seasons. After only three minutes, a shot from East was spilled on the six-yard line and Ted was on hand to slam the ball home. His second followed before half-time, Tony Powell's free kick being headed on by Stocks and East, then into the net by MacDougall. Then, after 70 minutes, Bournemouth were awarded a penalty and to the delight of the crowd, Ted strode up to complete his hat-trick and re-affirm his place among the division's top goalscorers.

MacDougall's scoring spree was hailed in the press as 'One Man's War Against Relegation'. It had certainly hoisted the Cherries to what seemed a position of comparative safety, comfortably clear of the relegation zone, but although he had scored all his side's goals in their last four games, he could not have done so without help from the rest of the side, 'I was lucky enough to get the goals, but I couldn't have done it on my own. Football is always a team game and the rest of the lads gave me all the support I needed. Ray Bumstead, Ralph Miller, Terry Gulliver and Keith East in particular were all good players.'

Cox and his team had worked hard to tighten up their game and performances began to suggest that they were perhaps a far better team than their league position indicated. After that initial settling-in period, MacDougall was now doing the job for which he was signed and doing it exceptionally well. That he should be doing it in a season when the team had been struggling was a tribute to his ability, and by now the supporters were very much on his side, despite fears that he may be the next player sold to balance the books. Inevitably scouts from other clubs had been alerted and continued to check on his progress, however, the presence of other clubs was not something that Ted allowed to affect his game, 'Originally, when I was at York and knew someone was watching me, I tried to impress them. It never worked, so after that I just got on with the job of scoring.'

After MacDougall scored in a fifth consecutive game against Bristol Rovers, albeit in a 5-2 defeat at Eastville, he drew comparisons with some of Bournemouth's most successful goalscorers of recent years. The goal against Rovers took him past the 18-goal mark established by Ken Hodgson in 1964/65 and put him in pursuit of the 28 league goals scored by Denis Coughlin a year earlier. More optimistic supporters were even beginning to wonder if Ted could eclipse that record haul of Ronnie Eyre – but that would have to wait until the following season.

Unfortunately, everything seemed to fall apart in mid-February. MacDougall now found himself a marked man and as a result was unable to find the net with the same regularity, triggering an agonising sequence of eight games without a win, which plunged Bournemouth back into serious danger of relegation. They managed just four more goals during this spell, with Ted grabbing what would prove to be his last two of the season, the first in a 3-1 defeat by Plymouth and the other a penalty in a 2-2 draw at home to Walsall. Another home draw at the end of the month, this time against Bradford City, left the Cherries just five places off the bottom of the table with only six games remaining, before wins at Stockport and against Bury at Dean Court raised hopes of avoiding the drop.

They were briefly enough to lift Bournemouth up to 19th, three points clear of the relegation zone, but although East brought his goal tally to four in three games when he was on target against Doncaster at Belle Vue, defeat there and in the following match at Shrewsbury put the Cherries back into serious difficulties.

Meanwhile off the pitch, Harold Walker had acquired sufficient shares in the club to enable him to take over as chairman from Doug Hayward, who was forced to step aside. The new chairman, whose business interests had made him a millionaire, was a lifelong fan of the club and had been appointed to the board two years earlier. He believed the club was in need of immediate restructuring and quickly set about his plans to turn it into a successful operation, but unfortunately his move came too late to save the Cherries from impending relegation.

A goal from Hartley was enough to bring a 1-0 victory at home to Mansfield, before the team travelled to relegation rivals Gillingham for their last game of the season, where they fought out a goalless draw. As a result, they found themselves lying precariously just outside the relegation zone, two points above Gillingham and one place above the bottom four. A late-season rally by the Kent club now seriously threatened to end Bournemouth's 46-year stay in the Third Division and crucially the Gills, with a better goal average, still had one fixture left to play. Remarkably, a few days later they won their final game away to champions Orient, relegating the Cherries for the first time in the club's history.

Relegation came as a terrible disappointment to all those associated with the club, says Ted, 'The players were devastated. At the time I thought I was some kind of a jinx. I'd done fairly well personally in each of the last three seasons, but each time the club I played for never seemed to make it. I was pleased I had managed to score goals regularly in the Third Division, but after one season, I was now back where I started. And, quite frankly, I was a bit choked about it all.'

Despite the loss of their Third Division status, MacDougall had actually provided Bournemouth with the kind of goal-getter they had missed for some time. He had become the first Cherries player to top 20 goals in a season since 1963/64 despite scoring only twice in the last 13 games. His final tally of 21 Football League goals, seven behind Macdonald, the division's leading scorer, was a remarkable achievement in a struggling side. Two further goals in the League Cup added to the belief that had the club had a more successful season, he might well have topped 30 mark.

Despite his modesty, for much of the campaign Ted was virtually a one-man strike force and, although East came along with some highly important goals late in the season, the side lacked depth to its scoring strength. Injuries too had caused great disruption to the side at vital stages of the season, particularly in defence where 71 goals had been conceded in league games alone.

Undoubtedly, MacDougall's goalscoring prowess, together with the emergence of a number of young players, many of whom now had valuable league experience, left Cox hopeful of a quick return to the Third Division. However, the question everyone was asking at Dean Court, was whether he would be given the opportunity to achieve it?

5

The Name's Bond, John Bond

THE future of Freddie Cox was quickly resolved as Harold Walker had already made up his mind to dispense with the manager's services, even before his team were relegated by courtesy of Gillingham. It was made public the following week and the search began for a new manager, someone able to feed the chairman's ambitious plans for the club, 'Freddie Cox, God bless him, he was a gentleman. It was such a shame, I really liked him, he was terrific to me during my time at Bournemouth.'

The search didn't last long and on 1 June 1970, 37-year-old John Bond was unveiled as the new manager of Bournemouth and Boscombe Athletic, having signed a five-year contract. Bond, a graduate of the West Ham United academy, had played nearly 400 league games during 17 illustrious years for the Hammers, in which time he helped them gain promotion from the Second Division in 1958 and won the FA Cup in 1964. He then played briefly for Torquay United, where he polished up his training for management by picking up tips from manager Frank O'Farrell, before gaining his first coaching appointment at Gillingham, the club he had ironically helped to relegate the Cherries the previous season.

Walker had attended the match at Leyton Orient which had sent the Cherries down, having already been impressed by the growing reputation of Gillingham's young coach. Bond had been interviewed for the assistant manager's position at Plymouth Argyle and was almost at the point of accepting when Walker contacted him to quickly arrange a meeting. The chairman found Bond to be a flamboyant man, someone who would have no fear in being courted by the media and exactly the person he needed to help him revitalise the club and change its sleepy image. He wasted no time in offering Bond the manager's job and they set off to find a formula that would bring instant success then, in the longer term, hopefully lead the club on in its quest to achieve previously unfulfilled ambitions. One of the first things Bond did was change the club's playing kit, dispensing with the famous cherry red shirts in favour of the famous red and black stripes of AC Milan.

Bond was delighted to join what he considered to be a fine club with great potential. His arrival, though, was greeted with a mixture of hope, apathy and even some resentment among the club's supporters. Cox, who had been seen as a failure, had also come to Dean Court via Gillingham and to some this was seen as a bad omen. But Bond, backed to the hilt by Walker, gradually transformed the club and made unhappy and dispirited players believe in themselves, as Ted recalls, 'John Bond came in with lots of new ideas but I didn't know quite what to make of him at first. In one of our early practice games he told me he wanted me to play on the right wing and to make diagonal runs. Now I had never played on the right wing and I didn't know what a diagonal run was! I believed that by this stage of my career, I had worked out the strengths of my game and they were all about getting into the penalty box and scoring goals.

'Needless to say it didn't work, I was taken off at half-time and John bombed into me telling me what I should be doing. I told him I hadn't a clue what he was talking about. I was a goalscorer, that's all I knew. Anyway I believed John was going to get rid of me because he thought I was trouble and too much for him to deal with as a new manager, but he turned out to be brilliant and soon found out how to handle me.'

Walker appointed the experienced former Ipswich Town chief scout Reg Tyrell as assistant manager, while Bond enlisted his former West Ham and Torquay team-mate Ken Brown as the Cherries' new trainer-coach. Tyrell had unearthed a wealth of young talent during his seven years at Portman Road, while Brown had become a close friend of Bond's during their 16 seasons as team-mates. Their aim was to provide the type of football that would win over the supporters as well as win matches. Bond later admitted that he had not been immediately impressed by MacDougall and had someone offered £15,000 for him, he would probably have accepted. However, he introduced modern coaching techniques aimed at developing teamwork, and these were to have a marked effect on a number of players, and most notably upon Ted. The sessions concentrated on getting the players thinking for themselves and encouraged an exchange of ideas on tactics with everyone invited to say his piece.

Bond quickly entered the transfer market and for his first two signings, he went back to two of his old clubs, taking defender Keith Miller from West Ham for £10,000 and outside-left Tony Scott from Torquay for a give-away £4,000. Scott, another former team-mate of Bond at both clubs, would prove to be an inspired signing and become the route of supply that MacDougall needed. In addition, experienced goalkeeper Fred Davies was signed from Cardiff City and the 30-year-old long-serving Reading forward Dennis Allen also joined him at Dean Court. Departures included Keith East, who joined Northampton Town, 'They all proved to be good signings for the club. Scotty in particular became invaluable to me, while Fred Davies was a steadying presence in goal and his experience was a great asset. Keith Miller took over from David Stocks as skipper a couple of months into the season and he played a real captain's role. Keith drove us on and became a tremendous influence on the team. He married his fiancée, Elizabeth, a short while after he moved down and they lived close to Joan and I at West Moors.'

Bond quickly created a great air of optimism around Dean Court as the season began, with a crowd of over 12,000 having already attended a pre-season friendly against West Ham, but early confidence received a jolt when, despite the presence of all four new signings, the Cherries suffered an opening day defeat at Aldershot. The reshaped Bournemouth side lined up for their first Fourth Division game with a 4-3-3 formation with Fred Davies in goal, Terry Gulliver and David Stocks as full-backs, Tony Powell and Keith Miller in the centre of defence, Dennis Allen, Trevor Hartley and John Meredith operating in midfield, with John Sainty and MacDougall up front, and Tony Scott operating wide on the left wing. Eddie Rowles was named as substitute.

Optimism was soon restored as the side won their next seven matches and MacDougall started finding the net. The cobwebs that had begun to settle around the club over the years were being blown away as the team's almost cavalier approach to matches was gaining the required results and they quickly emerged as serious promotion contenders. Ted had opened his account for the season with both goals in a 2-0 win at Newport County, a match which he regarded as a major turning point in his career, 'When Tony Scott came to the club we started working hard on crosses to the near post. John Bond came over to me at half-time and explained that I was making plenty of runs to the far post but not coming back into the space I had created at the near post. People understand this movement now, but in 1970 they didn't and it was quite revolutionary really. It seemed to make sense and I knew it was playing to the strength of my game, which was always to attack the ball. It sounds pretty basic but a lot of people didn't attack the ball, instead they waited for it to come to them.

'John didn't give me a bollocking, instead he told me I was doing great, but having created the space at the near post, why not come back into it? So I did, Scotty was playing balls in with the outside of his foot, and of course, I scored. It was like a light suddenly coming on, you know. Instead of just scoring 20 goals a season and not realising exactly how, if you know what you are doing then anyone scoring 20 is capable of getting 30. I know because that's exactly what happened to me.'

MacDougall followed that up with another goal against Peterborough and two against Stockport at Dean Court, in his 50th league game for the Cherries. The first strike came from the penalty spot but the second was more distinctive of Ted's play, his header flicking a high cross from Dennis Longhorn into the net.

Colchester felt the full force of 'Supermac' in mid-September, when he struck all four goals in Bournemouth's 4-1 win and in doing so he became the first Cherries player to score four goals in a game for 20 years. To the acclaim of the biggest league crowd at Dean Court so far that season, 7,769, the goals brought Ted's tally to eight in seven league matches. The 26th-minute effort which gave Bournemouth the lead was typical of MacDougall's ability to turn a half-chance into a goal. Colchester goalkeeper Graham Smith seemed in no trouble as he attempted a clearance despite a challenge from Allen, but the pressure was sufficient for Smith to drop the ball. That was enough for Ted, who moved in smartly and had the ball in the back of the net before the unfortunate goalkeeper had any chance of recovering. Two of MacDougall's other goals came from crosses by Scott, one a diving header, while the other was set up by a perfect pass from Stocks.

The Cherries' style of play was totally different from that of the previous season and early indications were that it was going to be successful. Under Cox, Bournemouth had at times displayed a rather negative outlook, but under Bond there was a far greater attacking style. The players had the belief that if the opposition scored three, then they could score four, and with MacDougall in this kind of form, there was a good chance they would.

The Cherries' winning sequence came to a halt at York, where Bond had the opportunity to have a close look at City's Phil Boyer, and it was MacDougall's former team-mate who put the home side ahead just before half-time. Ted was unable to mark his return to Bootham Crescent with a goal, although he did lay on a perfect cross for Rowles to land an equaliser in the second half. Bournemouth surprisingly lost the next game at home to Scunthorpe United, but then comfortably beat league newcomers Cambridge United 3-0 at Dean Court. Two classic MacDougall headers converted crosses from Scott and Allen respectively, with Hold also on the scoresheet in his first game of the season. It was enough to send the Cherries to the top of the table, ahead of Notts County on goal difference.

A goal in each of the next five games took MacDougall's total to 16 by the end of October, during which time he became the Football League's leading marksman, just ahead of Luton's Malcolm Macdonald. Ted's game was continuing to benefit greatly from both the new coaching techniques introduced by Bond and the stream of pinpoint crosses being delivered into the penalty area match after match by wingers Allen and Scott.

Meanwhile, Bond strengthened his squad once more by signing defender John Benson from Torquay for a club record fee of £15,000. Another former playing colleague of Bond's at Plainmoor, the former Manchester City player had no hesitation in leaving a Third Division club to join a side in a lower division because of his great respect for the manager, and the tremendous potential he felt existed at Dean Court, as Ted looks back, '"Benno" became another terrific influence on the rest of the side and he was one of those players who desperately wanted to do well for the club, and for himself.'

Bond then turned his attention to the forward line and having been impressed by Boyer's performance against Bournemouth a few weeks earlier, he made York a bid of £15,000 in an effort to sign him. The offer followed strong recommendation from MacDougall, 'I was certainly one of those who kept on to "Bondy" to sign "Charlie", I knew what a wonderful player he was then and I knew he could go on to become an even better one. That's why I recommended him to the boss on a number of occasions.'

While the Cherries were the first club to make a bid, Blackpool, Middlesbrough and Luton were also known to be watching Boyer's progress however, and the Yorkshire club opted to decline Bond's offer.

At the start of the season, the manager had introduced a concept of training known as the Coverdale System, much of which was centred on psychology and was extremely forward-thinking for the time. The radical training scheme had been brought to Harold Walker's attention by Ralph Coverdale, a business consultant, whose idea was to encourage people to look at their own approach to solving problems. It included exercises that did not appear to have much to do with football, such as writing essays, and building with toy bricks, but Bond firmly believed that the disciplines taught players a lot about their own strengths and also those of others around them.

Beyond this he actively encouraged the players to speak freely at meetings and also to play a full part in the club's public relations efforts. Essentially, Bond wanted the players to feel part of the town and the people of Bournemouth to feel part of the club. The initiatives did much to help Ted overcome his initial shyness, 'All the things John introduced were welcomed by the players and we tried hard to give him the encouragement that any new boss needs. I was a bit of an introvert at the time and could be a bit short-tempered with people, but gradually John brought me out of my shell.'

Team spirit inevitably grew stronger and Bond also took the opportunity to take his players to the much-acclaimed Lilleshall Sports Centre to continue the Coverdale training, together with a week's concentrated coaching. They were accompanied by a film crew from the BBC TV current affairs programme *Panorama*, which was to feature an item about the new training methods. It was all helping to lift the profile of the club of course, although it failed to prevent a single-goal defeat at Darlington upon the conclusion of their stay in Shropshire.

The Cherries quickly returned to winning ways by beating Southport and Hartlepool, with Ted netting the winner at Haig Avenue and grabbing the team's third goal against the Pools at Dean Court. It was another goal which stemmed from a cross by Scott, after Ted had twice combined well with Rowles, to enable the former youth team prodigy to claim two goals himself.

Bournemouth had been knocked out of the League Cup by Torquay in a first round replay back in August, so they hoped for rather more success when the FA Cup came around in November. However, they were drawn away at Isthmian League part-timers Oxford City in the first round and struggled to find any fluency in an under-par performance, where they were frequently beaten to the ball by their opponents and created few scoring opportunities. Bond was somewhat relieved when MacDougall came to Bournemouth's rescue with an equaliser four minutes from the end of the game, his late header ensuring the teams would meet again at Dean Court the following Wednesday.

Just 1,600 spectators had seen the first match at the White House ground but the replay eventually captured the attention of a much greater audience and created headlines in the national press. Having earned the Cherries a reprieve, Ted celebrated with a personal six-goal haul in their 8-1 win, to create a new club FA Cup scoring record. This match was all about MacDougall. His scoring flair lit up the night and brought about a procession of goals against brave, but outclassed opponents. Ted was magnificent and poor Alan Goucher, the City defender who had marshalled him well in the first game, was left gasping. Not only did MacDougall's six goals establish a new record for the club, it took his total for the season to an amazing 25.

The goals that night came from three headers, as well as three shots – one prodded low inside the post, another rocketed into the roof of the net and a left-footer perfectly placed into the far corner. Ted started the demolition of City as early as the seventh minute, and scored five in the second half in the space of 35 minutes. Bournemouth's other goals by Longhorn and Rowles were almost incidental in a game that was dominated by one man. Afterwards City manager Ron Humpson remarked that without MacDougall, his side may have made a reasonable game of it. He was the latest in a growing list of managers who were left wondering how to deal with a player of Ted's ability in front of goal.

MacDougall's knack for scoring with such regularity inevitably began to attract the attention of a number of bigger clubs. Goals have always spoken for themselves in football, and Ted quickly became one of the hottest properties in the English game with scouts being despatched to Dean Court or wherever the Cherries were in action. Bond knew that if they so desired, Bournemouth could quickly raise a considerable sum by putting the striker up for sale together with an emerging defender, 22-year-old Tony Powell, and highly talented teenagers David Jones and Eddie Rowles. But with the chairman's financial backing, the club was no longer forced to sell and Bond wanted his players to achieve success at Dean Court. Despite admitting he would have taken as little as £15,000 for MacDougall when he first arrived at the club, by now even a £50,000 bid would not have interested him. Ted had quickly become an integral part of the long-term success Bond was trying to achieve and there was every indication that he would go on to make an even bigger impact, 'I was quite happy at Bournemouth, I was enjoying my football more than I had ever done before and didn't really think about a change of clubs. The prospect of being a key player in a successful side appealed to me. I'd had two seasons at York and the club had to seek re-election to the league at the end of both these, then the Cherries had been relegated in my first season here. I thought it would be quite nice to be in a successful side for a change!'

The team travelled to Meadow Lane in early December, only to suffer a 2-1 defeat against their big promotion rivals Notts County in front of a crowd of over 11,000. The manager was critical of County's tough tactics afterwards, following a match that saw MacDougall head home his 26th goal of the season and the Cherries debut of 24-year-old former Gillingham full-back Mel Machin, who Bond had swooped to sign from his previous club in a £9,000 deal. Always keeping a keen eye on the transfer market, the manager now had the strong foundation he wanted in defence to launch a further assault up the table, 'Mel reckoned that, when he came to Dean Court, he had lost a bit of confidence. But I had never seen a full-back with as much ability on the ball as him.'

In the same week that Machin arrived, Bond made a second approach to York regarding Boyer and increased his offer to £20,000. City were among the promotion contenders themselves and their manager Tom Johnston was naturally reluctant to part with someone of Boyer's ability at this stage of the season, so for the moment the player remained at York. Meanwhile, Manchester City were the first of a number of leading clubs to express an interest in signing MacDougall, although no firm offer was ever received.

While negotiations continued with York, the Cherries suffered two further defeats – the first an embarrassing FA Cup exit at home to famed non-league giant-killers Yeovil Town. After his six-goal haul against Oxford City in the first round, neither MacDougall nor any of his team-mates could muster even a solitary goal against the Southern League side. Lacking adequate support, Ted was strangely subdued and seldom looked likely to add to his scoring tally, 'John Bond went spare after the game and the following Monday he took us down to Bournemouth Pier. I thought he was going to throw us off, which wouldn't have been good for me because I can't swim! But instead he made us run to Sandbanks, about four miles along the coast, and up and down the groynes on the beach. That was one of my least favourite memories of the FA Cup.'

The defeat came as a blow but the cup exit only served to make everyone even more determined to gain the main objective of promotion. Still looking to improve the quality of supply to MacDougall, West Ham winger Harry Redknapp, another ex-team-mate of Bond, travelled down to Bournemouth for talks with the Cherries manager after the club had made a £32,000 bid for his services. However, Redknapp was not keen to drop down to the Fourth Division and with First Division clubs like Coventry and Tottenham also showing an interest, he rejected the move.

When the FA Cup exit was followed by another single-goal defeat at Grimsby, Bond knew he had to act quickly to strengthen his hand and after further negotiations, York finally accepted Bournemouth's offer of £20,000 for Boyer. The player came to Dean Court after having scored 34 goals in 126 league games for City, including 14 that season. His arrival as the club's latest most expensive player did not seem to trouble him, and the fact that Ted was already at the club played an important part in making up his mind to sign for the Cherries, 'We had met up after the match at Bootham Crescent earlier in the season and I told him what a good club Bournemouth was and how ambitious they were. Naturally I was delighted when he decided to sign.'

The transfer fee further emphasised the chairman's determination to get Bournemouth out of the Fourth Division as quickly as possible. It brought the club's spending for the season to around £80,000, a considerable amount for a Fourth Division club in 1970, with little player movement out to balance the books. It was no surprise therefore, when Walker launched a new share issue in an attempt to try and bring further investment into the club. Meanwhile, following the postponement of the Boxing Day match against Exeter City, the Cherries lost their place in the top four promotion bracket and Boyer's debut had to wait until Bournemouth travelled to face Barrow early in the New Year, 'Before the Barrow game we were staying up in Blackpool and the boss called me in to see him. After the number of goals I had scored by this time, John said that he had expected me to be knocking his door down asking for a pay rise. I was still on £28 a week and I knew some of the other lads were on £35, but it didn't bother me because it wasn't just about the money. Anyway John asked if I would like to sign a new contract at £35 a week, with an additional £2,000 if I stayed until the end of the season. At this time in my life, if I had £200 in the bank then I had a lot of money, so I asked him, "Which wall do you want me to run through to sign it?"'

The Cherries won 2-1 at Holker Street thanks to two MacDougall penalties, ending a run of four games without a victory. The victory saw the side halfway towards their season's objective of 60 points, a little short of what Bond had originally hoped to have achieved by this stage, but with the MacDougall–Boyer partnership re-established the Cherries went unbeaten in the next seven games. In the first of these, a hard-fought 1-1 draw at Scunthorpe, a young Kevin Keegan lined up against the Cherries but despite proving a handful throughout, there were no goals for the future England captain on this occasion, although Bournemouth were grateful to Rowles, who headed home Sainty's cross to grab a point 15 minutes from time, 'Eddie Rowles had a lot of ability, he just needed to believe in himself a bit, while nobody worked harder than John Sainty to make himself a good player. John switched from being a striker to a midfield role and it gave him a fresh lease of life and more confidence in his own ability.'

A five-goal demolition of fellow promotion contenders Oldham marked the home debuts of Machin and Boyer, the latter celebrating the occasion in style by scoring two of Bournemouth's goals. MacDougall scored another, Rowles got the other two and the supporters went home thrilled by the quality of the attacking play they had witnessed. More was to follow, first when MacDougall was twice on target and Boyer once as Northampton were put to the sword on the south coast, then Ted struck two more goals as Exeter left Dean Court pointless. The attacking style of play was reaping its reward, and alongside it home attendances were steadily increasing and the visit of the Grecians attracted a crowd in excess of 9,000, the highest of the season so far. West Ham manager Ron Greenwood, looking to add extra striking power to his First Division side, was among that number and after chatting to Bond afterwards, must have left the ground impressed with what he had seen.

MacDougall had taken his tally to 33 goals in 32 matches in all competitions, out of a team total of 51. He still believes that much of the credit for this was down to the manager, 'Up until I met John I'd always been just a far-post player, a bit greedy perhaps, looking for goals. Suddenly now everything we practised seemed to come off, and it was all about playing me in. I revelled in it and I loved all the attention. John did wonders for everyone's confidence and made every player think he was really someone. Each day we learnt, we didn't just train. That's why so many of us became better players. We were all going out with the feeling that the team would score goals – and win!'

MacDougall's finishing power was again a key factor in a six-goal thriller at Crewe, where he was twice on target after Boyer had originally put the Cherries in front. The first goal was a header from a Scott cross while his second came when he pounced upon a poor back pass to put Bournemouth briefly 3-2 in front. On this occasion though, the Cherries had to be content with a point as a certain Stan Bowles popped up ten minutes from time to volley the Alex level. MacDougall was certainly reaping the benefits of Scott's regular supply of accurate, early crosses. The 29-year-old winger was encouraged to play his natural game and in doing so, it meant he was able to provide many openings for MacDougall to strike, 'Tony Scott always gave me great service from the wing which helped to provide a number of my goals. Nobody appreciated him more than I did. Unfortunately he suffered with injuries throughout his career but on his day he could be unstoppable. I certainly missed him when he was not in the team.'

Ted's two goals at Crewe brought his league total to 28, within four of Fred Eyre's club record, and strengthened his position as the country's top goal-getter. For the past two seasons the top scorer in the league had finished with 27 goals, with Albert Kinsey of Wrexham on this mark in 1969/70 and Tottenham's Jimmy Greaves reaching the same number in 1968/69. Amazingly, MacDougall had already beaten this figure with 18 games of the season remaining. Speculation concerning his future grew each week and Ted's name was by now linked in the press with a dozen First Division clubs, as well as a batch of Second Division outfits. His value in the transfer market was fast increasing too and there was a real prospect of the club receiving a six-figure fee if they should decide to cash in their most valuable asset – not that they had any intention of doing so.

Early in February came the much-awaited visit of top-of-the-table Notts County to second-placed Bournemouth. A fantastic crowd of 15,430 saw the two sides fight out a 1-1 draw in a game that had all the drama which could have been expected from such a contest. County maintained the tough approach that had been a feature of their game all season and again the Cherries had to endure some over-eager tackling from the outset. They lost full-back Stocks early on with a gashed forehead which needed several stitches and took some time to establish any sort of rhythm to their game.

County eventually went ahead on the hour through the former Liverpool, Coventry and Birmingham forward Tony Hateley but soon afterwards Boyer was brought down in the penalty area and MacDougall immediately stepped up to take the spot-kick. Goalkeeper Barry Watling dived the wrong way but managed to save the ball with his feet, the first occasion Ted had failed to score from a penalty for Bournemouth. Eight minutes from time though, Boyer dived bravely to head home a perfect cross from Benson to a tremendous roar from the home supporters. Bond was unhappy about the treatment MacDougall received from the County defenders, alleging that he had been spat at and then as he went for the ball, had two fingers pushed into his eye.

After the game Ted still could not see properly and it left more than a little bad feeling between the two clubs, 'I got beaten up a bit in this game but as I became more experienced I soon learned to look after myself, and if there was something between me and another player I would see that through while the game was going on. That can be a good thing but it can become a bad thing, however I made sure I protected myself.

'I picked a poor time to miss my first penalty but it never put me off taking another as I saw them as a great opportunity to score. The following week, I wanted to practise penalties after everyone had finished training but to do it properly, I had to have someone go in goal so I persuaded our groundsman, John Harriss to stand there while I thumped the ball either side of him into the back of the net.'

The extra practice paid off as in the following match, a 3-2 victory at Northampton, MacDougall gave the Cherries the lead from the spot, then scored the 100th league goal of his career shortly afterwards with a glancing header low into the far corner of the Cobblers' net. Boyer added the third early in the second half before the home side rallied with two goals in the last 25 minutes. Arsenal had now become the latest club to show an interest in Ted and sent a scout along to watch him at Northampton, while another interested observer was Leicester manager Frank O'Farrell, who had renewed his earlier interest.

However, O'Farrell was soon informed by his former protégé Bond that the striker would be staying to help Bournemouth's bid for promotion and, to protect their asset, the club quickly insured him against serious injury to the tune of £85,000, the equivalent of more than £1m today.

The team's unbeaten run came to an end when Southport surprisingly gained a 1-0 victory at Dean Court. But the Cherries immediately bounced back with victories over Lincoln and Chester. Ted equalled Ronnie Eyre's tally of 32 league goals in a season by converting a penalty at Sincil Bank and then climbing high to head home a Scott corner against visiting Chester. Earlier in the match he had provided a pass to lay on a fourth-minute goal for Boyer and later completed the passing movement which enabled his strike partner to score his second and Bournemouth's third. The scoring partnership of MacDougall and Boyer was again top of the bill, 'You couldn't get more opposite characters than me and Charlie, we were the odd couple but we just complemented each other perfectly. More often than not Charlie did all the running for me, all the work, while I took all the glory. Mind you he got his share of goals though, and it got better and better once we learned to work in tandem. I used to look at him and nod my head or something, and he knew exactly what I was going to do and what he had to do.'

Ted was now just one goal short of Eyre's record of 40 goals in all competitions, 'I really wanted to beat this and I set myself a target of 50 for the season. If I could manage that I felt that I would have really achieved something.'

MacDougall continued to be the subject of increasing transfer talk but deadline day ended with him still a Bournemouth player. By now, even an offer of £100,000 would not tempt the club to sell and Bond did not believe that by keeping him at Dean Court, he was hampering MacDougall's progress at this stage of his career, 'John was quite correct, he was still helping me learn more about the game and improving my play. There were lots of rumours circulating about my future and newspapers linked my name with a number clubs. It was all very flattering, of course, and it was nice to think that they were showing this interest in me. But I was happy and content with Bournemouth at that time and the club obviously felt the same.'

To further strengthen the team as the transfer deadline approached, Bond went back to West Ham and took 20-year-old winger Pat Holland on loan for the remainder of the season, 'Pat made a slow start, but gradually settled to some good form, particularly in away games.'

In the meantime, MacDougall was crowned as the town's 'Sportsman of the Year' by readers of the *Bournemouth Times* but then failed to score for three games as the Cherries put in some disappointing performances. They lost to Workington and Hartlepool, and stumbled to a goalless draw with Barrow in a match played in a deluge of rain. Finally in the home game against Darlington, he scored the only goal of the game to equal Eyre's record, stabbing the ball home from close range following good work by Holland and Sainty. It proved enough to maintain Bournemouth's hold on second place in the league table.

The goal that gave MacDougall a new club record came on Friday 26 March, when he scored the opener in the Cherries' 1-1 draw at Stockport. On a wet night, Ted struck after 70 minutes with probably one of his best goals for the club. It certainly deserved a greater audience than the meagre gate of 1,732 at Edgeley Park and of these, only a handful of spectators at the Cheadle End got a close-up of what a superb goal it was. Having been thwarted on several near-post runs by County defenders, MacDougall asked Sainty to aim for the far post with a corner from the right. There he leapt and met the ball perfectly, his header screaming through the night air and into the County net before rebounding viciously back out off the stanchion. The power in the header left it hard to imagine how anyone could have even kicked the ball harder.

Unfortunately the evening ended in something of an anti-climax when Stockport grabbed an undeserved equaliser five minutes from time and it was not until 6am the following day that Ted got back home, where the local press were waiting to greet the club's new record goalscorer before he shared breakfast with Joan, 'I don't remember doing anything special to celebrate. We probably just went shopping! But, I do remember the board of directors later presented me with a silver tea set in recognition.'

Eyre went on to score 250 goals for Bournemouth and Cherries supporters were no doubt hoping MacDougall would remain at the club long enough to have a chance of beating that too. Going into the final run-in, he simply could not stop scoring and with 8,000 supporters turning out at Dean Court to salute him, he responded with two more goals against visitors Newport County. Both were directly laid on by the hard-working Boyer and lashed into the net by the deadly marksman's right foot. Ted's ability to score vital goals when the team was not at its best had again proved important, as costly defensive mistakes allowed second-bottom County to snatch a point at the death. Bond was worried that his side had now dropped vital points to the three bottom teams in the division in the space of three weeks but his concerns would soon be swept aside as the Cherries went on to gain promotion in style – losing just one of their remaining seven games.

First came a performance full of aggression that produced four goals to see off visitors Southend on Good Friday. This time MacDougall was overshadowed by Boyer, who scored two of the goals in a superb display of front-running and opportunism. Determined not to be left out though, Ted finally got his name on the scoresheet when he prodded the ball over the line following up a shot by Boyer ten minutes from time. The following day saw the Cherries draw a blank but still pick up a point at Exeter, before the club's leading marksman was on target again in a two-goal victory over Cambridge United, taking his league and cup tally for the season to within five of his 50-goal target.

Promotion finally came when challengers Chester lost at Exeter on a day when the Cherries didn't even kick a ball. They had fought out a draw at rain-sodden Colchester the night before, Ted's diving header ensuring they brought home the point that would eventually ensure they would be heading back up to the Third Division at the first attempt, 'Promotion came as quite a relief to me after what had happened in the previous three seasons. John had brought in all these new ideas, and very quickly the disappointment of the previous season was turned into a determination to hit back. We gave it a go from the start and he made us all better players, while Ken Brown's knowledge of the game and cheerful disposition was also very valuable. We knew we had full backing from everyone at the top and that it was up to us to get the club back up.

'For me personally, the manager had shown me ways that I could score even more goals and because I was not an enormously gifted player I had to understand about the 18-yard box, about angles and movements and stuff like that and understand how to score goals – and I got that through John.

'It was just a superb season as far as I was concerned. The goals kept coming all through the year and that was my line of business. Any striker who is able to score regularly can have no complaints. He's doing the job he is there to perform for the team's benefit and I was delighted that my goals helped Bournemouth achieve promotion. At certain times it had reached the point where if I didn't score it made the newspaper headlines. It was crazy but that's how it was! I thought I could score two or three goals every game and it all stemmed from confidence gained on the training ground. Everything was centred around me – the end product, forward play and things like that. It was fantastic.

'But of course I couldn't have done my job successfully without the rest of the side who gave me wonderful support throughout the season. I wasn't the best player, I just scored goals and goalscorers usually grab the headlines, but often the players who back you up do not always get the credit they deserve.'

Bournemouth still had two games left to play and in the first of these, at Peterborough, although Ted tucked home another penalty, they lost 3-1. However, their final game had a touch of irony for both MacDougall and Boyer, as York City, also ensured of a promotion place, were the visitors to Dean Court. Notts County had already clinched the Fourth Division championship but the Cherries would be guaranteed to finish as runners-up if they won their last match, while Ted needed three more goals to reach his 50-goal target.

Before kick-off there was a tremendous response from a crowd in excess of 12,000, when Ted was presented with the Jack Paterson Memorial Trophy as the Dean Court Supporters' Club Player of the Year. When the game got under way on a hard, bumpy pitch, play was scrappy in the early stages but as the first half progressed the visitors found themselves coming under increasing pressure and eventually the Cherries went ahead. In the 28th minute, after a handball offence in the York penalty area, MacDougall stepped up to strike home goal number 48 from the spot. Soon after, a mix-up in the City defence let Ted in again. This time he stretched out his right leg to stab the ball towards goal and much to the consternation of the defenders, the ball slowly trickled into the net. Scott added a third goal before the break and the match was over as a contest. The only question remaining was whether MacDougall could reach his half-century.

The second half was all-out attack from the Cherries with everyone doing their utmost to help Ted find the net once more. He came very close when a cross from Miller flicked off the inside of his heel in the closing minutes, only for City keeper Hillyard to pounce on it at the last second. Try as he might though, MacDougall could not find that elusive 50th goal, although he did play a part in setting up Boyer for Bournemouth's fourth as they romped home to victory. After the game, the Cherries' players and management left Dean Court on an open-top bus and headed off to celebrate the club's first promotion with their exuberant supporters, 'And don't forget the players from York City. Remember, their club hadn't arranged a celebration for them, so after the game they asked if they could come to ours!'

The celebrations did not end there however, as earlier in the year Bournemouth-based holiday tycoon Fred Pontin offered the Cherries an all-inclusive break if they should achieve promotion, and the team duly jetted off to Majorca in early May. Football was not altogether forgotten about though, as they still found time to play a friendly fixture against local side Manacor during their stay on the 'Holiday Isle'.

MacDougall's 42 league goals during the 1970/71 season had only been exceeded on four occasions in post-war football and equalled on just one occasion since. They came in a total of 81 goals scored by the team in all. Remarkably, considering the kind of attention and close marking he received from opposition defenders, Ted remained clear of serious injury and did not miss a single game throughout the season, 'I was the most successful scorer in the Football League by quite a distance, but if I'm honest, what I really would have loved to do was to break Dixie Dean's record and get over 60 in all competitions. I always loved scoring and, when the goals came, my confidence quickly grew and I became a better all-round player that season. After it ended I signed a new four-year contract which meant my wages rose to £100 per week. Bear in mind most First Division players were only on £50 to £60 then. It was incredible! But at the time the whole town was buzzing, if you haven't lived it you can't explain it. It seemed like every day there was national press and television down, something going on, stories to report, and we all revelled in it in fact! We couldn't wait for the next season to begin.'

6

Goal Crazy

DURING the summer of 1971, Bournemouth's football team had become the talk of the town and the name of Ted MacDougall had become synonymous with all that was good about it. Season ticket sales at Dean Court had trebled in 12 months and as supporters looked forward to the new season, John Bond signed a new five-year contract as manager, ending speculation that he would succeed Frank O'Farrell at Leicester City. O'Farrell had decided to take over the reins of Manchester United and the job at Filbert Street was reported to have been worth nearly twice the salary Bond was receiving at Dean Court, but the boss was keen to try and bring Bournemouth back-to-back promotions.

Defender Bill Kitchener and forward Micky Cave both arrived from Torquay for £15,000 fees, adding to the contingent that Bond had already assembled from his former club. In addition, midfielder Ian Davidson came from York in an exchange deal that took striker Eddie Rowles in the opposite direction. As the players headed off for a pre-season trip to Cornwall, they were offered a bonus of £800 a man to gain promotion to the Second Division, £250 up on their reward for promotion the previous season, and MacDougall shared the club's optimistic outlook for the season ahead, 'I set my personal target for the new season at 30 goals, but stated at the outset I would be happy to get 25. I believed that the determination, skill and team spirit which served us so well in the Fourth Division would enable the team to make

59

a challenge in the Third Division. I expected to receive tighter marking following my scoring success the previous season but was confident that, with more of the same assistance I had received from the other lads, I would continue to score goals.'

The Cherries were certainly not going into the Third Division to be a mid-table side. Bond set his team a 60-point target in the days of two points for a win and promised the team would continue to play the attractive way they had during the previous campaign. While he could not expect MacDougall to score as many goals at the higher level, his performance in a pre-season win against First Division Southampton suggested an exciting season lay ahead, 'It was a boost to my ego at the time to notch a couple of goals against Southampton. A player always wants to do well against opponents from a higher division even though it was only in a friendly match.'

Immediately before the opening league game, MacDougall received the Football League, Divisional Player of the Year award for his exploits during the previous season. The poll was conducted among league managers and Ted was the first Bournemouth player to have received such an honour. It set the tone for the afternoon ahead as the Cherries got off to a flying start with a 3-1 victory against Shrewsbury. All three new signings made their debuts for the club and inside the first half-hour Miller and Boyer had put Bournemouth ahead, then after a reply from the visitors, MacDougall scored the goal that the 11,000 home crowd had been expecting. It came 11 minutes from time, when Ted met Scott's cross with a perfect diving header.

A hard-earned draw at Bolton was followed by home wins over Rotherham and Blackburn which sent the Cherries to the top of the table. Against the Millers, MacDougall converted a cross by Cave to send his side on their way to another 3-1 victory, his powerful header from around eight yards out striking visiting goalkeeper Roy Tunks before bouncing off his legs and into the net. Three days later it was Cave's turn to score the only goal to claim the points against Rovers.

It was not just on the pitch that Ted was making his mark though, as off it he was now displaying all the style the early 1970s demanded – a chic perm-haired, flared-trousered image which looked every bit as smart as a men's fashion model! It was the perfect time for him to go into business with George and Megan Webb, and together they opened a sports shop in Christchurch Road, Boscombe. Ted MacDougall Sports was officially opened at the end of August, 'It was something I had been thinking about for a while, the football was going great but I wanted to develop an interest away from the game itself. George was a nice guy and his wife Megan was a lovely person. Our partnership worked very well and we went on to open five sports shops in the Bournemouth and Poole area, and at one time we also owned a toy shop and a drug store.'

The Cherries lost their top spot following a 1-0 defeat at Halifax and were then knocked out of the League Cup by Blackpool, although earlier in the competition they had come from a goal behind to beat fellow Second Division side Portsmouth at Dean Court, with MacDougall striking twice inside seven minutes. They returned to their best with a convincing 4-1 victory at home to Rochdale and having gone three games without scoring, MacDougall twice hit the woodwork with superb headers before finding the target with a third shortly before half-time. Five minutes earlier Boyer had given Bournemouth the lead, slotting home a fine pass from MacDougall, who later converted a penalty before completing his hat-trick with a telling shot from ten yards out. Despite receiving closer attention from defenders, the MacDougall/Boyer partnership was continuing to make its mark.

A brilliantly executed win at Wrexham sent the Cherries back to the top of the table, and although Eddie May kept Ted relatively quiet on this occasion, goals from midfielders Cave and Miller proved that the team could score from elsewhere when needed. A MacDougall penalty then ensured a victory against Chesterfield ahead of a clash with their old rivals Notts County at Meadow Lane. County were again among the early pacesetters and their initial success again owed much to the goals of Hateley. Against Bournemouth however, he was particularly well shackled by 19-year-old defender David Jones. At the opposite end MacDougall applied the finishing touch to Benson's goal-bound header to give the Cherries a half-time lead, although the match ended all square after Don Masson converted a second-half penalty for the hosts, 'I always believed David Jones was going to be a really good player and he was improving with every game he played. Unusually for a centre-half in those days he possessed tremendous balance and technique. It was such a shame he suffered badly with injuries later in his career.'

Bournemouth maintained their challenge throughout October, losing just once at Shrewsbury, where despite two goals from MacDougall, Alan Groves, the long-striding left-winger, set the home side alight with a spectacular performance which duly impressed John Bond – who signed him for the Cherries the following season. Ron Greenwood was a spectator at Gay Meadow, among a group of First and Second Division managers, fuelling more speculation that the Hammers boss was about to take MacDougall to Upton Park, with Harry Redknapp and Bobby Howe possibly travelling in the opposite direction. Greenwood had already rejected Bond's second offer in the region of £30,000 for Redknapp, while the Bournemouth manager had also shown an interest in Howe for some time.

Meanwhile, Ted continued to knock in the goals and a penalty in a 3-2 home win over Port Vale chalked up his 12th of the season, despite him not having felt his best in recent games, 'I remember suffering from a series of colds, stomach problems and niggling back trouble for a time. I also went a few games without scoring which always made me anxious but thankfully these spells usually didn't last for too long!'

A defining moment in Bournemouth's season came with the visit of Aston Villa in late October, when the Cherries completed a comprehensive 3-0 victory and confirmed their position as worthy Third Division leaders. 'Magnificent Boscombe Crush Villa' proclaimed the local *Sports Echo* after Villa were all but killed off in a 20-minute burst during which Boyer and MacDougall both hammered first-half goals, Ted heading home following another pinpoint cross from Scott.

Throughout the game Boyer was able to open up the Villa defence at will, and having supplied the cross for Ted to score earlier, Scott supplied another for Tony Powell to convert late in the second half and adequately reflect the Cherries' total dominance in the game. The crowd, 20,305, was almost double the previous home gate and those that may once have questioned the club's potential for promotion, were surely now left in little doubt.

MacDougall's goal against Villa brought his total to a phenomenal 63 since the beginning of the previous season, a scoring rate unmatched by any other contemporary striker. It had not gone unnoticed by Scotland manager Tommy Docherty, who had openly stated that he did not care in which division Ted played, as long as he could score a few goals for Scotland. Bond had already assured Docherty that he believed Ted was good enough to get goals in any class of football and the 'Doc' continued to look closely at the Cherries' leading scorer. The possibility of becoming the first Third Division player to be capped by Scotland excited MacDougall, 'I would have liked that yes, it would have been a great achievement for me while playing at that level and of course a great honour, as it still was when the call eventually came a few years later.'

To further enhance their promotion credentials, Bournemouth followed up their win against Villa with an emphatic victory at Mansfield. Playing with poise and authority, their five-goal flurry at Field Mill brought their season's total of league and cup goals to 32, the highest in any of the four divisions at the time, and kept them clear at the top. Boyer and Jones had given the Cherries a two-goal interval lead before MacDougall took over, smashing a 24-minute hat-trick. First he headed home a Scott cross, then minutes later he timed his movement to perfection to side-foot home a centre from full-back Kitchener. The third came after he had received the ball in midfield and with Boyer moving to the right to attract the attention of the home defence, he played the ball to Scott who was unmarked out on the left. MacDougall then raced fully 25 yards to meet the winger's cross and head powerfully downwards and into the net. It was a classic move which ended in a trademark MacDougall goal, 'Phil and I seemed to have an ability to anticipate what the other one was about to do. It was something unique. He loved going down the wing, although he was often the one who linked play in the centre. He had a great appetite for the game and a terrific ability and willingness to work and work, and he would run his socks off. He had to because more often than not he had to do my running as well! Actually we used to do sprints together in training and I was quicker than him, but 25 to 30 yards was like a marathon to me and he was much quicker over that distance!'

Coventry manager Noel Cantwell, a close friend of Bond, was among a posse of First Division representatives in attendance at Field Mill. However, it was not just MacDougall the scouts were watching, as Boyer too was also attracting an increasing amount of attention. Bond dismissed any transfer talk when interviewed by Fred Dinneage for ITV's *World of Sport* programme aboard the club's new luxury coach en route to Mansfield. He also spoke of the club's intention of challenging for a First Division place within five or six years and was backed up by Walker, who issued a statement reaffirming the club's ambition in the wake of growing transfer rumours regarding MacDougall. He made reference to unwelcome 'illegal approaches' made by other clubs but admitted that although the club wanted to keep their leading goalscorer, it would not stand in the way of any player whose interests demanded that he be allowed to move to a bigger club. In the meantime, the latest compliment paid to Ted's scoring ability came from new Manchester United manager Frank O'Farrell who, during a television interview, named him at this time as the game's most exciting player, 'We went from sports programmes to news programmes and were mentioned again on *Panorama*! Bournemouth was big and everybody knew who we were. We were getting similar crowds to Southampton down the road and they were in the First Division. It was electrifying to be part of the whole thing.'

To the frustration of many a disappointed manager, the only move Ted planned to make in November 1971, was to a new home in Ashley Drive at nearby Ringwood, 'The house cost me £20,000. It was situated in an acre of land and I bought it at the time as an investment for the day I retired!'

Back on the pitch, Torquay's visit to Dean Court was no doubt an opportunity to renew a number of old acquaintances, but the game was eventually settled by a fine solo run and finish by MacDougall. Two more goals followed at Bradford City to earn the Cherries a draw and leave them two points clear at the top, with 26 points from 17 games, as attention turned to the FA Cup.

It was Saturday 20 November 1971 when Bournemouth met Southern League Margate in the first round of the competition at Dean Court. By now already recognised as one of the most lethal marksmen in the business, Ted was about to enter the record books.

The two teams lined up as follows:

Bournemouth: Davies; Machin, Kitchener, Benson, Jones, Powell, Cave, Boyer, MacDougall, Miller, Scott. Substitute: De Garis.

Margate: Brodie; Yorath, Butterfield, Clayton, Paton, R. Wickens, Jarman, J. Wickens, Brown, Kearns, Baber. Substitute: Summers.

Ten years earlier, the Kent part-timers had produced an act of FA Cup giant-killing by toppling the Cherries on their own turf but their hopes of a repeat lasted just 90 seconds, the time it took for MacDougall to stab home the first of his nine goals as Bournemouth massacred them 11-0, the club's best FA Cup victory.

Ted's remarkable display of ruthless finishing shattered his own FA Cup record of six goals the previous season and the overall individual scoring record for the competition, which had stood since 1922 when St Albans amateur Billy Minter scored seven goals against Dulwich Hamlet in a game St Albans amazingly lost 8-7.

The Margate side included a number of players with Football League experience, the most notable being Eddie Clayton who had spent more than ten successful seasons with Tottenham during the 1960s, and Chic Brodie, a vastly experienced Scottish goalkeeper who had also seen service with Manchester City, Wolves, Aldershot, Gillingham, Northampton and Brentford. His league career had ended the previous year when he broke a kneecap in a collision with a dog that ran on to the pitch at Colchester.

Prior to the match, Margate manager Les Riggs made it clear that his side had no special plans to deal with MacDougall and gave former Southampton and Aldershot defender Dave Paton the unenviable job of marking him. Paton was optimistic that if he could hold Ted in check for the first 15 minutes of the match, it would give his side a chance. However, after the game the same player sat disconsolately in the visitors' dressing room shaking his head and wondering just what more he could have done to stop a player with MacDougall's goalscoring ability.

By half-time 'Supermac' had rattled in four of the Cherries' five goals with Cave nipping in for the other to shatter Margate's resistance. In the second half they were completely mesmerised by MacDougall and company as the score mounted. Machin struck his first goal for the club, then came four more goals from Ted, the eighth, a penalty, taking the score into double figures. A number of young fans rushed on to the pitch to celebrate with their hero, then as soon as the pitch was cleared, he scored again. MacDougall's ninth goal was his 28th of the season and brought up his century in two and a half years with the Cherries. It provided a fitting end to the game, much to the delight of the crowd of 12,000, 'They weren't all good goals, or the most satisfying of my career but it was always nice to see the ball hit the net. I had become a right greedy sod. Whenever I scored one, I wanted two; when I scored two, I wanted a hat-trick. Once I had completed my hat-trick I made up my mind to try and score a double hat-trick before half-time. It was a wet afternoon and the ball zipped quickly across the grass, it was perfect for forwards because defenders couldn't get tight to you and I know this sounds big-headed, but it was just one of those games when I felt every time that I got the ball I could score.

'I knew the story of "Ten-Goal Joe Payne" and wanted to emulate him. When the eighth went in against Margate, I thought, "Two more for the magic ten." It sounds silly I know, but I was disappointed with the nine because I wanted that ten. "Ten-Goal Ted MacDougall" has a great ring to it. Mind you, "Nine-Goal Ted MacDougall" isn't bad!

'I was still trying as hard when I scored the ninth as I was when I got the first. That's what I was there for. Everything went right that day and it was just one of those things. Chic Brodie told me afterwards that he was the unluckiest goalkeeper in the world. Apart from having his professional career ended by that dog, also while he was playing for Brentford, he had placed his cap by the goal post at Millwall one sunny afternoon, only to find a grenade inside it when he went to pick it up! Then more recently, a crossbar had fallen on his head!'

For the record MacDougall's goals came in the second, 20th, 27th, 43rd, 56th, 75th, 80th, 85th and 88th minutes. It was a performance unlikely to ever be repeated and the Bournemouth supporters on the popular South End terrace paid their own tribute by adapting the lyrics from the theme of the popular *Banana Splits* television show and sang out, 'One MacDougall, two MacDougall, three MacDougall, four. Five MacDougall scores the goals and so do many more!'

It emerged after the game that Riggs had light-heartedly asked Bond if he would take MacDougall off at half-time. Bond, not surprisingly, refused as he believed to have done so would have been disrespectful and suggest that he felt sorry for them. Instead, he praised his side afterwards for not easing up at any stage of the game.

With the Sunday papers screaming headlines of 'Supermac Hits Nine', Ted became a household name overnight, yet it took him some time to appreciate the impact his new record would make in English football circles, 'I didn't realise just how phenomenal it was at first. At the time I didn't think cup goals were all that important because what mattered was that we kept scoring them in the league, as promotion was our real target. Nobody knew it was a record of any description while we were playing, I certainly didn't think about it, funny that! I got four goals in the first half and five in the second but I was just disappointed that I didn't get the other two! Mickey Cave, a lovely guy who died so tragically in 1984, nicked that one in the first half, then when Mel Machin scored with a diving header, he was in a position I normally occupied, so I should have definitely had that one!

'People ask me if I got to keep the match ball but I didn't. I wasn't really interested in having mementos like that, besides the club probably needed it for the next game. Anyway, I went home afterwards and of course there was no internet or anything like that to check these things, then the telephone started to ring. It was the BBC saying did I know I had created a new record? I told them I hadn't realised that, thanked them for their call and didn't give it another thought at the time, because Joan and I were travelling up to London that evening with George and Megan Webb to attend a sports trade fair.

'We went into a restaurant in Central London to have dinner and left around 11pm. On the way to our hotel we bought copies of the early editions of the Sunday newspapers. Wow! There it was in thick black print – I couldn't believe it, I suddenly realised this seemed pretty big!

'When we went to the trade fair the next day the public address announcer kept going on about me and what had happened in the game that afternoon, and I'm meeting players like Martin Chivers and he's shaking my hand, and the press want to do an interview! Remember I was a Third Division player and I didn't appreciate the significance of all this publicity. Meanwhile there were press running all round the place trying to find me!

'For a few days afterwards I found it difficult to handle really, but Bondy was brilliant throughout and helped me enormously. It's hard to believe all this happened more than 40 years ago now. Whenever I tell the kids I coach today about the time I scored nine goals in the FA Cup – which I do with monotonous regularity – I tell them I was only eight years old at the time!

'The following Monday, John called me over at training and said he had received a call from Geoff Hurst, the former England international, who had his testimonial match at Upton Park on the Wednesday, and he would like me to play. I asked John who else was playing and he told me I would be part of a European XI together with the likes of Eusebio, Simoes, Uwe Seeler, Jimmy Johnstone, Tommy Gemmell, Willi Shulz, Jimmy Greaves, Dave Mackay – top players I had only seen on television. Again I thought, "Wow!" These were massive players and I was just a kid from the Third Division! We were to assemble at the Hilton Hotel in Park Lane, London, so I drove there after training in my beat-up, second-hand car and found myself stood in the hotel lobby rubbing shoulders with all these great players thinking, "What the hell am I doing here?" I was the only player I'd never heard of!'

The press made a lot of Ted's selection in the European XI as Scotland team boss Tommy Docherty was to take charge of the side. There were also false rumours spreading around Upton Park on the night of the game that MacDougall was going to sign for the Hammers, so when he walked out on to the pitch the crowd of close to 30,000 cheered and sung his name. He started the game, scored a goal and gave a good account of himself before being substituted at half-time, 'It was the first time I had met Tommy Docherty and of course we went on to have a bit of history! It was a night game in London, a full house and I'm in this European XI in a testimonial match for the only guy ever to score a hat-trick in a World Cup Final!

'I'm sure I was a bit in awe of my team-mates that night but I had a great time and I was chuffed to bits to have scored. Docherty took me off at half-time but that didn't matter, I was there, I wasn't overawed and I was so excited. I got on well with Geoff Hurst and he agreed to make an appearance at my sports shop later in the season.'

Increasing speculation suggested that Ted would soon become Britain's first £250,000 player, with plenty of clubs apparently prepared to splash out a giant-sized fee for him, 'At this particular time it didn't bother me because I was settled, we were top of the Third Division and I wanted to see if we could get promotion. I had just opened the shop, had a new home, Joan was expecting our first child and I was enjoying life. Of course I was ambitious, but as long as the goals kept coming and the club was successful, I was more than happy to stay. The press were regularly asking me what my latest goal target was. I just used to laugh and tell them that I would wait until I achieved my original target before setting a new one. The fact they kept asking meant I was scoring goals regularly though and that was all I really wanted to do!'

By now, the top names in football were commenting on the Cherries' scoring sensation. In his weekly column in *Goal*, Manchester United's Bobby Charlton told readers he could not remember the last time the press and TV kicked up the sort of fuss that they were now making about Ted. Although Charlton admitted that he had not seen MacDougall play a full game, he sensed it was very obvious that Ted loved to score goals and had an instinctive knack for it. He did, however, suspect there may be some limitations within Ted's game otherwise he would have already been snapped up. Nonetheless, England's record international goalscorer believed that if MacDougall could keep on banging in the goals, it would not be too long before one of the First Division clubs would be in for him, 'That was probably true, I was scoring goals but I still knew that technically, I was not a good player. I didn't have a good style and I couldn't run properly, and I had already worked out that without that ability to get goals regularly there was no way I would progress in football.'

Bill Shankly was next to comment on MacDougall's scoring prowess in the pages of the weekly newspaper *Inside Football*. The Liverpool manager told readers how delighted he was for Ted to score his nine goals against Margate and to see him proving to be so successful. Shankly believed that only time would tell whether the striker would one day shine in a higher division, as he believed the gap between the First and Third Divisions was vast. However, The British Beermat Collectors' Society already considered MacDougall to be of sufficient stature to select him in the top ten personalities it would like to see on a beermat in 1972! Top of the poll was former Prime Minister Harold Wilson with Ted coming fourth behind the Labour Party leader, top model Vivien Neves and singer Frank Ifield. Closer to home, Harold Walker presented him with a gold watch, suitably inscribed to commemorate his FA Cup record.

Such was the level of interest in MacDougall and his goalscoring partnership with Boyer that a few weeks later they were asked to guest for First Division Coventry in a friendly match against the Polish side Gornik, in a bid to boost the attendance at Highfield Road. It is hard to imagine that a Premier League club would today ask to borrow two League 1 strikers to increase their gate! But back in 1971 with Bond's blessing, the two Cherries players not only played but were two of the outstanding players on show.

Despite the bright and breezy attacking style that had made them into one of the most entertaining and talked about teams in the country, Bournemouth announced a working loss of £166,000 for the previous season and expected to have another deficit, albeit much smaller during the current campaign. Walker continued to bear the brunt of the costs in pursuing his promotion dream, which continued at Barnsley, where the side fought out a goalless draw, then dropped their first home point of the season against York. Despite being played in swirling fog, the game started brightly when MacDougall was soon perfectly placed to head home a cross from Scott, but City struck back twice, one of the goals coming from former Cherries forward Eddie Rowles, before Ted was on hand again to equalise following a corner on the left by Scott. It was his 100th goal for Bournemouth in only his 124th appearance. The result meant the Cherries surrendered the top spot to Notts County on goal average however, as the previous season's

Fourth Division promotion rivals now contested the top two places in the Third Division.

After Bournemouth's dominance against Margate, Fourth Division Southend kept them at bay for more than an hour in the next round of the FA Cup until MacDougall and Boyer eventually found a way through. Boyer struck first with a brilliant header from his partner's pass before MacDougall headed home a second goal ten minutes from time. The following week, Halifax were defeated on the south coast before the big Christmas match came at promotion rivals Brighton. The game attracted a crowd of over 30,000 but disappointingly, the Cherries went down to a two-goal defeat and dropped out of the top two.

Concerned over the loss, Bond further strengthened his squad, returning once again to Torquay to complete the signing of their former Sunderland, Mansfield and Aston Villa midfielder Tommy Mitchinson for a fee of £23,000. Mitchinson made his debut on New Year's Day as Bournemouth bounced back to form, with Boyer scoring his first hat-trick for the club as they smashed four goals past Wrexham at Dean Court.

Five days later Bond entered the transfer market again, this time signing 27-year-old West Ham utility player Bobby Howe. Howe's club record £33,000 transfer fee brought the club's expenditure to over £200,000 in 18 months, the equivalent of more than £2m today. The arrival of Howe left the way open for David Stocks's departure and, perhaps not surprisingly, he moved to Torquay soon afterwards. Howe made his debut against Rotherham at Millmoor, where Bournemouth absorbed heavy pressure before emerging with a goalless draw.

The Cherries missed out on a money-spinning tie in the third round of the FA Cup and instead travelled to Third Division rivals Walsall where they suffered a surprise defeat, the home side's teenage striker Bernie Wright scoring the game's only goal. Bond admitted afterwards that his team's performance had been below its usual standard, for which he accepted responsibility having reshuffled his side to operate without the injured Scott, as Ted recalls, 'We just didn't perform without Tony at Fellowes Park that day. People sometimes forgot just how much he contributed to the side. He set up so many of my chances, but unfortunately he didn't have a strong physique and his fragile legs attracted some wincing tackles, which meant he spent a good deal of the season injured. Tony was coming to the end of a career that had started at West Ham and also taken him to Aston Villa. He wasn't super quick and didn't do much running, but he was one of the best crossers of a ball I ever saw. Although he was right-footed, he played on the left for us and had this great ability to cut the ball across his foot so that it moved away from the goalkeeper. All I had to do was to get on the end of it.'

With Scott fit again, the Cherries were back to their best against Notts County in a thrilling match played in front of the biggest league crowd at Dean Court for ten years, 21,154, which included Derby County manager Brian Clough. It was decided by two great goals within the space of five minutes midway through the first half by MacDougall and Boyer. The first came when Machin, Scott, Kitchener and MacDougall opened up the County defence to enable Boyer to score with a wonderful left-footed strike. Then Ted jumped perfectly to meet a well-flighted cross from Mitchinson and headed home his first goal in six matches, much to the crowd's delight and the striker's relief.

In the second half MacDougall came close to scoring again, heading a cross from Kitchener against the County post, and then watched Mitchinson hit the ball across the face of the goal as it rebounded to him. It was a game worthy of two sides challenging at the top of the table and despite five bookings by referee Clive Thomas, it was by no means tough or bad-tempered as some previous meetings between the two clubs had been, 'That goal came as a great relief to me at the time, as I had not scored for over a month! But whenever I expressed a concern about not scoring, John Bond would tell me every striker in football has a spell when things do not go right and not to worry. He had such confidence in me. County were a good side with a very strong midfield. We put John Benson on Don Masson, and Tony Powell on Willie Carlin though and they took care of them.'

It was no surprise that MacDougall was the subject of another week's transfer speculation following Clough's appearance at Dean Court. Seemingly unfazed though, he ended the week by playing a part in Howe's first Cherries goal to earn a draw at Port Vale. Seven days later Ted scored the solitary goal that beat Plymouth Argyle on a saturated pitch following a week of heavy rain and a torrential downpour just before kick-off. The all-important strike came just before the hour mark when a Scott corner was headed on by Howe, before MacDougall leaned back into a left-footed shot which gave young Plymouth goalkeeper Peta Bala'c no chance. His 33rd goal of the season ensured Bournemouth remained in the second promotion place, two points behind league leaders Aston Villa, who were growing in strength as the season progressed.

Such was the interest in the Cherries' visit to Villa Park in February that it drew a record Third Division attendance of 48,110. Well over 3,000 Bournemouth supporters were believed to have travelled to the game by road and air, but later estimates suggested it was more likely to have been between as many as five and seven thousand. The match was also televised by the BBC and highlights were shown on *Match Of The Day* later that evening. The atmosphere inside the ground was electric and two goals in two second-half minutes by the home side dramatically altered the course of the game, after Ted had given the Cherries the lead on 27 minutes with a classic diving header. Bournemouth had attacked Villa from start to finish, not once opting to fall back and defend, with the menacing MacDougall always a threat to a rather cumbersome Villa defence. Had his brilliant shot on the turn early in the second half not gone narrowly wide, it is very doubtful whether Villa would have recovered. But an equaliser by Geoff Vowden after 72 minutes set Villa Park alight and the ability of the fanatical home fans to lift their side proved a vital factor in the latter stages of the game. To thunderous roars from the frenzied crowd, Villa continued to press forward and soon afterwards Andy Lochhead was on hand to hook in the winning goal.

MacDougall's effort at Villa Park was immediately shortlisted as a contender for goal of the season and has since become an iconic image in the club's history. Ted recalls the goal vividly, 'Our defence cleared a Villa attack and Tony Powell played the ball up to me in the middle of the park. I've no idea what I was doing there but anyway I sent it out to Tony Scott on the wing. Tony made progress down the right flank while Phil Boyer took all the defenders to the near post and I raced towards goal into the space behind him. When Scotty crossed the ball I met it with a full-length diving header from about 12 yards past goalkeeper Jim Cumbes. It was a superb team goal, exactly what we practised doing on the training ground. It really delighted me – even though we ended up losing.

'I regarded every goal I got as a good one, but I suppose this one gave me the most pleasure of any I scored. With both teams going for promotion and such a large crowd inside the ground, it produced a real life or death atmosphere. The goal said everything about these times at

Bournemouth and thankfully the BBC were there to film it, as there is so little footage available from this period in the club's history, and of course there is no footage at all of the Margate game.'

Many neutrals present believed the better team lost at Villa Park, having been impressed with the Cherries' imaginative and intelligent football. Bond's side played more first-time passes than would have been seen in many First Division games at the time but there was a school of thought that believed the team were sometimes encouraged to attack too much and that this was not always the best tactic. For his part, Bond spoke about the 'ridiculous' result of a game in which his players worked so hard and played so impressively only to gain nothing but sympathy for a defeat they did not deserve. Although he still believed his side were the best in the Third Division and a class above Villa for most of the match, the defeat had left them with a disappointing away record with only two wins from 13 league games, 'I think at times we did perhaps try to attack too much away from home but that was the way John liked to play the game. Sometimes the pitches were so poor that it was difficult to pass the ball and at times we got ourselves into problems against teams that adopted a more direct approach, but we should have seen these games out and picked up more points from them. When you're at the top, of course everybody wants to beat you, but we were a bit like "soft southerners" when we went up to the frozen north! We were the "Flash Harrys" in the league, I still remember Bondy's suits and kipper ties!'

The foundations of Bournemouth's promotion push lay in their impressive 14-game unbeaten home record, but together with injury and suspension to key players, their failure to win matches they had dominated became a matter of some concern. Machin scored his first league goal for the Cherries against lowly Mansfield but significantly Scott damaged a shin in an early collision with former Cherries team-mate Dennis Longhorn and took no further part in the game. Then, with the country gripped by a power shortage as a result of the miners' industrial action, Bournemouth were forced to stage their midweek fixture against Walsall in the afternoon as the use of floodlights was forbidden.

Nonetheless, a crowd in the region of 10,000 still managed to attend in extremely cold conditions at Dean Court, only to see their team 'frozen out' by the visitors' defence in a dour goalless draw. Again the absence of Scott proved a vital factor and to make matters worse,

MacDougall even missed a penalty midway through the first half. The Cherries were also without defender Powell, one of the side's most competitive players but whose style of play did not always find favour with referees, and he was serving a 28-day suspension. As a result he would be missing for six vital games, as Ted remembers, '"Knocker" was a great man to have in midfield or defence and a great player to have in your side. He came from Bath and was originally a boxer in his youth. He was a strong player and a real character, who became very popular with the supporters because he always gave total commitment, took no prisoners and played with great determination. He had been sent off earlier in the season, but his disciplinary record was not that bad and the suspension he got was harsh.'

Bond moved quickly to strengthen the service to MacDougall and Boyer, signing the experienced former Southampton and Middlesbrough winger Dave Chadwick from Halifax Town for a fee of around £10,000. The move met with instant success as Bournemouth won their next four games in convincing style to enter the final stages of the season with 48 points from 33 games and still in a commanding position for promotion. He had immediately taken the chance to play both Chadwick and Scott against Torquay at Plainmoor, where Ted converted a cross from each player to secure a well-deserved victory. Together with Chadwick and Mitchinson, he was again on target as the Cherries beat Bradford City 3-0 at Dean Court, a win that was quickly followed by another home success, this time against Bristol Rovers, which included a goal apiece from MacDougall and Boyer. The team's fourth successive victory came at the Vetch Field, where Kitchener followed in a MacDougall header to score against Swansea, after Boyer's opening goal had been cancelled out by the Welsh side.

On the back of these results, the team was set a revised 66-point target which Bond believed would be enough for them to take the league title. Inexplicably though, they faltered badly in mid-March, vital decisions going against them as they failed to win any of their next six games. First, they were denied at Walsall, despite having made a great start when, after home goalkeeper Bob Wesson lost a Kitchener cross, MacDougall met the loose ball with his shoulder and directed it into the net. Boyer smashed a shot against the woodwork soon afterwards but the home side fought back to claim a point.

Prior to Bournemouth's next match at home to Bolton, Ted received the May Baily Trophy as the town's Sports Personality of the Year from singer and entertainer Sacha Distel. Once the game began though, the Cherries were unable to strike the right note and found the going tough against a resolute Wanderers side. Former England World Cup star Roger Hunt gave the visitors an early lead with a 20-yard shot that left Davies helpless and although the 15,000-strong crowd did their best to try and lift the side, they found it difficult to break down the visitors' defence. Those who had resigned themselves to defeat and left the ground early missed a bizarre ending to the match when, following a corner, the Cherries were denied an equaliser despite players claiming the ball had crossed the goal line before being hooked out by a defender. Referee Tom Reynolds would have none of it and while the argument raged, Bolton got on with the game and Hunt scored again with just 90 seconds of the match remaining. The home side immediately struck back when directly from the restart, MacDougall headed home his 40th goal of the season, but unfortunately this was the game's last meaningful action and Bournemouth's proud undefeated home record had gone after 18 matches.

A second successive defeat followed against Oldham, where Bournemouth went down 3-1 after taking the lead at Boundary Park through Chadwick, but fortunately the other sides left in the promotion race, Aston Villa, Brighton and Notts County, also dropped points as the season entered its final stages, although Villa still had a two-point cushion at the top of the table. Bond remained confident that the players would pick themselves up, but found it hard to stomach a further blow four days later at Rochdale. With the side playing positive attacking football from the start at Spotland, they took the lead with a goal just after the half-hour when, after a series of imaginative attacks, MacDougall prodded the ball in from close range after a throw-in on the left taken by Howe had been hooked across to the centre by Kitchener.

Earlier in the game the referee had been forced to retire with a back injury, the senior linesman taking over after a four-minute delay while a substitute linesman was found among the crowd. The spectator-turned-linesman took centre stage early in the second half and to Bournemouth's fury appeared to disallow what seemed a perfectly good goal that would have given them a two-goal lead. To make matters worse, Rochdale equalised soon afterwards and the Cherries were eventually grateful for a penalty save by Davies to help them return with a point. After the game Bond was extremely critical about the performance of the substitute linesman, describing the decision to disallow his side's second goal as 'the most ridiculous and cruel decision the team had yet had to encounter'.

As April dawned, Brighton's visit to Dean Court was to prove vital in deciding the final promotion places. The all-ticket match attracted a crowd of 22,540, the largest at the ground for ten years. Bournemouth welcomed Powell back after his suspension while Brighton manager Pat Saward included forward Ken Beamish, a recent signing from Tranmere who Bournemouth had tried to sign earlier in the season. Tension was evident in both teams but the game soon came to life with Ted's aerial presence causing all kind of havoc for the visitors, while the daring Boyer tore great holes in the Brighton defence. Their pressure finally told shortly before half-time, when the packed ground erupted after a Mitchinson through ball was picked up by MacDougall, who ran through to score. The second half saw the home side under tremendous pressure but they held on agonisingly until five minutes from the end, when Beamish snatched an equaliser.

For once, there was criticism among supporters that Bournemouth had played very defensively in the second half but Bond later denied he had given them any specific instruction to do so, 'I think there was a feeling of anxiety among the supporters that we were going to blow it. Remember the club had joined the Football League in 1923 and never been anywhere other than the Third Division. Many of them had seen a number of previous promotion bids come to nothing. Some felt John made too many changes to the side and perhaps because he had so many good players at his disposal, he was more inclined to make changes, but I think there was a feeling around the place that Lady Luck had deserted us and things had started to go against us a little bit. The game at Rochdale was a perfect example and Bondy's reaction typified our frustration.'

A goalless draw followed in midweek at Chesterfield, where goalkeeper Ron Tilsed, released by Bournemouth only a few weeks before, was instrumental in keeping his former colleagues at bay. Nonetheless, a narrow victory at relegation-threatened Tranmere meant the Cherries still held on to second place on 54 points with six games left to play. They were now five points behind leaders Villa but equal on points with Brighton, who had a game in hand, and three points ahead of Notts County who had three games in hand. The game at Prenton Park was a very physical one and Bournemouth had shown plenty of courage, character and determination to fight their way back after going a goal down in the first half. Ted found himself being marked by his former Liverpool colleague Ron Yeats, who had ended his distinguished career at Anfield to become Rovers' player-assistant manager and behind him was another ex-Liverpool man in goalkeeper Tommy Lawrence.

The home side played with a rugged approach which the Cherries took time to overcome, Scott suffering most as Rovers tried to deny MacDougall any service, but they responded magnificently and 20 minutes from time Ted shook off the attention of Yeats to finish off a simple but effective move. It was started by Jones on the left, whose pass to Boyer drew the home defence hopelessly off balance and although he was falling as the ball arrived across goal from his fellow striker, MacDougall still managed to slot the ball in with Lawrence beaten. Two minutes later he struck again after substitute Chadwick ran through to cross to the waiting striker who rose in splendour at the far post to head a great 44th goal of the season, 'Earlier in my career I would fade out of a match like this because I wouldn't have known how to deal with it, but by now I had learnt how to look after myself and was not easily intimidated. Although past his prime, Ron Yeats was still a colossus of a man and knew every trick in the book, but I wore him down and had the satisfaction of scoring twice as a result.'

Bournemouth faced another tough battle when relegation-threatened Barnsley travelled south and the well-drilled Yorkshiremen proved to be a nut the Cherries couldn't crack, returning north with a precious point taken from the home side's grasp in a goalless draw. The result meant they dropped two places and their performance had shown signs of fatigue and anxiety, although it was only the second league game of the season in which the team had failed to score at Dean Court. With promotion seemingly slipping from the Cherries' grasp, newspaper speculation turned from MacDougall towards Bond and having already turned down approaches from Leicester and Coventry earlier in the season, the manager now rejected Everton's approach to join the management team at Goodison Park as assistant to manager Harry Catterick.

The speculation was hardly what the club needed at such a vital stage in the season, but two brilliant away victories at Bristol Rovers and York suggested that the players had every intention of carrying their promotion bid all the way to the very end. A reshuffled side at

Eastville saw Cave recalled for the first time since returning from a loan spell at Plymouth and also included John Sainty, who had not started a game since New Year's Day. Goals from Chadwick and Boyer proved enough to restore the Cherries to second place, but the spot was straightaway conceded to Brighton, who were home winners the following night.

At Bootham Crescent, with the York defenders expecting a pass to Boyer, Ted accepted a loose ball in the centre circle and raced through unchallenged to score with a crisp left-foot shot. Then, after Bournemouth had absorbed heavy pressure from the home side Boyer, captain for the day, slotted home Chadwick's low cross one minute from time to guarantee victory. The two goals took MacDougall and Boyer's combined total for the season to 60.

Sadly though, as April drew to a close so did Bournemouth's last hopes of gaining promotion. A harsh penalty and a goal scored from a double deflection meant their first visit to Blackburn ended in a disappointing defeat, despite MacDougall initially putting them ahead. With Brighton winning the same evening, the Sussex side were now three points clear in second place with just two more games to play, and looked increasingly likely to join Aston Villa in gaining promotion.

The Cherries had to beat Oldham at Dean Court in their penultimate game and hope other results went their way. It proved to be a fiery affair, ignited midway through the first half when Machin was sent off immediately before a cross from Scott was calmly controlled and steered home by Boyer. Soon afterwards the same player carved a great hole in the visitors' defence, Scott made the final centre and true to form, MacDougall was there to grab goal number 47. But, as the final whistle blew, news agonisingly filtered around the ground that Brighton had won against Torquay which put them beyond the Cherries' reach.

Throughout the season Bournemouth had played exciting football, scored goals, had been feted by the media and were probably the best side in the Third Division. It would not be an exaggeration to say that MacDougall's presence in the side drew many extra thousands to Third Division grounds up and down the country and it was no surprise when The *Daily Express* voted Bournemouth the most entertaining team in the division. They had one of the most outspoken and sought-after young managers and facilities that were better than at many First Division clubs, yet when the season's excitement had ended, and the promotion places settled, they were still in the Third Division. That they finished third with a record number of points (62) for a club that failed to gain promotion was of no consolation, as a place in the Second Division had been snatched away from them by Brighton in the final weeks of the season. Back in October when the Cherries demolished eventual champions Aston Villa by playing simple and direct football they had looked the more likely to achieve their ambitions.

Supporters were left wondering how a side with a millionaire's backing failed to gain promotion and many felt the manager's mistake was to keep trying to improve an already very good side to the extent that by the end of the campaign, the team which played so magnificently against Villa was not the side that completed the club's fixtures. The big buys, brought in to try and guarantee promotion, seemed to disrupt the team's rhythm and they were never as impressive again as that day against Villa. In his defence, Bond could argue to some extent that he was forced to try a different form of approach once opponents began to work out that the best way to stop MacDougall and Boyer from scoring was to cut out the service supplied to them by Tony Scott.

Undoubtedly, the manager and players suffered considerable personal disappointment but their sympathies were with the chairman and also with the club's supporters. To this day, even allowing for the Cherries' recent success, many of those supporters still believe the 1971/72 team to have been one of the best Bournemouth sides to have graced the Dean Court pitch. As Ted admits, 'It was such a shame we didn't get promotion because the nucleus of the side would have stayed together for a crack at Division Two and who knows, the club may have gone on even further. The team was full of good players – Bondy improved every one of us and we played some great football. In terms of quality, we were pretty much a First Division side but we were playing in the Third.

'You only have to look at how many of that team eventually made it into the top level with Norwich City. But it was a major turning point at Bournemouth because it slowed all the momentum down. We had the players and if it had been three up we would have been there. The chairman invested a lot of money in the club and we all wanted to repay him but it just wasn't to be.'

7

A Point to Prove

DESPITE attracting interest from a host of First and Second Division clubs during the 1971/72 season, when it drew to a close Ted quickly re-affirmed his intention to remain with Bournemouth and to have another crack at promotion. As soon as it became clear his side would be remaining in the Third Division, John Bond had informed MacDougall of exactly what contact there had been from other clubs and then left Ted and Joan to make their own decision, 'Joan and I were expecting our first child in July so it was important to try and keep things settled. I still believed the club would develop into one of the best in the country and I wanted to help them get promotion the next season because at the time that's where I saw my future.

'I had already learnt to take little notice of any transfer talk I read about in the papers. It was flattering to read that big First Division clubs were after me, but I still felt that my football future was at Dean Court. I knew people would say that I lacked the self-confidence to accept the challenge of top-flight football, but that wasn't true. John knew I had a desire to play at the highest level and perhaps get a Scottish cap, so the door was open for a transfer at the end of the previous season if the right offer had come along. Although there was interest, it didn't. One First Division club who inquired about me wanted me to go along on trial. What a bloody insult!

'Our new house was almost finished and I was opening a second sports shop in Poole. Although my contract would make me one of the highest-paid players outside the top division, it was never a question of money really, more a matter of happiness and contentment. Unfortunately things did not quite work out that way in the end sadly.'

The news that Ted had decided to stay with Bournemouth, rather than be put up for auction among half a dozen clubs, was the finest start to the summer on the south coast. In mid-May, the Cherries squad had flown to Turkey for a four-match tour, based in Istanbul, the ten-day adventure including fixtures against Galatasaray, Fenerbahce, and a national representative team. Meanwhile, back at home, the board of directors successfully approached the Football League for permission to change the club's name to AFC Bournemouth, 'to present it in a more up to date image both nationally and locally'. Later in the summer, an exciting £1m ground development scheme was announced, with building work phased over a five-year period to provide a sports complex housed beneath an all-seater stand. Despite having just missed out on promotion there was clearly not going to be any let-up in the club's ambitious plans for success on or off the field.

Upon the team's return from Turkey, another busy summer followed, inevitably still surrounded by plenty of speculation regarding transfer activity. After rejecting an offer to become manager of Coventry City, Bond looked to further strengthen the Cherries' squad for the forthcoming season. Perhaps surprisingly though, Tony Scott was allowed to leave Dean Court, his susceptibility to injuries finally making up Bond's mind to allow the winger to leave on a free transfer in appreciation of the contribution he had made in restoring the club to the Third Division, 'I cannot emphasise too much, how important Scotty's wing play and crosses were in everything I had achieved at Bournemouth. He was exactly the sort of player I needed alongside me. He had so much ability but although he was a very intelligent player, he couldn't really look after himself. Had he been blessed with a bigger physique, he would have achieved considerably greater success in the game. I was sad to see him go.'

When Bond learnt that his long-time target, Harry Redknapp, had been transfer-listed by West Ham, he made another attempt to lure him down to the south coast. This time it was successful and the winger joined the Cherries in the close season following a £35,000 deal. He was joined at Dean Court by former Southampton and Everton defender Jimmy Gabriel, who arrived for a fee of £20,000. Bond also wanted a player who would command the middle of the park and made enquiries regarding Tottenham's former England international Alan Mullery. However, Fulham got in first and Spurs snapped up their offer of £65,000, so Mullery went back to his old club. Bond also openly expressed an interest in West Ham and England star Geoff Hurst which aroused further speculation that Ted might be leaving Dean Court after all. Wolves, West Ham, Coventry and Crystal Palace continued to chase MacDougall over the summer months but having already pledged his loyalty to Bournemouth, Ted was in no rush to change his mind, nor to set himself a goalscoring target for the new season, 'After scoring 47 goals the previous season and 49 in the season before that, understandably the media kept asking me what total I would be chasing the next time. My answer was always as many as possible, but I didn't put extra pressure on myself by setting any massive target. My job was to score goals and so long as I could hit about 25 in a season I always felt I was doing my job. There were some games when clubs would put two or even three men on me making it increasingly hard but of course every time they did that they left others with extra freedom to exploit.'

Remarkably, MacDougall managed to remain level-headed about life while his name remained prominent on the back pages of the national press. He could have been forgiven for believing some of the things that were written about him, but fortunately a wise Scottish head ruled his heart, 'It did affect me at first. I felt I had to do things just to please the press because I liked to read about myself. Everyone is vain in some way and I thought it was great to keep reading my name on the back pages.

'I still think you have to be born with a talent for scoring goals. It's purely instinctive to have a crack at anything in the penalty area. With me, nine times out of ten it seemed to go in, I never forgot that I was not the best of players outside the box but I was there to score goals, and I was doing it.'

Pre-season visits by Tottenham and Manchester United evoked memories among supporters of Bournemouth's 1956/57 FA Cup run, when they beat Spurs in the fifth round before losing to United in the quarter-finals. This time however, they went down 4-2 to Bill Nicholson's side in the first fixture, during which Ted was kept well in check by Tottenham's Welsh international centre-half Mike England, who allowed him few opportunities on goal either in the air or on the ground.

A Point to Prove

United manager Frank O'Farrell knew an all-out drive for one of the major honours was the least that would be expected by the United hierarchy in the coming season.

Nonetheless, the match at Dean Court did little to suggest the team would be capable of achieving it, as MacDougall scored two great goals to begin yet another round of gossip about his chances of a £200,000 move to the First Division. With United chairman Louis Edwards and director Sir Matt Busby looking on from the stands, they could only reflect on a dismal south coast tour that had seen their side gain an unimpressive goalless draw at Fourth Division Torquay and then suffer a 3-1 defeat at Bournemouth. Even their goal against the Cherries came from a penalty.

Ted had three clear scoring chances in the first half and scored with the third. Sainty started the move, Chadwick nipped past Tony Dunne before crossing the ball, and there was Ted accelerating into space to head home. United were without George Best who was under a club suspension, but after Charlton had levelled, Martin Buchan, O'Farrell's £120,000 signing from Aberdeen, headed the ball into his own goal under pressure from Micky Cave to restore the Cherries' lead. Then late in the game, MacDougall delighted the 17,000 crowd by sliding in his second goal from a cross by Cave.

Before kick-off, Bobby Charlton, United's captain that evening, had told reporters he looked forward to seeing if Ted was as good a player as he looked on television. Afterwards, he praised the Bournemouth striker, believing he would give a lot of defences plenty of trouble again in the new season, as he appeared to have a similar gift to players like Jimmy Greaves and Roger Hunt – the knack of being in the right place to knock the ball into the back of the net. Like MacDougall, Charlton also believed the knack for scoring goals is not something you lose by moving into a higher division, 'High praise indeed! But I don't believe he ever thought I was good enough for a club like Manchester United!'

As the new season beckoned, Bournemouth's fluent attacking football again made them favourites for promotion, although some analysts cast doubt upon the strength of the team's defence, 'A new season always worried me a little. I always wondered whether I would be able to emulate the last one. I suppose it's like falling off a bike and wanting to get back on again to make sure you can still ride! By this stage of my career I had a reputation to live up to. The reputation of being a goalscorer could be a bit of a millstone around your neck.

People almost demanded goals from me. When I had a bad goalless game it was making just as big headlines as when I got a hat-trick!

'Obviously I loved to score goals. If I failed to score in a game I felt rough all weekend even though we might have won. I wasn't happy until I'd banged in ten to 15 goals each season. That was the psychological barrier. Until I broke it, I probably used to try too hard. I made that mistake in the friendly against Spurs. I got myself too tensed up so I decided to change this against Manchester United a few days later. It worked. I grabbed two goals and had a great game. Scoring against teams like United gave me back the confidence I sometimes thought I was losing.

'People had been harping on for ages about all my goals coming in the Third and Fourth Divisions. But apart from those two against United I scored another in the all-star team that played against West Ham in Geoff Hurst's testimonial. I felt this was proof enough that I could score goals in any company. But I was still only 25 at this time and was prepared to wait for my chance to play in the First Division. My heart hoped I might even get there with Bournemouth.

'Remember it was only just over two years before that I was playing for York earning £21 a week. I was poor then and in comparison I was wealthy now. I'd bought a house and invested some money for the future because you're only at the top in this game for a short while. I had also just become a father, my daughter Alison having recently been born.'

Surprisingly, Bournemouth made a very indifferent start to the new campaign. After three games they had gained just one point and lay third from bottom of the league table. Bond described their 3-0 defeat at newly relegated Bolton on the opening day of the season as 'shameful' and this was followed by a disappointing 2-2 draw at home to Chesterfield. Immediately prior to kick-off, MacDougall was presented with the 1971/72 Football League Third Division Player of the Year trophy by Harold Walker, to follow up his similar award for the Fourth Division the previous year, but unfortunately he could not mark the occasion with a goal, being well-shackled by the strong Chesterfield defence.

At Watford the following Saturday, Redknapp made his much awaited debut and his 16th-minute corner led to MacDougall putting the Cherries ahead. Soon afterwards he pounced again, coolly sweeping Machin's low cross into the net after his original header had struck the crossbar. The Cherries' suspect defence then fell to pieces, causing a complete turnaround as the home side went on to win 3-2.

There was a winning start in the League Cup however, a 2-0 success against Plymouth at Home Park, where Ted showed just how ruthless a finisher he could be, clinically taking advantage of defensive errors to score both goals within a space of 15 second-half minutes as well as hitting the bar with two headers, one in each half. Bond refused to panic about the league form but was no doubt relieved when the Cherries' first win of the season came, albeit by a single Machin goal, against Halifax at Dean Court. The overall performance was far from convincing however, and when Scunthorpe travelled to the south coast four days later, it took a late goal from MacDougall to rescue a point.

Despite their disappointing start to their season, there was no shortage of visiting scouts keeping an eye on MacDougall and his colleagues. Ted had as many as eight First Division scouts watching him on occasions, including Birmingham, Coventry, West Bromwich Albion and Newcastle, while interest was growing in other members of the talented Bournemouth side. Right-back Machin was attracting the attentions of Manchester City and Wolves had been checking on centre-half David Jones, while Cardiff were keen on the captain Miller.

MacDougall certainly made the trip worthwhile for those watching the replay of Bournemouth's League Cup tie against Second Division Blackpool, after the teams had fought out a goalless draw at Dean Court. Throughout the evening, MacDougall was magnificent at Bloomfield Road, three times having headers stopped on the goal line, but it was ultimately as a decoy that he proved most lethal. With the entire Blackpool defence concentrating on his run to meet a Bobby Howe free kick, Powell moved behind him to score the Cherries' goal in a 1-1 draw, although the team were denied a clear-cut penalty when Ted was pulled down during extra time.

Meanwhile, the Cherries' league campaign began to pick up and they gained their first away point of the season in a lively but goalless game at York and followed this with a 2-0 home victory against Southend, in which Miller not only provided the midfield inspiration but also scored both goals. The first seven league fixtures had brought MacDougall only three goals of his own, although he had also hit two in the League Cup at Plymouth. By any normal yardstick this would still be a satisfactory situation, but for Ted, to whom goals meant happiness, it was not good enough and after the Southend match he stunned his manager and the media alike when he expressed a dramatic change of heart over his future, 'I told the manager and the press that I had become unsettled as the goals were not coming as freely as I wanted, and when that happens to a striker things start to go a bit flat. I just felt that it was now time to move and to prove to myself that I could succeed at a higher level. Really you could sum it up with one word – ambition. I wanted to give myself the chance of playing in the First Division while other clubs wanted me in case I didn't get another opportunity. I guess I had become insecure.

'I didn't want to go, it would have suited me better if we had been promoted as I had all my business interests in the area. I loved Bournemouth and it certainly wasn't about money. I had many regrets about leaving a club which had always been good to me. I hoped the supporters would appreciate that it was a matter of personal challenge.'

MacDougall had always been honest enough to admit he was nothing without his goals and Bournemouth's slow start to the new season had made him anxious about his future, particularly as the goals had not been coming as he felt they should. Ted's change of heart was the signal that started a furious chase for his signature.

Finance was not a vital factor because although of course any move would make him one of the best-paid footballers in the country, he was by this time earning £150 per week at Bournemouth, the equivalent of around £2,000 today.

Bond initially sought to reassure MacDougall, fully understanding his player's disappointment in not scoring as often as he would wish, but he felt Ted was contributing a lot more to the overall team performance and, in this respect, his game had found a new dimension. In his heart Bond knew it was always likely that one day an offer of around £200,000 would come in and MacDougall would decide he wanted to move. Once Ted had expressed a burning ambition to make his name in the First Division, much as Bond desperately wanted to convince his prize asset that he should stay at Dean Court a little longer, the manager also felt obliged to honour a promise not to stand in the player's way should he decide to move on.

As news broke about MacDougall's likely departure, the interest shown by pursuing clubs intensified in the hope that a transfer was imminent, and with penalty shootouts not yet the accepted format for settling such stalemates as Bournemouth's League Cup saga against Blackpool, another posse of First Division representatives gathered at

Villa Park, the neutral venue chosen for a farcical second replay. The attendance itself was only 2,337 and although again stretching to extra time, the game failed to match the quality of the previous matches, with Blackpool running out 2-1 winners. The interested observers included Wolves manager Bill McGarry who had originally made a £100,000 offer for MacDougall a year previously and Jimmy Andrews from Spurs but it was not a night on which Ted enhanced his reputation.

However, as speculation escalated about his future, Ted did turn in an impressive all-round display a few days later, scoring the Cherries equaliser in a 1-1 draw at Brentford. Bournemouth were a goal down after just 90 seconds, before MacDougall hit back in the tenth minute when from a Redknapp cross, he headed powerfully against the upright and as the ball came back to him from the rebound, he hooked it into the net in spectacular style. Moments earlier he had swerved past a pack of defenders and hammered a close-range shot that almost cut a hole through the Bees' goalkeeper Paul Priddy, who later went to hospital for a check-up. MacDougall also did his fair share of defensive work and troubled Brentford throughout the game, despite having to go it alone for much of the second half as the Cherries appeared content to settle for a point.

The Sunday newspapers were full of transfer talk the following day. Their columns reported that Spurs assistant manager Eddie Bailey was among those watching Ted at Brentford. He had apparently been joined by Crystal Palace chairman Arthur Wait and Bill Dodgin, who was scouting for West Ham. There were also suggestions that with the likelihood of money to spend from the impending sale of MacDougall, Bournemouth were poised to bid again for Notts County midfielder Don Masson, having already had one bid of £100,000 turned down. As the media circus speculated on where MacDougall's immediate future might lie, Bond received a call from Frank O'Farrell.

Typically, the Manchester United manager had not given any public indication of his recent interest in the player, although he had previously been an admirer when manager at Leicester and must have been impressed when Ted scored twice against his side in the summer. Unknown to the press, O'Farrell had also watched MacDougall from the terraces at Griffin Park the previous day and a meeting was arranged for the Monday. Bournemouth assistant manager Reg Tyrell met O'Farrell in Salisbury and drove him down for further talks with Bond and Walker at the chairman's home, where discussions continued all day, and after the United boss had returned to Manchester, talks continued at Dean Court, all without the knowledge of MacDougall.

Amid all the transfer talk, the Cherries faced a home fixture against Port Vale the following evening, a game O'Farrell returned to Bournemouth to watch. Despite the intense speculation surrounding his future, MacDougall managed to compose himself sufficiently to not only take the field but also score the first goal in a comprehensive 4-0 victory, 'I remember after one of my last games, maybe the last game, I was in John Bond's office and I was crying, physically crying. I couldn't handle the pressure and the tension, it had become too much for me and I was distraught. All the press were outside, national as well as local, it was like you get in the Premier League today but this was in the Third Division and I just broke down. Fortunately John and I had developed a camaraderie, like father and son really, I believed in him after all he had done for me personally and he handled things for me.'

Palace manager Bert Head was also present at Dean Court, still trying to persuade Bond that it would be in MacDougall's best interests to move to Selhurst Park. But not even the money and players offered in exchange – believed to be in the region of £150,000 plus Bobby Bell and either Bobby Tambling or Bobby Kellard – worked in their favour as Bond felt that Head was trying to get MacDougall 'on the cheap' and eventually told him that the players he had offered in part-exchange were not those he wanted. More discussions with O'Farrell then took place at Tyrell's Christchurch home after the game, where the United boss stayed overnight.

At 9am on 27 September 1972, MacDougall was informed of United's offer prior to a meeting with O'Farrell, where they discussed terms, 'When I was told it was United and Frank O'Farrell wanted to talk to me I was thrilled – and decided immediately. Remember there were no financial advisors or agents in those days – none of that crap! John knew Frank well from their days together at West Ham and Torquay, and the three of us met at Reg's home. Frank was very pleasant and he asked me what sort of money I would be looking for. I told him I was on £150 per week and he took a sharp intake of breath. He thought about it and then said he couldn't give me more than £160 because that was what Best, Law and Charlton were on!

'As I always said, it wasn't about money really as Bournemouth more than looked after me. The average First Division player was on about £60 a week at the time, and I was on £150 in the Third. After it was all agreed I felt numb. I couldn't believe it had happened. Any footballer wants to play at the highest level possible, and when a club like United wants you, well it was almost too good to be true. I knew there would be tremendous pressure on me. I was 26 years old, which was a bit late to move into the First Division, but I believed I could make the grade and Manchester United were the only other club I really wanted to join.'

After scoring 126 goals in 165 appearances for the Cherries, MacDougall was on his way to Old Trafford. His transfer fee was widely quoted as £200,000, the equivalent of £1.8m today, although Bournemouth's club records show that he moved for £194,455 with a further contingency sum of £27,777 payable when he had scored 20 goals in competitive first-team football for United. Either way, it was a record sum at the time for a Third Division player and shattered the highest transfer fee the Cherries had previously received, the £30,000 Freddie Cox had obtained for Roger Jones in January 1970. Bournemouth bookmakers George Sims had opened a book the previous day on Ted's transfer fee and had been inundated with bets. The initial odds were 6/4 on a fee between £176,000 and £200,000, although these were wisely later shortened to 4/6.

A disconsolate Bond released the news to the press shortly afterwards and, such was his connection with MacDougall, he described his feelings as similar to those when a father loses a son. After the transfer was concluded the manager admitted that once he knew Ted's feelings about wanting to get into the First Division, he got in touch with a number of clubs and informed them that Bournemouth would be prepared to sell. He did so having always maintained that he would do his best for MacDougall should he wish to leave Dean Court but despite rumours to the contrary, there had never been any question of O'Farrell having an option. The United manager came in with a straight offer and that was it. Upon completing what he considered as the worst day's work he had ever done, Bond reaffirmed his opinion that Ted would get goals at any level and would soon be the leading striker in the First Division, 'One thing I still regret is that I didn't get a hat-trick in that last game against Port Vale. I really wanted to turn it on to say "goodbye" in the best way to all the wonderful people who made my stay with Bournemouth so happy. I had got what I thought I wanted, I was off to Manchester, Old Trafford and the First Division, but Bournemouth still meant an awful lot to me. Sometimes I blame myself for leaving because I loved the place, I loved the people as they had always been very kind to me but there comes a time when you have to move on and try to prove yourself.

'John Bond had worked so hard to establish a fine team of players at Dean Court and morale among us was still really high – although, of course, everyone was so disappointed when we just failed to go up the previous season. It stopped all the impetus around the club. I think if we had gone up everyone would have stayed – I certainly would have. John had been really terrific to me and I sincerely hoped everyone understood how I felt at the time and that no one thought I had let the club down by moving.'

There was no doubt that Bournemouth and their supporters felt a great sense of loss when MacDougall left Dean Court. How on earth could the club possibly replace him? He was adulated throughout the town but well before he left, everyone knew that his transfer was inevitable and the general opinion was that the club had done well to keep him for so long. Most supporters seemed to appreciate that there comes a time in most people's career when contentment must end if ambition is bubbling just beneath the surface, and they wished Ted well. Many took the attitude that if he couldn't be scoring goals for the Cherries then it would be fine by them for him to do so for Manchester United. They were quite rightly proud of him and he became the town's prodigal son.

Now both the football club and its prodigal son had a huge challenge ahead. The most astonishing goalscorer ever to play in the lower reaches of the Football League had traded his enviable lifestyle in Bournemouth for a place in the dog-eat-dog world of the First Division.

8

Nightmare at the Theatre of Dreams

S O Ted was apparently set to become the darling of the Stretford End at Old Trafford. Allowed to leave Liverpool by Bill Shankly, recruited by Freddie Cox from York and groomed by John Bond at Bournemouth, 'Supermac' was now about to rub shoulders with George Best, Bobby Charlton and the rest of the greats at Manchester United. Described at the time as the biggest gamble in British football history, Frank O'Farrell had staked his managerial future on MacDougall making good in the First Division.

The day after the transfer had been agreed, Ted travelled to Manchester to undergo a medical before officially signing his contract. His arrival brought O'Farrell's spending in the previous six months to over £500,000, an extremely large amount for the time but although equivalent to almost ten times as much today, a drop in the ocean given current transfer values. In fact, it's hard to imagine the sort of fee an out and out goalscorer like MacDougall would command these days, but the United manager believed Ted's style of play would reap major rewards at United and maintain the Old Trafford club's tradition for scoring goals. Joining them may have seemed a dream come true for MacDougall, but September 1972 was not a good time to be starting a new chapter of his career in Manchester.

The club was struggling badly to replace legendary manager Sir Matt Busby, who had relinquished control to Wilf McGuinness in 1969, then when results dipped, returned the following year before handing over to O'Farrell in June 1971. The softly-spoken Irishman had enjoyed a playing career which had started at his hometown club Cork United, before he moved to West Ham in 1948. A polished wing-half, he established himself in the first team a couple of years later and became part of the West Ham 'Academy' of managers, which would eventually include Malcolm Allison, Noel Cantwell, Dave Sexton, John Bond, Ken Brown and Malcolm Musgrove, who later became O'Farrell's assistant at Leicester and Manchester United. He played 210 league and cup games for the Hammers before moving to Preston in 1956. A further 118 league appearances followed before O'Farrell moved to Weymouth as player-manager in 1961.

After O'Farrell guided the Dorset club to the Southern League championship, Torquay United offered him the manager's job in 1965 and they gained promotion from the Fourth Division at the end of his first season in charge. His style of management brought discipline to the club and despite having little money available, he managed to sign former colleagues Bond and Brown among others from West Ham, and was able to consolidate the Gulls' position at the higher level. In December 1968 he was enticed away to become manager of relegation-threatened Leicester City, and guided them to a losing FA Cup Final appearance the following year, but could not stave off relegation to the Second Division. After reshaping the club, he brought them back up two years later before being invited to take over at Old Trafford.

O'Farrell spent a comparatively large amount of money in a short period of time as he sought to rebuild an ageing team which still included great players such as Bobby Charlton and Denis Law. And if that was not difficult enough, he also had to deal with the off-the-pitch antics of the wayward genius George Best, which caused much unwanted media attention. As well as Buchan, notable signings had included £200,000 England winger Ian Storey-Moore from Nottingham Forest and the £65,000 capture of Manchester City's Welsh international forward Wyn Davies. The 30-year-old Davies had endured a relatively lean spell at Maine Road after enjoying plenty of scoring success at Newcastle in the sixties, and his arrival at Old Trafford was seen as something of a gamble. Two weeks after Davies moved across the city, O'Farrell moved for MacDougall, but buying a Third Division striker was undoubtedly his biggest gamble of all.

Initially United did well under O'Farrell's leadership. The team were five points clear at the top of the First Division by Christmas 1971. Sadly, in the second half of the season they went on a disastrous run of defeats and ended up finishing in eighth position. They had made a dreadful start to the 1972/73 season, confidence was low, the atmosphere around the club had become negative and they were now dangerously placed near the bottom of the table. In to this turmoil stepped MacDougall, saddled with a massive transfer fee and charged with the task of winning over the country's biggest support, 'Unfortunately I joined the worst club at the worst time I could ever have done. Anyway, Joan and I, together with our two-month-old daughter Alison, stayed with Joan's parents at Widnes while we looked for a house in the Manchester area. Initially, I was still over the moon a club like United should want me. I just hoped the fans weren't expecting miracles, although deep in my heart I knew I could make the grade. All I needed was time to settle in, but they were down the bottom, Law and Charlton were finishing and Best was about to go AWOL. Phew!'

The jury was certainly out among the country's leading football pundits. Those who thought Ted would be a success in the First Division acknowledged that he could only be regarded as such if people were satisfied for him to simply score goals, and not expect him to start producing other touches which he hadn't shown before. His aerial ability was certainly the equal of anyone and he had more agility than might have been expected. He was brave enough but he would need support, and a supply of the ball in the right areas. At United there were players such as Best and Moore who would demand attention from defenders in their own right, which might give MacDougall more room, although whereas it might have taken two defenders to mark him in the Third Division, defenders in the First were much better, and one against one could be quite enough. Most importantly of all, he would need to be given time to adapt and settle into his new surroundings.

Doubters questioned the wisdom of United's gamble after Tottenham and West Ham, admittedly comfortably placed in the league, had shied away from a deal. Had they possibly seen something lacking in Ted's game and come to the conclusion that discretion was the better part of valour? There were also concerns whether Davies and MacDougall would be a successful strike pairing. The tactic of Davies flicking the ball on with his head for Ted to run on to seemed so obvious that everyone would be ready for it, but what other variants of play might they achieve together? Only time would tell.

Inevitably comparisons were drawn between MacDougall's transfer and the move made by the other 'Supermac', 22-year-old Malcolm Macdonald, who had joined Newcastle United from Luton in a £180,000 deal three years previously. Newcastle had taken the plunge at the time when several other clubs had similarly held back and Macdonald's success had already more than justified his price tag. The two strikers were different types of player of course, Macdonald being the forcing type of centre-forward with the run and shot while Ted's game hinged on his predatory nature in the opposition penalty area. Nonetheless, comparisons continued to be made by the media although it remained of little interest to Ted and the least of his worries at the time.

O'Farrell wanted to give MacDougall a chance to settle in to the training regime at Old Trafford, so left him out of the side to play Sheffield United the weekend after he signed. He watched from the bench at Bramall Lane as United lost to a late Alan Woodward penalty, then having played for Bournemouth in the League Cup earlier in the season, he was forced to miss the third round tie against Bristol Rovers at Eastville a few days later, from which United were somewhat fortunate to return with a draw.

Ted's debut came on 8 October against West Bromwich Albion at The Hawthorns, for which United's starting XI was Stepney, Donald, Dunne, Young, James, Buchan, Morgan, MacDougall, Davies, Best and Storey-Moore.

MacDougall had a quiet game and understandably looked a little unfamiliar with United's style of play. However, a Best penalty and a second-half equaliser from Storey-Moore earned them a point in a 2-2 draw. Further pressure fell on O'Farrell when Bristol Rovers sensationally knocked United out of the League Cup in the replay at Old Trafford. With tensions still running high the following Saturday, Ted marked his home debut with a superb match-winner against Birmingham in front of a crowd of 52,104, 'It was a tremendous feeling to score on my home debut, but I remember feeling mentally shattered during the match. I suppose it was due to the pressure that built up before the game. It was a much greater ordeal than my first game because I wanted to prove myself to the fans and the team. Quite frankly I didn't feel at all sharp and felt I could do a lot better once I had settled in, but that goal certainly gave me a lift as I desperately wanted to score. It was a near-post header from a Tony Dunne cross, Wyn Davies made a great run to draw their defenders away and when I saw my header cross the line, I could have jumped over the stands! Wonderful! I still remember it well.

'Afterwards I felt absolutely drained but Besty insisted on taking me out on the town that night! He was never short of glamorous company and that evening he introduced me to these two women, one was Miss Wales and the other Miss Germany – it was that type of scene shall we say!

'A couple of weeks later we played a friendly match up at Aberdeen and we stayed overnight at the Railway Hotel in Princes Street, Edinburgh. We met a guy who ran a couple of nightclubs nearby, one for the general public and another underneath one for the VIPs, so to speak. We all went downstairs of course and this same guy was vetting everybody who came in, especially the women. I stayed a couple of hours, then went back to the hotel to go to bed.

'Anyway, George being George, the door to my room burst open around 3am and he storms in and ask where the women are. I told him I didn't know anything about any women, but Frank O'Farrell had been awakened by all the rumpus and told us we were all in trouble now because the newspapers had got hold of the story. I didn't know what the hell was going on but it turned out that George had tried to bring two women back to his room but the night porter had said they couldn't come in to the hotel. So George told him where to get off, the porter called the police and as a result there's a detective and a sergeant downstairs, with George effing and blinding all over the place after being found in bed with the two women. But that was Manchester United – imagine all the fuss if something like that happened today!'

Unfortunately the win against Birmingham was to prove something of a false dawn as United lost their next two games. A goal from Charlton could not prevent a 2-1 reverse at Newcastle which was followed by a disastrous 4-1 home defeat by Spurs, a game which saw Martin Peters score all four Spurs goals, with only Charlton on target again for United. The result left them rock bottom of the First Division and O'Farrell's days appeared to be numbered. While the press and supporters were calling for his head, he was also suffering increasing resentment from some of the club's senior players, 'I quickly found that most of the players had no respect for Frank O'Farrell. There were two camps, those that the manager had brought to the club like Buchan, Storey-Moore and myself and those that were still living in the Busby era. A definite "them and us" mentality existed. We used to train at the Cliff in those days and the three of us "newcomers" had to get changed in the reserve-team dressing room, while the rest of them changed in the first-team room round the corner. I never thought to ask why that was, but Manchester United was all about "I wanna be top dog" and it was difficult. I once asked Bobby Charlton for directions to the training ground and I'm still waiting for the answer!

'It wasn't that United was such a big club which gave me a problem, it was simply that I was in a team where everybody wanted to be "The Man", "The Star". Most of the 1968 European Cup-winning team were still there and some were clearly in the latter stages of their careers. Best was fading and they were all vying for his position, none more so than Willie Morgan. He had the long hair and would do his tricks, of course he really wanted to be George. Do you think any of them were going to worry about me and going to give me the ball when I made a run? They just thought, "Who are you? I'm not going to give you the ball." No, they'll take an extra touch, do a drag back or a Cruyff turn – they'll do something else and the crowd will cheer them. By this time I've made about three runs and I still don't get the ball but nobody saw that!

'My game was simple because it was defined but if I didn't get the ball I might as well sit up in the stand! The difference when I was at Bournemouth was that they got the ball to me. If I missed chances, then the others could have a go at me but they never worried because they knew I would get the next one, and I had confidence in my ability. If I'm not getting the service but I'm still making the runs what more can I do? If the manager is not on my side and doesn't see this and is more affected by other things then I've got no chance.'

Many critics believed United's position stemmed largely from defensive problems following the sale of Nobby Stiles to Middlesbrough 18 months previously, shortly before O'Farrell became manager. Although he was beset by injury problems at the time, and may have looked past his best as a First Division player, it was felt that Stiles's experience and infectious personality would still have proved invaluable. Looking around United's opponents at the time and the impact players such as Jack Charlton (Leeds), Tommy Smith

(Liverpool), Frank McLintock (Arsenal) and Mike Bailey (Wolves) were having on those around them, the critics appeared to have a case.

While Busby was manager, United played the game largely off the cuff, relying on sparkling individualism rather than teamwork. But United no longer had enough great players to make this approach work, and this had led to a more methodical style of play. O'Farrell wanted players running off the ball, which he considered to be a necessity in modern football rather than playing the ball to feet in the style that United had previously played the game. Old habits died hard and one or two of the club's senior players were still finding it difficult to adjust. There was little rapport between the players and management and indeed, Charlton later admitted that the team were not fully receptive to O'Farrell's ideas or those of his coach, Malcolm Musgrove, and were not always able to grasp what they were required to do.

Not one to throw in the towel, O'Farrell took his side to Leicester in early November, where goals from Best and Davies secured a 2-2 draw against his former club. The following weekend United hauled themselves off the bottom of the table with only their third win of the season, and the fact that it was against league leaders Liverpool made it doubly sweet. Despite the yawning gap between the two clubs, another crowd in excess of 50,000 packed into Old Trafford to see Davies and MacDougall score the goals that gave them a massive victory.

The match was not without its contentious moments as Liverpool argued that they were denied a penalty when Stepney had brought down Steve Heighway and also that Ted handled the ball before setting up the first goal for Davies. Afterwards, as Bill Shankly sportingly conceded that the best team had won, O'Farrell and MacDougall beamed into the television cameras enthusing over the team's performance. Believing that the press had been having a ball at United's expense in recent weeks and responsible for much of the enormous pressure he had been under, the manager vowed to continue his efforts to find the right mixture for long-term success. 'I definitely didn't handle before Davies scored!' insisted Ted. 'To be fair the press were good to me when I first joined. They didn't demand anything special and gave me time to settle in for which I was grateful. They could have become impatient because I was keeping Brian Kidd and Denis Law out of the team and they were still big stars at Old Trafford. I would relate myself going to Manchester United as similar to an actor who had previously only appeared in the provinces, suddenly going to the

West End stage. Everything was magnified, highlighted – you screw up and it's never forgotten.'

United were unable to produce a similar performance a week later though, when they suffered a three-goal defeat in the Manchester derby at Maine Road, however in the next match, Ted was back on the scoresheet, his second-half winner bringing a 2-1 home victory against Southampton. The result lifted United up to 19th place and was followed by their first away win of the season at Norwich. Best was an absentee at Carrow Road, having apparently walked away from football, but once again MacDougall was on target together with Storey-Moore to end a run of home victories for the Canaries, 'I loved Bestie, he was fantastic with me, although I didn't really understand quite what was happening, but everybody at the club had been taking a fair amount of stick. That was one of the things about being with a club like United, you were expected to do well and the pressure was always intense. The victory at Norwich was good for our morale, then we lost at Stoke and went to Palace.'

United's plight had undoubtedly had a detrimental effect on Best, whose enthusiasm for the game had appeared to be diminishing for some time. Despite his efforts to avoid the kind of distractions that had blighted his later days at Old Trafford, the opportunities to succumb were never far away. Earlier in the season he had failed to turn up for training and as a result had been dropped from the side. This time he had gone to London and had still not returned when United went down 2-0 to lowly Stoke at the Victoria Ground. Having finally lost his patience, O'Farrell suspended and transfer-listed Best upon his eventual return, which prompted John Bond to make an unsuccessful effort to tempt the wayward Irishman to join Bournemouth. Bond had offered United £250,000 to sign him while the now-disgraced former disc jockey Jimmy Savile offered Best £500 a week for him to become resident DJ at Savile's Le Cardinal discotheque in the town.

Ted recalls, 'I remember George was sent to join me in the reserve dressing room at the Cliff upon his return. It was typical of what was wrong at United, but thinking back there was so much that was wrong really, although I didn't question it at the time. I loved George but I remember one matchday he had a business deal worth around £20,000 to sign in London so United sent a private plane down to bring him back for the game. Unfortunately he failed to show up at the airport and went to a wine bar instead.'

Following a meeting with directors Sir Matt Busby and Louis Edwards, Best was removed from the transfer list. O'Farrell was left furious and with his authority having been severely undermined, his future was clearly in serious doubt. The row had widened the split among the very same players he desperately needed a response from in the next game at bottom-of-the-table Crystal Palace. Sadly they let him down and instead gave a performance that showed some staggering deficiencies in individual technique and teamwork. After falling two goals behind in the first half, they collapsed totally after the interval and eventually lost 5-0. The result was the club's biggest defeat in four years and revealed the enormity of United's plight. It proved to be the last straw for the directors and signalled the dismissal of O'Farrell, Musgrove and chief scout John Aston Senior, 'It was an awful performance, Don Rogers scored three or four goals for Palace I think and coming home basically Frank got fired. I felt sorry for him. Perhaps he did not communicate with the players as well as he should have done but there were too many people against him rather than for him. When Willie Morgan told me Tommy Docherty had got the job before it was officially announced, I said, "That's it then, I'll be gone by March!"

'Even if Frank had stayed longer at Manchester United I don't believe he would have brought the best out of me, although he was a very nice guy. He'd learnt his trade before he came to Old Trafford but he wasn't a big enough character. He was not strong enough to deal with the two factions. He had to deal the players from the Busby era, the players he brought in and the results going against them. He had too many problems of his own to worry about mine. It needed somebody with a lot of character, like Ron Atkinson when he came in some years later to sort things out.'

O'Farrell later acknowledged that he felt MacDougall was not accepted by a number of the other players at Old Trafford. He believed they had prejudices from the start about the way Ted played and decided that he was not one of their sort, so they gave him the cold shoulder treatment as a result. Musgrove shared much the same opinion although he doubted that United had the players capable of getting the ball to MacDougall in the penalty area anyway. Both agreed that as a result the supporters never saw the player's full potential.

Youth team coach Pat Crerand, who had retired from playing at the end of the previous season, was briefly put in temporary charge and was assisted by former defender Bill Foulkes. Both had been members of the club's European Cup-winning team and they held the fort until the ebullient but volatile Tommy Docherty was appointed as the new manager a few days later. The 44-year-old Scotsman had been managing his country's national side with some success since his appointment in August 1971, but wasted no time in agreeing to take the reins at Old Trafford.

He had previously enjoyed a playing career at Celtic, Preston and Arsenal, while winning 25 full caps for Scotland in the meantime, before becoming player-coach at Chelsea in 1961. He took over as manager the following year and despite suffering relegation in his first season in charge, he brought the club back to the First Division the following year and took them to the FA Cup Final in 1967. Life was never dull with 'the Doc' around and his strong opinions on the game sometimes led to confrontations with players and directors, which eventually brought about his departure from Stamford Bridge later the same year.

After spending an unsuccessful 12 months at Rotherham United, Docherty was lured to Queens Park Rangers, only for him to quit after just 29 days. He joined Aston Villa soon afterwards and despite initially reviving the club's fortunes, he was dismissed after they slumped to the bottom of the Second Division in January 1970. Docherty then spent 15 months in Portugal as manager of Porto, his side narrowly missing out on the Portuguese championship, before his return to England as assistant to Terry Neill at Hull City.

Docherty soon discovered that while skill and enthusiasm was not in short supply at Old Trafford, unfortunately a number of players were past their best and the team was nowhere near good enough. He appointed Crerand as his assistant and met the players for the first time at Mottram Hall in Cheshire on the eve of his first game in charge. The team the following day was picked by Crerand and Foulkes and included MacDougall, who gave a United an early lead, an advantage they held until Allan Clarke equalised for Leeds in the dying seconds of the game. Sadly, it would turn out to be Ted's last goal for United. Meanwhile, an open letter from George Best was printed in the match programme in which Best wished United the best of luck for the rest of the season but reaffirmed that he had decided not to play football again, although he did subsequently re-appear for United the following season before finally quitting the club for good.

A 3-1 defeat against Derby brought Docherty's side down to earth and with no league fixture scheduled for the following weekend, the manager took the opportunity to arrange a friendly match at Second Division Hull. Docherty announced that he would be fielding what he believed to be his strongest side and when neither Davies nor MacDougall's names appeared on the team sheet, the press quickly latched on to their absence. Davies would eventually be offloaded to Blackpool for £14,000 in the summer and while MacDougall sat disconsolately in the stands watching old-established stars Charlton and Law grab the goals that defeated the Tigers, the rumour mill began circulating news that he would also soon be leaving Old Trafford. Ted was a strong character, but few in the game at that time were as forthright and headstrong as Docherty, who wasted no time in fashioning a new United.

Soon after the match at Hull, Docherty appointed Tommy Cavanagh as his first-team coach. Cavanagh, not a man to stand any nonsense from any player, was the man who goaded the fine Nottingham Forest team of 1966 to 1968, when he was coach at the City Ground under manager Johnny Carey. Docherty had already begun his search for new players and his first addition was young full-back Alex Forsyth, who joined United in a £100,000 deal from Partick Thistle. Then the Doc leapt back into the transfer market and paid £120,000 for Arsenal's 28-year-old Scottish international midfielder George Graham in time for him to make his debut against his former club. There was to be no starting place for MacDougall at Highbury though, nor was it a happy start for Graham as the Gunners ran out 3-1 winners.

The following Saturday, a second-minute goal by Wolves captain Mike Bailey was enough to put United out of the FA Cup at the third round stage. Substitute Tony Dunne was sent off to add to United's woes and Docherty was now left with just one overriding target for the rest of the season – to stay in the First Division, 'Tommy Docherty was a larger-than-life character though he never rated me, but I didn't have a problem with that – football is an opinionated game. Mind you he could be very sarcastic. Obviously some players fit in with some managers, and don't with others. I didn't want to leave Manchester United, it was the club I idolised as a kid, but if the manager didn't pick me and my face didn't fit, then it was out of my hands.'

By the time MacDougall regained a place in the side for West Ham's visit to Old Trafford, the team also included the highly regarded

21-year-old Scottish centre-half Jim Holton, who Docherty had signed from Shrewsbury for £80,000, and 23-year-old Scottish international forward Lou Macari, who had joined United from Celtic for £200,000. A self-confessed competitor who excelled when the chips were down, Macari had impressed Docherty with his willingness to work hard for the team and possessed exactly what the manager was looking for in a front-runner. He made his mark immediately by scoring a point-saving goal on his debut to earn them a 2-2 draw to the delight of another crowd in excess of 50,000, many of whom wore tartan scarves and headwear to embrace the strong Scottish element now prevalent within the club, 'Lou was a great player and he went on to have a very good career, but unfortunately there was no chance of us forming a partnership like I had with Phil Boyer because he was a totally different player. I can't say we really became mates but I respected him for the player he was.

'The mood among the players at this time depended on whether you were either part of the old regime or part of the new. Tommy brought in a number of Scottish lads and they were good players. They were part of the new guard and I was now definitely part of the old, and the new boss made it clear he didn't want me long-term. It's very difficult in these situations, the same happened to Charlton, Law, Sadler etc, when O'Farrell took over because they were Busby's players, although they were also international stars which made it a bit different.

'Martin Buchan became a friend and you're looking for friends when you're a big name with a big price tag and there's nobody there to help you really. It wasn't a case of being big-headed on my part, I needed help at this time and I didn't get any. Unfortunately, I was the type of player that relied on other people to make things happen, my runs and movement were good but I still needed people to recognise this and get the right balls in to me.

'It was a hopeless situation. One day the press wanted a picture of all the Scottish contingent at the club and I was told to make sure I was on the end so that when I left, it would be easier to cut me out! But I'm over it now, it's all history, it was just that I needed encouragement and support at the time.'

When Everton came to Old Trafford four days later, United gave a debut to 21-year-old Irish international midfielder Mick Martin, a £20,000 Docherty signing from Bohemians. Ted remained in the starting 11 but after an ineffective performance he was replaced by

Kidd as United struggled to break down the visitors' defence. The change had little effect as Everton held on for a goalless draw and with little else to report upon, the press centred their attention on the wrong sort of headlines for MacDougall, 'There were about 60,000 inside the ground, it was the biggest home crowd of the season I think. I was substituted after about an hour and when I came off I went straight to the dressing room. Denis Law was injured so he didn't play and he was there in the dressing room. He asked me if I wanted to get changed quickly and get away before the crowd came out, then go and have a pint with him. The press reported that I had stormed out but we had just gone off to a hotel for a quiet pint! Law was my idol, I loved him and he was one person who was trying to look after me.

'Bobby Charlton was a different sort of character. He was better after he had drunk a couple of beers and loosened up a bit. The only time he ever spoke to me was when I roomed with him once before an away game and he asked me to turn the light off! Not strictly true, but it goes down well on the after-dinner circuit! Let's just say we didn't have any rapport between us – he was just different.'

Despite his lack of confidence in MacDougall's ability, Docherty kept him in the side for United's visit to Coventry the following Saturday. With the team now being dubbed as 'Little Scotland', Docherty's successor as national team manager Willie Ormond was at Highfield Road to watch the 1-1 draw that ensued. Unfortunately, Ted had a quiet game and did little to enhance his own international aspirations, however, the point helped the club climb away from the bottom two places in the league table. Nonetheless, the Doc was still searching for his first win since taking over from O'Farrell and it had not escaped his attention that the three clubs now below United each had games in hand, 'Although I played under Docherty he never gave me an opportunity as such – he played me because he had to, he couldn't just put me in the reserves after United had paid a huge transfer fee for me. One day, I went into his office to ask if there had been any offers for me and he asked me if I would be willing to move down to the Second or Third Division. But the way he asked me, it was as if he was taking the piss – that was the sarcastic side of him coming out.'

Ted met up with John Bond and the Bournemouth team at Rochdale a few days later, where he watched the Cherries gain a narrow victory. Then, the following day, while English football was looking forward to all the thrills and drama of the FA Cup, United were flying miles away from the action, as Docherty sped them off on what would today be called a 'team bonding' mission. Out of the cup and without a fixture for two weeks, the manager took his squad over to Ireland for a friendly against Bohemians, then on to Portugal where they played his former club Porto. The trip brought some success as United comfortably beat Bohemians, while the match against Porto ended goalless, then upon their return to league action, the manager got his first victory after six weeks in charge. Charlton was the main inspiration behind the home win against Wolves, with the former England veteran scoring both of United's goals. However the joy again proved to be short-lived, as it was followed by a heavy away defeat against Ipswich Town, 'Before the Ipswich game I was watching BBC television's *Grandstand* at the hotel and they showed a feature on that day's Bournemouth v Bolton match. I would have given anything to have been there and playing in that match. I was so pleased to hear they had won afterwards that I forgot about being beaten 4-1 at Ipswich! But I knew deep down I couldn't return to Bournemouth because I had reached a stage where I had to establish myself and to return to Dean Court would have been a backward step. It would have played into the hands of all those in the press who said I couldn't make it at the top level and suggest that I had opted for the safe route.'

Although selected in Docherty's starting XI on two further occasions, MacDougall was still unable to break the goal famine which had not seen him on the scoresheet for almost two months. Although his courage and effort was never in doubt, and appreciated by United's Stretford End supporters, Ted's record showed just five goals in 18 appearances for United and the longer he went without scoring, the more depressed he became, but thankfully his Old Trafford agony was about to come to an end, 'At times I wasn't even allowed to train with the first team and I knew my time was up – it had been six months of hell really! I was Frank O'Farrell's man and the Doc didn't fancy me. I have never regretted going to Old Trafford but I do wish I had been able to spend a little longer there and given a bit of a run in the team. Nonetheless it was a great opportunity and an honour, now when people ask me who I played for, when I tell them Manchester United, they say, "Wow!"

'However, I cannot tell you how pleased I was to get away from United in the end.'

9

Under Greenwood's Wing

DESPITE inconsistent results over the years, West Ham United had continued to serve up football to delight the purists during Ron Greenwood's tenure as manager, with attacking play, skilful players and football to enthral even the most difficult-to-please fans. Greenwood himself had a reputation as one of the football world's leading thinkers.

After a successful playing career during which he won the First Division with Chelsea in 1955/56, he turned to management and initially became coach to Oxford University before continuing his apprenticeship at Isthmian League Walthamstow Avenue. He then became manager of Eastbourne United and also England's youth team before joining Arsenal as assistant manager and coach, and for over two years, was also coach to England's under-23 side. Greenwood was appointed manager/coach at West Ham in April 1961 and he was one of the technical advisers appointed by FIFA for the World Cups in 1966 and 1970. Later in his career he was of course destined to enjoy a spell as full England manager between 1977 and 1982.

Few who saw the 1965 European Cup Winners' Cup Final at Wembley between the Hammers and TSV Munich 1860 will have seen a better exhibition of competitive and highly entertaining football. Yet following that success, which came after winning the FA Cup the previous season, the Hammers had not succeeded in taking any major titles. Greenwood's pride in the quality of football served up at Upton

Park ensured that style became synonymous with West Ham and it was a quality that many of the players reared under Greenwood took with them in their own managerial careers. And the Greenwood style was reflected in the club's England World Cup-winning trio from 1966, Bobby Moore, Geoff Hurst and Martin Peters, of whom only Moore remained at the club in February 1973.

Before the 1972/73 season had started Hurst had been sold to Stoke for £80,000 after 14 years at Upton Park, during which time he had played nearly 500 games and scored 248 goals. However, the team had made their best start to a season for four years and following a win at Everton in Moore's 500th league game, West Ham occupied eighth position in the First Division at the end of November.

The goalscoring of 27-year-old Bryan 'Pop' Robson had been a large factor in the team's albeit modest success and by New Year the Sunderland-born striker topped the scoring charts with 17 goals in 25 league games. With Trevor Brooking and Bermudan international Clyde Best regularly chipping in, the team looked to have solved the threat of a goal drought after the sale of Hurst. Nonetheless, transfer talk was still rife and Greenwood, a long-standing admirer of MacDougall's goalscoring ability, had been monitoring the situation at Old Trafford having missed out on the signatures of players such as George Graham, Derek Possee and Bill Garner, who had all changed clubs in recent months. Speculation increased when Robson fell out with Greenwood after protesting about being played in midfield during a 1-0 home defeat against league leaders Liverpool.

As well as being renowned for their entertaining style of football, West Ham had often shown an alarming inconsistency and once again this now began to cast a shadow over their season. Typically, after having beaten Chelsea 3-1 at Upton Park one weekend, the following weekend they allowed Hull City, then a mid-table Second Division side to outpace, outplay and outthink them in slipping to a one-goal FA Cup defeat. As February drew to a close Greenwood decided to add a fresh face to his side and made his move to bring MacDougall to the East End of London, 'I met Ron in the car park of the Post House Hotel in Stoke, he had driven up from London and I had driven down in my car with Paddy Crerand. John Bond had advised me to join West Ham as he felt they would serve my strengths well and get balls in to the box which was what I needed to re-establish myself. It was similar to the type of football I had been used to at Bournemouth and I believe John would have liked me to have gone to West Ham in the first place. So I took a drop of £60 in wages and accepted £100 a week – don't forget I had been on £150 a week at Bournemouth – and shook hands on it with Ron that day. With agents around, that would never happen today!

'That night I was lying in bed around 10pm when I had a phone call from the Tottenham manager, Bill Nicholson. He asked me if Ron and I had agreed a deal, and if so whether we had shaken hands on it. I said we had, so he wished me good luck as long as I didn't score too many goals against Spurs! Bill said he had wanted to sign me but his reaction was fabulous, he was a true gent – I should have gone to Spurs really!'

West Ham agreed a fee of £150,000 with Manchester United to secure MacDougall's signature and he became the first British player to have had almost £350,000 spent on him in one season. Ted received criticism in the media for collecting five per cent of the transfer fee, which he was quite entitled to do as, despite having made it clear how unhappy he was at Old Trafford, he had technically not requested a move.

Hammers fans looked forward to the addition of MacDougall in attack alongside Robson, and with Moore having one of his best seasons together with Billy Bonds linking up well with Brooking in the middle of the park, they had hopes of achieving their highest finishing position in the league and securing a UEFA Cup place for the following season. Unfortunately they were forced to wait a little longer than expected for Ted's first appearance, his registration being delayed by a week when the forms failed to reach the Football League's Lytham St Annes headquarters in time, as the post was delayed due to an ongoing rail strike.

MacDougall's debut eventually came when he wore the number nine shirt in a goalless draw against Sheffield United at Bramall Lane on 11 March 1973. The Hammers lined up as follows: Ferguson, McDowell, Lampard, Bonds, Taylor, Moore, Best, Lock, MacDougall, Brooking and Robson. Substitute: Holland.

In a match where chances were at a premium, they were eventually grateful to keeper Bobby Ferguson for two saves from Alan Woodward's twice-taken penalty to come away with a point, 'I hoped that at West Ham I would get a chance to get out of the spotlight a little and settle down to my football. I knew what people were saying, that I wasn't good enough for the First Division and all that. I admit my goalscoring record at United had been poor but I didn't really take much notice of the criticism because when you had a crowd of 50,000 at a game, you could never please everyone! Even when I scored the nine goals for Bournemouth against Margate some people said afterwards, "Ah yes, but what about the ones he missed?" I could never satisfy them all so I didn't intend trying!'

A few days later MacDougall returned to Bournemouth in the West Ham side for former team-mate Bill Kitchener's testimonial match. A back injury had forced Kitchener, himself a former Hammer, to retire and appropriately enough Ted found his scoring touch back at Dean Court, grabbing his first goal for the Hammers with a diving header, typical of many goals he had scored during his time with the Cherries. The match ended in a 3-3 draw, and as well as recapturing his appetite for finding the back of the net, MacDougall looked comfortable playing alongside his new colleagues. His first league goal since Christmas followed, in his home debut for the Hammers against Manchester City, where he slipped past City's Tony Book to strike the ball into the net. Cheered on by a crowd of just under 30,000, Robson added a second goal and West Ham eventually ran out 2-1 winners to move up to seventh in the table.

A week later, MacDougall was on target again, this time in an ill-tempered 3-1 win at Crystal Palace. Palace's battle against relegation gave the match an unwelcome, violent undercurrent, which eventually saw Ted laid out by Palace defender Bobby Bell. Earlier, Robson had given West Ham a 1-0 interval lead, which MacDougall then doubled, wrong-footing Palace's defenders after receiving a pass from Moore, before Brooking scored a third, 'He must have hit me hard because I don't remember much about the incident with Bell! It was probably just as well he laid me out, otherwise I would have probably thumped him back and been in trouble myself!'

Further victories followed, first at home to Everton, where Brooking's run set up Robson's 25th goal of the season, which was followed just before the final whistle by Kevin Lock's first league goal. Then against Newcastle at St James' Park, a gale force wind made conditions difficult, but didn't prevent MacDougall netting two superb headed goals, both set up by Brooking, to give the Hammers a 2-1 win.

Greenwood had told Ted when he arrived that his job would be to attack from close to the flanks, rather than going straight down the middle where Robson was playing and doing so well. With four goals in his first five games, MacDougall had made a great start to life at Upton

Park and the team had risen to fifth in the table, 'Ron Greenwood was good on the game, probably ahead of his time as a manager back then, but he didn't believe in central strikers because he thought central defenders were poor players when they didn't have anyone to mark. He had a system which was quite unique, he'd got Clyde Best playing as a right-winger and me as a left-winger. Then he got Pop Robson, who was the best finisher I ever played with by the way, and Trevor Brooking coming late through the centre from midfield.

'As a result the big centre-halves didn't know what to do as they didn't have anyone to mark because Pop and Trevor would stay deep and Clyde and I used to whip these crosses in for them to run on to. It worked great, I was crossing these balls with my left foot, pinging them in and I thought, "This is good!"

'Ron was obviously happy with me, the team was doing well and my touch started to improve – it had to playing in tight situations against better players. I was never frightened of using my left foot and I would cross balls with it to avoid having to keep pulling the ball back on to my right. My control and confidence levels also got better by playing this different role and I realise now it did me good because it made me a better footballer. Ron told Bondy he was impressed with me, he didn't realise I could play like that. The training at West Ham helped, we practised a lot of two against one and three against two situations and doing this with people like Brooking, my touch improved a lot.'

In April, Ted was back at Dean Court again for former Cherries player Alan Green's testimonial against Leicester. Green's brief but promising career had been ended by a heart condition, and together with fellow Hammer Frank Lampard, MacDougall guested for Bournemouth in a match which they won 2-1. Reunited with Phil Boyer in attack, Ted's goal was the first-half highlight. Picking up a pass from Lampard, he hit a low shot inside the post, beyond the reach of goalkeeper Peter Shilton. It proved to be his last goal of the season however, although he featured in each of West Ham's remaining five matches.

Just one victory in those last five games ended the Hammers' hopes of securing a UEFA Cup place. Against Leeds at Upton Park, John McDowell collided with Ferguson, causing play to be held up for ten minutes before the goalkeeper left the field suffering from concussion. Best took over in goal but was unable to keep out a header from Allan Clarke, although Pat Holland replied with a last-minute equaliser. On

Good Friday, a Robson hat-trick, together with a goal from Brooking, brought an exciting 4-3 victory against Southampton.

Then the following day, with five regular players injured, Robson was forced to play in defence against Derby, where the normally placid Greenwood marched out of the Baseball Ground in response to a late penalty decision which rescued a point for the home side. Another draw followed against Birmingham at St Andrew's, before Arsenal came to Upton Park for the final game of the season. Ray Kennedy and John Radford gave the Gunners a two-goal lead in the first half before an own goal from Pat Rice brought West Ham back into the game. Try as he might, Robson failed to score the one goal he needed to equal Hurst's post-war Hammers record of 29 as West Ham slipped to their first defeat in ten games. The result meant the Hammers slipped back to finish sixth but it still constituted their highest position in Ron Greenwood's 12 years at the helm.

The club then embarked on a series of end-of-season friendlies, which saw them visit Israel, Norway and Spain, 'We were due to play against an Israel National XI in Tel Aviv and on the day of the game I went out for a walk with Bobby Moore, Clyde Best and Frank Lampard – the usual reprobates! We were in this street called Dizengoff, a big thoroughfare with cafes and bars and the temperature was about 90 degrees Fahrenheit. We were strolling along and Bob said he wouldn't mind a drink, so we nipped in to a bar and he ordered a round of beers… then another and another, and then on the other side of the street we saw Ron Greenwood. We quickly called the waiter over and asked him to take away all these bottles of beer before Ron spotted them. Anyway we played the match and it was probably one of my better games for West Ham!'

MacDougall could now justifiably take a deep breath and look back at the 1972/73 season with the air of a man who had just flown halfway across the world! When the campaign opened, he was the focal point of a talented Bournemouth side gearing itself up for another attack at promotion from the Third Division. Within weeks he had left in a blaze of publicity to become a Manchester United player, tasting life in the top flight for the first time. Then, when his stay at Old Trafford had become troubled and turbulent, West Ham had stepped in to seemingly relaunch his career.

For their part, Manchester United escaped relegation and Bobby Charlton announced his retirement as a player before accepting the manager's position at Preston. The Bournemouth players missed out again in their bid for promotion but had miraculously walked away from the wreck of their team coach following a road accident on their way home from a game at Scunthorpe in January. Assistant manager Ken Brown was not so lucky however, suffering a broken thigh, while Boyer and Alan Groves, although not seriously hurt, had both been initially trapped in the wreckage, 'The boys certainly had a lucky escape because the coach skidded on ice and ploughed through a garage wall and into a house. I certainly hoped my travels were over though, I found it good to begin with at West Ham and the lads really helped me to settle down in the last few weeks of the season. I thought they were a great club with great prospects.

'It took a bit of time and character on my part to get over the troubled period I had gone through, but I always felt things would gradually sort themselves out. However, I still had one major concern, although the manager's tactics had proved to me that I could do other things in the game apart from scoring goals, the problem was scoring goals was really all I wanted to do. I wasn't really going to be satisfied crossing balls for others to score all the time and I don't think Ron Greenwood understood that. Unfortunately as a result things started to turn sour again the following season.'

10

Coming to Blows

FOR almost a decade West Ham had been tipped as pre-season favourites to win a trophy, but since 1965 honours had constantly eluded them. The club had flattered to deceive despite the quality of its players often being enough to prevail against any First Division opposition on their day. Once again though, they were among the bookmakers' favourites for success in 1973/74.

There were no major additions to Greenwood's squad during the close season, but there was already no shortage of ability, youth and experience at the club. Firstly there was the goalscoring threat of MacDougall and Robson, then, the presence of emerging defender Kevin Lock would enable captain Bobby Moore to link up in midfield. Add to these the ability of Ferguson in goal and the tremendous work rate of Bonds in the middle of the park, and there was good reason for optimism. Ferguson, Moore, Lampard and Best were all full internationals, while McDowell, Lock, Taylor, Robson, Bonds and Brooking had all represented England at under-23 level.

At its summer conference, the Football League had voted in favour of a new three up, three down arrangement between the First and Second Divisions, hoping it would mean fewer meaningless, end-of-season games. Another off-field change was the government's decision to introduce VAT, which meant that football supporters across the country would be hit by an increase in ticket prices. However, MacDougall was struck by a problem of his own when he returned from the summer break, 'Unfortunately I suffered a bout of hay fever in the summer and the first day back for pre-season training, we went out for a run in Epping Forest, which didn't help me much. There's me and Clyde Best, who looked like the boxer Sonny Liston as he had come back about four stone overweight – and that was just his right leg! We went on this long run, and soon the two of us and Bobby Moore were so far behind the others were out of sight, and we had no idea which direction they had gone. So Clyde puts his ear to the ground, then looks up, points into the distance and says, "I think they went that way!" Ron had to send a runner back for us in the end.

'I didn't know it was hay fever at the time, but the problem started when I joined Bournemouth. Maybe it was all the pine trees down there, I don't know but it had become a bit of a problem and I was sent to the clinic down West Ham High Street. Here they got me running up and down steps, then blowing into a bag and the doctor gave me all these injections to see what I was allergic to. Eventually he sent a letter to Ron Greenwood telling him that this player he had just bought from Manchester United was allergic to two things – grass and running! Hence the reason when people tell me I was a lazy player I say, "Yes, but I was allergic to it." It wasn't that I didn't want to run, I just couldn't! That was my get out of jail card.'

By virtue of their free-scoring approach the previous season, West Ham qualified for the pre-season Watney Cup competition where they met the previous winners, Bristol Rovers. Though MacDougall was fit enough to score his first goal of the season at Eastville, the Hammers put in a poor display, the Third Division side eventually winning the tie on penalties after the scores finished level at 1-1. Sadly just before the new league season got under way, former Bournemouth manager Freddie Cox died in Poole Hospital aged just 52 after collapsing at home with a heart attack. After parting company with the Cherries, the man who had originally brought MacDougall to Dean Court had concentrated on running his family newsagents business in the town, 'I was so sorry to hear the news. Freddie still had so much to offer the game and I shall never forget the kindness he showed myself and Joan.'

A crowd of 28,169 at Upton Park saw the Hammers start brightly before slipping to a 2-1 defeat in their opening league game against Newcastle. With MacDougall still playing out on the left wing, Robson had put them ahead but Malcolm Macdonald replied with two for the visitors, his winning goal coming when Ferguson allowed a tame shot to enter the net. With Ferguson then indisposed, 18-year-old Mervyn Day made his debut at home to Ipswich two days later, in a game which started brightly with Bonds and Brooking both scoring within the first seven minutes, but then turned in the visitors' favour, and in the end the Hammers were grateful to a late Best goal to rescue a point.

If the first two games had been disappointing, those that followed showed little improvement as the Hammers failed to win any of their first 11 league games, picking up only four draws and scoring only ten goals in the process. Desperate to try and turn things around, Greenwood continually made changes to the side, a number of which were not popular with his senior players and MacDougall was one who could no longer be sure of a regular place, 'Although things went well for the team when I first joined West Ham, I didn't get on particularly well with Ron Greenwood and he seemed to have little idea of how to handle players. He would never have survived today. I needed geeing up because I wasn't scoring enough goals but Ron was never one to do that. I got on very well with Bobby Moore though, who always had a word of encouragement for me and we quickly became friends. As results started to go against us I was in and out of the side and unfortunately my relationship with the manager just got progressively worse.'

Despite twice leading at Norwich thanks to headers from Best and Robson, the Hammers eventually had to settle for a share of the spoils before grabbing a more fortuitous point in a goalless draw at Queens Park Rangers, in which the home side had three goals disallowed. MacDougall had been left out of the side at Loftus Road but returned for the visit of Tottenham to Upton Park, but still unable to find his first league goal of the season, he was substituted as Spurs grabbed victory through a goal from Martin Chivers.

Angered by their team's performance, hundreds of disillusioned Hammers supporters left the ground before the end of the game. Two days later Ted was left out again, as they slipped to a 3-2 defeat in the return fixture with Queens Park Rangers, where McDowell and Taylor were both guilty of bad errors which each cost their team goals. Still trying to find his best team and formation, Greenwood had now given starts to a total of 17 different players in six games, 'The second half of the previous season had gone pretty well for us and we thought we could keep it going but it just didn't work. Defensively we started badly, Ron tried playing three at the back but that didn't work, so Bobby

Moore came out of midfield and went back into the defence because we were conceding too many goals. Then we got stuck in a dreadful run of results and team spirit suffered greatly as a result.'

A falling-out between Greenwood and Moore soon made matters worse and led to the latter's apparent request for a transfer. Greenwood left the England skipper out of the side for the next game at Manchester United because of 'unexpected adverse publicity that was bad for morale'. This fuelled speculation that Moore, who had achieved a record total of 107 appearances for England during the summer, was about to join Brian Clough's Derby County and created more unrest at Upton Park.

With Bonds leading the side, MacDougall returned at Old Trafford but again had no joy in front of goal during a comfortable 3-1 victory for United. Greenwood restored Moore to the team which faced Leicester at Upton Park the following week however, when a rare error from Peter Shilton allowed Robson to put the Hammers in front, but once again they were unable to hold on to their lead, a mistake by Lock this time leading to Frank Worthington's equaliser. MacDougall started the game but, for all his aggressive running, his shooting was wayward and he was eventually replaced by young striker Ade Coker.

September drew to a close with a defeat at Stoke, whose first win of the season included a headed goal from ex-Hammer Geoff Hurst that left his former club just one place off the bottom of the league. The team were again guilty of playing some poor football, while MacDougall turned in arguably his worst performance since joining the club. Greenwood's biggest headache continued to be the defence though, which rarely looked comfortable and always likely to make a crucial mistake. Ferguson was dropped from the side for the visit of Burnley and transfer-listed after making disparaging comments about his team-mates. Day again stepped in but could do nothing to prevent Colin Waldron's winning goal for the Clarets. Soon afterwards came a flashpoint which saw MacDougall sent off for the first time in his professional career after head-butting Burnley's Doug Collins in an off-the-ball incident, 'I was never a shrinking violet and could be a real piece of work at times. On this occasion I let my anger and frustration get the better of me. With me, things were either right or wrong and if they were wrong I had to put them right, even during a game, and at this point in time things at West Ham were going badly wrong. I was my own worst enemy when things were not going well for me. I was a difficult person to deal with when I wasn't hitting the back of the net and Ron Greenwood had no idea how to handle me, mind you he had plenty of other problems at the club to deal with – most of which I seemed to get the blame for!

'We had a bad run of results, I lost form and unfortunately it all reached a head one Friday morning at the ground when Greenwood was stood in front of everyone speaking about the next day's game and this, that and the other. Meanwhile I've got my head down and I'm not really looking at him so he says, "I want you to look at me when I'm talking to you." I just shook my head and told him I was sick of looking at him. That wasn't good!

'Bobby Moore told me not to worry about what Greenwood had said and to just go out, play my natural game and score a goal. But it was the beginning of the end really, Ron certainly did not have the ability to pull it all together. I stayed at Bobby's house on several occasions while I was at West Ham. He was terrific with me and the world is certainly a poorer place since he left us.'

Ted's first goal in almost two months eventually came in a hard-fought 2-2 draw against Liverpool in the League Cup at Upton Park, in which the Hammers had twice fought back from being a goal behind but unfortunately things sank to a new low following a league defeat at Everton. MacDougall had struck a shot against the post at Goodison Park, before a poor back-pass by Keith Coleman allowed Everton's Joe Harper to nip in for what proved to be the only goal of the game.

When Best, returning to the side after injury, missed a simple chance to equalise near the end it left West Ham rock bottom of the First Division and the knives were out for the manager. Greenwood refused to quit but despite receiving his chairman's backing, speculation remained that it was only a matter of time before he moved up to general manager, relinquishing his involvement in the day-to-day running of the side.

Suspended for the next three games following his sending-off against Burnley, Ted took the opportunity to watch his former Bournemouth team-mates in action against Aldershot where a Sainty hat-trick gave the Cherries a comfortable victory. It also gave him a chance to talk with John Bond about the problems at Upton Park. Not for the first time, Bond, who was then among the names being linked with a managerial vacancy at Nottingham Forest, gave MacDougall just the encouragement he was looking for, 'John knew better than anyone that I needed reassurance and he told me that he still believed I was one of the best goalscorers in the country and on a par with any other striker in the game. That was all I needed to hear.'

In Ted's absence, a goal from McDowell, who had now been moved in to midfield, gave the Hammers their first victory of the season at Coventry. But the following week, without the injured Robson, Brooking was forced to play up front in a goalless draw at home to Derby and the absence of a serious goal threat in the League Cup replay at Anfield saw the game settled by a superb diving header by Liverpool's John Toshack.

With Bond's message foremost in his mind, MacDougall returned for the trip to league leaders Leeds in early November. The Yorkshire side had dropped just three points all season and predictably, the match went according to the form. After Paul Madeley's cross had struck the crossbar, Mick Bates was first to the rebound and put the home side in front, before Mick Jones added a second before half-time. Jones grabbed another after the break and Allan Clarke added a fourth, while MacDougall's 83rd-minute header from Bonds's cross was nothing more than a consolation. The action did not end at the final whistle though, as a dressing-room bust-up between the two players after the game brought problems within the club to a head, 'We were a goal down and Billy Bonds plays a ball short towards me and he thinks I should have come off my man to get it, so it's my fault. "You fucking so and so!" he says. Anyway Norman Hunter nipped in, the ball breaks to Lorimer and he crosses it in to Jones who scores. This is still the first half and as we're making our way back for the restart he's still going on about it. "I'm gonna have you, you fucking so and so!" Anyway I told him to piss off and nothing was said in the dressing room at half-time.

'Then near the end of the game I scored so I'm happy and I didn't give a shit. Back in the dressing room, I'm in the shower washing my hair and Bonzo, who was a big lad, was in the middle of the communal bath having a right go at me again. So I said to him, "Why don't you do something about it instead of talking about it all the time?" So he took one step forward and I really wellied him, I hit him straight across the chest and he fell back into the bath! Some of the players got hold of him, thank God, and in comes Ron Greenwood and assistant manager John Lyall and they've got hold of me with my arms pinned across my back and I said, "That's what wrong with your so and so club, it's full of cliques." Nothing more was said but from that point on West Ham just wanted to get rid of me because by this time I was real, real trouble.

'There were two main cliques at West Ham, the "Half of Lager Lads" which I was part of and it also included Moore, Best and Lampard. Then there was the "Golfing Clan" which included Brooking, Robson, Day and McDowell. Although most of us got on all right, it had started to disunite us as a team. Those players that were not part of either of these groups became very isolated, except for Bonzo who used to wash windows after training! Mind you he was a winner, and I always thought he was decent until we had this altercation. So that was me gone – great way to get a move I suppose!'

Not for the first time, MacDougall faced criticism among supporters and in the press for failing to come back and help out the overworked Hammers defence during the game, opting instead to remain on the halfway line, 'My whole demeanour hinged totally on whether or not I was scoring goals. That's why people got pissed off with me. If people gave me grief about not dropping back and helping defend I would just ask them when they last helped me up front? Anyone who had a go at me needed some ammunition to come back with, because I would always come back and have a go at them. I wouldn't sit back and just take it.'

While the press continued to speculate on the consequences of the fall-out at Elland Road, MacDougall remained in the starting XI for the game against Sheffield United at Upton Park the following Saturday. To deepen the gloom, two goals from Alan Woodward gave the visitors a 2-0 interval lead, but a second-half fightback brought goals from Bonds and Brooking and a share of the spoils. However, Greenwood's appearance at Bournemouth's game against Charlton four days later, renewed speculation that Ted could be about to return to his old club.

Optimistic Cherries supporters began to chant his name during the match, but even if Bond wanted to bring their former striker back to Dean Court, the club did not have the finance available without the need to sell players first. It would not prove to be a long-lasting dilemma for the Cherries manager though, as events elsewhere would soon dramatically change the landscape for himself, MacDougall and the south coast club.

It was the resignation of Norwich City manager Ron Saunders that triggered a series of events which would have great significance to both Bournemouth and West Ham. Anxious to strengthen his squad,

Greenwood had been strongly linked with City's Graham Paddon but Saunders's departure came before the Hammers boss had been able to complete a deal to bring the player to Upton Park.

In the meantime, still searching for a second league win of the season, Greenwood had again shuffled his pack without much success, switching Robson from his preferred attacking role to play in midfield and pushing Brooking forward. Best, another player reported to be looking for a move away from Upton Park, and MacDougall had joined Brooking up front but with little sign of improvement, although a precious point was collected from a goalless draw at fourth-bottom Wolves.

Then, as November drew to a close, Greenwood completed the signing of striker Bobby Gould for £70,000 from Bristol City. Similar in style to MacDougall, the much-travelled Gould made his debut alongside him, against one of Gould's former clubs, Arsenal, at Upton Park. Neither player was able to make much impression and the ensuing 3-1 defeat meant that after 17 games, West Ham were one place off the bottom of the table, with only one win and just nine points to their name. Cries for Greenwood's dismissal could be heard throughout the match but it was MacDougall who sensed his time at Upton Park might be nearing its end, 'When Ron brought in Bobby Gould it hammered home to me (no pun intended!), that my time was just about up at Upton Park.'

Meanwhile something of a wrangle was taking place between Bournemouth and Norwich, the outcome of which was to shape Ted's future career. John Bond had been given permission to speak to City chairman Arthur South, who in turn had offered him the manager's job at Carrow Road. Bond, although torn between loyalty to Bournemouth and his strong ambition to manage in the First Division, had apparently indicated that he was ready to accept the job, subject to being released from his contract at Dean Court. The following day though, it seemed he was not going to Norwich after all, when Harold Walker refused to release him from his existing contract and instead offered him a new ten-year contract to stay at the Third Division club.

Bond's response was apparently to resign so that he could then apply for the Norwich vacancy, at which point Walker felt he had no alternative but to agree to Bond's departure, although he believed Norwich had got him 'on the cheap'. The whole matter left a nasty taste between the two clubs. After South had spent much of the day considering other names on his shortlist, he was no doubt delighted to eventually obtain the services of his first choice and Bond agreed a four-year contract. Cherries coach Ken Brown joined him at Carrow Road, while Bournemouth received £10,000 in settlement of Bond's contract.

Bond had clearly been frustrated having narrowly missed out on promotion at Dean Court for a second consecutive season. Again, critics were quick to point to the number of team changes he had made, but perhaps of more significance were the number of points dropped against struggling teams, and the loss of the coaching influence of Brown at a critical stage of the season. Bond left hoping his next three and a half years of football management would be as happy as the time he had spent at Bournemouth, but his departure would nonetheless rip the heart out of the club, 'I know John was genuinely grateful to Mr Walker and the club for giving him his first management opportunity, and I know just how much he wanted to get the club into the Second Division at the time. The team had made a disappointing start to the 1973/74 season, but had strung together an unbeaten run which had brought them back into the promotion picture. But John was an ambitious manager and he always said his aim was to manage a First Division club. Bournemouth was probably the most ambitious and progressive club outside the First Division at this time, but football being what it was, there was never any guarantee that they would make it and in football you have to accept the opportunities when they are presented to you.'

As soon as Bond knew he would be taking over at Norwich his first priority was to get MacDougall to join him at Carrow Road and negotiations with Greenwood were soon under way. The talks were made easier because Paddon wanted to leave Norwich and West Ham wanted to sign him. Despite MacDougall's singular lack of scoring success in 14 months with Manchester United and West Ham, Bond firmly believed that Ted's recent troubles were as much off the field as on it, knowing he was the sort of person who easily got depressed, and remained convinced his goal touch would soon reappear.

What proved to be MacDougall's last appearance for West Ham came in a 1-0 defeat against Liverpool at Anfield and soon after his return to London, he was on his way to Norfolk in a club record £140,000 deal, while Paddon travelled in the opposite direction for £30,000 less. It meant that Ted had become the first player in Britain to command over half a million pounds in transfer fees. West Ham were happy, Bond couldn't believe his luck and Ted couldn't wait to join him, '"Budgie" came to West Ham and he did a great job for them, and I was off to Norwich – it was the best thing that ever happened really. I just wanted away because Ron Greenwood was never capable of getting the best out of me. But I knew that if I could get back with Bondy, I could continue where I left off at Bournemouth. My time at West Ham proved to me that I could do something else apart from just score goals but it wasn't what I wanted to do, so I left feeling that it had been pretty much a waste of time really and the whole experience didn't do me much good.'

11

Back in the Old Routine

RON Saunders resigned as Norwich City manager following a 3-1 home defeat against Everton on 17 November 1973. With the crowd voicing their disapproval for his tactics and amid speculation linking him with the manager's job at Manchester City, a bust-up with City chairman Arthur South after the game led to Saunders resigning before storming out. The Canaries had won just twice in 16 matches and were third from bottom of the league table, nonetheless within a week Saunders was unveiled as manager at Maine Road.

He had succeeded Lol Morgan in the Carrow Road hot seat in July 1969, having already earned a reputation as a hard man during his time as manager of Oxford United. While in charge at Norwich, he had signed some quality players such as Graham Paddon, Peter Silvester and Doug Livermore to complement the imposing presence of centre-half Duncan Forbes, locally born Peter Stringer – another no-nonsense defender – and talented goalkeeper Kevin Keelan in what was basically a hard-working Second Division outfit.

Saunders, a great believer in organisation and discipline, enjoyed his finest achievement at the end of the 1971/72 season when, after so long in the wilderness, Norwich were crowned Second Division champions. He then embarked on one of the most significant seasons in the Canaries history and the club's first campaign in the First Division. A winning goal in the dying seconds of their final home match ensured they retained their First Division status for the following season, while

122

they also reached Wembley for the first time in the final of the League Cup, although losing by the only goal against Tottenham Hotspur.

During the summer of 1973, chairman Geoffrey Watling stepped down and was replaced by Arthur South – soon to become Sir Arthur upon his knighthood the following year. South was a former Lord Mayor of Norwich and had previously fronted a public appeal to save the Norfolk club in 1957. City looked to be in good hands, albeit those of a very different character than its previous chairman. Popularly known as 'Citizen South of Norwich', he was the straight-talking Labour leader of the City Council with a passion for local politics and football. Few who knew him well were probably surprised when, within three months, his relationship with the blunt and unyielding Saunders ended in such dramatic and very public fashion.

City had made a horrendous start to 1973/74 and whoever succeeded Saunders faced a huge task in keeping City up. The £150,000 sale of the popular David Cross to Coventry City had left them woefully short of any proven ability in attack and the only notable success had again been their progress in the League Cup, where they had reached the quarter-finals. The man given the task of reviving the club's fortunes was the East Anglian-born John Bond. Like his new chairman, he could be outspoken and at times flamboyant but his positive outlook came as a breath of fresh air at Carrow Road.

Immediately given the go-ahead to bring in fresh blood, before his first match in charge, Bond quickly completed the deal that reunited him with his former Bournemouth 'goal machine'. Many supporters questioned the new manager's remarkable faith in MacDougall after he had managed just five goals in 24 appearances at West Ham. Did he still have that rare knack of finding, and using, space in the penalty area? Were his poor results with Manchester United and West Ham really just a reflection on the overall performance of those teams and their inability to provide him with the service he needed? Bond believed so, and immediately instructed MacDougall to once again make his mark in the box, and to get in as many headers and shots on goal as possible. Just like at Bournemouth, the manager concentrated all his team's attacking intent upon feeding his striker's appetite for goals, 'I had had a crap 15 months and I needed to get back with someone who believed in what I did. I was a very complex character at this time and if I was given crap nobody was going to get anything out of me. I needed to be understood and unless a person understood how my complexity worked, they would never get the best out of me. I still knew I had it in me to score goals but I needed somebody to believe in me and someone to give me the ball. John told the lads at Norwich that they had one of the best finishers in the country in their team and to play me in, to give me the ball where I wanted it. It was pretty simple really and music to my ears!'

Ted wore a Norwich shirt for the first time against Burnley on 8 December 1973, the City team at Turf Moor being Keelan, Butler, Wilson, Stringer, Forbes, Prophett, Briggs, O'Donnell, MacDougall, Suggett and Mellor. Substitute: Howard.

It did not prove to be a particularly memorable debut for MacDougall, the Clarets' Billy Ingham scoring the only goal to send City to the bottom of the First Division. MacDougall's best chance came after Colin Suggett took the ball to the byline, then having created space for himself by checking inside, Ted moved back into the space to receive Suggett's pass. It was a classic MacDougall manoeuvre but unfortunately on this occasion, his final shot was blocked.

Four days later, Burnley were again the opponents in Bond's first home match in charge at Carrow Road. On the day he was appointed, the Lancashire club established a two-goal advantage in the home leg of their semi-final in the Texaco Cup, a competition which involved 16 English and Scottish clubs who had not qualified to play in Europe. City had reached the final the previous season and had already enjoyed victories over St Johnstone and Motherwell this time around. A crowd of just below 12,000 turned out to see MacDougall mark his home debut with two goals, although a 3-2 victory on the night gave Burnley a comfortable aggregate victory and ensured their progress to the final.

The signing of MacDougall was the first of several moves Bond made to transform Norwich's style of play. He made no secret that his long-term aim was to make them as adventurous and skilful as his Bournemouth team had been, and he wasted no time in persuading Fred Davies, Mel Machin and John Benson to leave the south coast and join him in East Anglia. Harold Walker had pleaded with the players not to leave but such was the influence Bond had over them, his pleas were ignored. Goalkeeper Davies ended his playing career having been offered a coaching position at Carrow Road, while popular City full-back Clive Payne travelled to Dean Court as part of a combined deal which netted the Cherries a sum of £50,000 but led to more bad feeling between the two clubs, 'Bondy started to get everyone playing just the same as we did at Bournemouth. Kenny and Fred were doing the coaching, and with Benno and Mel there too I quickly settled in and off we went. The trouble was we had a lot of ground to make up.'

MacDougall, Machin and Benson lined up together at Carrow Road in City's first league match under Bond's management, more than 20,000 supporters braving wintry conditions to see them take on second-placed Liverpool on a snow-covered pitch. The game started sensationally when in the first minute, with defenders struggling in the snow, 20-year-old City striker Paul Cheesley ran through to shoot past the advancing goalkeeper Ray Clemence. The crowd's delight was relatively short-lived though, as Liverpool levelled less than 20 minutes later when Peter Cormack slipped the ball past Keelan. As conditions worsened, the players continued to struggle on the snow-covered pitch but City held on for a well-deserved point, MacDougall had displayed some neat touches in the difficult conditions, Machin looked stylish in linking up the attack, as he had done so well at Bournemouth, and above all, the supporters went home satisfied with what they had seen.

Looking to improve the service to MacDougall, Bond included young winger Steve Grapes in his side at Leeds the following week. Although ultimately beaten by a goal from Terry Yorath, City emerged from the game with a good deal of credit, their attacking football having given the runaway league leaders a more difficult afternoon than they had become accustomed to. Ted's first league goal for the Canaries came four days later, on Boxing Day in the East Anglian derby at Carrow Road. It arrived after a miscued clearance from Ipswich's former Bournemouth goalkeeper David Best had fallen straight to City debutant Billy Steele. Steele's shot then hit the crossbar and before anyone else could react, MacDougall put the rebound in the net. Yet it was Norwich who eventually lost the game, their local rivals hitting back with two second-half goals and Bond's third defeat in four games meant that the Canaries slipped back to the bottom of the pile and a further winless run of five games soon followed.

It began three days later, when Ron Saunders brought his Manchester City side to Norfolk. After a bright start, Grapes crossed for MacDougall to put the Canaries in front but by half-time the lead had been lost, with Denis Law snatching a goal back, to the very apparent delight of his new manager. By now, Bond knew he had to try and rebuild his side but was also aware that there was little opportunity for experimentation when every point was needed in the fight against relegation. He retained the core of City's defence, with Stringer and Forbes staying together in the middle, and Keelan looking better than ever as he approached 500 games in goal.

Having allowed Cheesley to join Bristol City, Bond completed the £30,000 signing of Sheffield Wednesday's former West Ham winger John Sissons ahead of City's visit to Upton Park on New Year's Day. Sissons had played with both Bond and assistant Ken Brown when the Hammers had won the FA Cup and European Cup Winners' Cup in the mid-1960s. It was another example of his preference for signing players known to him previously. Ten of Bond's principal signings at Bournemouth had been from his former clubs and testament to his belief that when signing a player it was essential not only to know how a man played, but what his attitude to the game was both on and off the field, 'John liked to bring in players he knew he could rely on and who wouldn't let him down and in return he showed a lot of faith in those players. He wanted us to play an open and exciting style of football and he would go for players he knew could help him to achieve this.'

MacDougall's re-emergence was certainly paying off and he left his mark upon his return to Upton Park with two second-half goals. The only problem was that West Ham hit back with four, including two from Paddon, and the result left Norwich even further adrift at the bottom. Further defeats followed against Arsenal, first in the FA Cup at Carrow Road and then in the league at Highbury the following week, before City's next point came from a 1-1 draw at home to Wolves. MacDougall gave them a first-half lead when he netted a classic diving header following a cross from Benson, but another precious point was lost when Derek Dougan equalised midway through the second half, leaving Bond still searching for his first league win.

Amid all of their struggles in the league, Norwich could take some encouragement from their progress in the League Cup, where they were unfortunate to eventually be defeated by Wolves in the semi-final. Unable to take part, having already played for West Ham in that season's competition, MacDougall could only look on as City just missed out on a second successive appearance at Wembley, going down by the only goal at Molineux after the first leg had resulted in a draw.

In the meantime, down in Bournemouth, Phil Boyer had stunned Cherries supporters by submitting a transfer request. Although the request was not accepted by Harold Walker, the beleaguered chairman agreed to consider the matter at the club's next board meeting. As soon as Bond became aware of the situation he tabled a £100,000 bid, which was immediately rejected, and then increased his offer to £145,000. Relations between the two clubs were already at an all-time low and Bournemouth, having alleged that Norwich had made an illegal approach to Davies earlier in the season, now asked the Football League to intervene in the matter. Walker refused to negotiate with Bond and stated categorically that Boyer would not be going to Norwich.

As the saga continued, MacDougall made an unlucky return to Anfield, twice coming close to putting the Canaries ahead, before having a goal disallowed for offside. Having kept Liverpool out for 89 minutes, City's hopes of a point were finally sunk when Peter Cormack popped up to head in Ian Callaghan's cross. Bond's first league win as manager finally came at his tenth attempt against Queens Park Rangers at Loftus Road. Two goals in as many first-half minutes saw City race ahead, Trevor Howard netting first with a smart near-post header, then Benson firing in a thunderous long-distance shot. Although Keelan saved a penalty from Gerry Francis, Stan Bowles eventually reduced the arrears for Rangers, but despite being under considerable pressure, City held on for their first away win of the season.

In a dramatic turnaround in events at Bournemouth, Norwich completed the signing of Boyer for a new club record fee of £145,000. Despite interest from other clubs, including Chelsea, who had offered £80,000 plus striker Tommy Baldwin in exchange, the Cherries board finally agreed to allow Boyer to link up again with MacDougall. Many Cherries supporters were left baffled by it all after the chairman had given assurances that no more players would be leaving the club. The circumstances behind the transfer were eventually investigated by the Football League and City were fined £5,000 for a breach of regulations. Perhaps not surprisingly, the League also insisted that any further transfers from Bournemouth to Norwich until the end of the following season must first gain their approval, 'From the moment I arrived at Norwich, there was never any doubt that John would move in for Phil Boyer again. Unfortunately this caused some unpleasantness at Bournemouth which was a shame. Mind you, I think Bondy had a bit of a job convincing the Norwich board that they should smash their transfer record to get him. "Charlie" thought he was going to QPR, so I phoned him and said you're not going there, you're coming to Norwich with me! Obviously I was delighted because I loved him as a person and knew his presence would result in more opportunities for me. We went on to room together all over the world, it was just like being married – I bossed him around and he just accepted it! In all seriousness, he became a very influential person in my life, we always got on well and I can't ever remember having an argument with him.'

Bond had told his club's board of directors that he believed MacDougall would only ever be 70 per cent as successful without Boyer alongside him. It was something that neither Frank O'Farrell nor Ron Greenwood had perhaps fully appreciated, preferring instead to find somebody else to undertake Boyer's role. Had they signed him instead, then the careers of both players could have been very different. Now, after scoring 46 goals in 140 league games for the Cherries, he was reunited with his old strike partner and produced a typically Boyer-like performance on his City debut against Sheffield United at Carrow Road, his all-action front-running quickly winning over the fans and adding a new dimension to the Norwich attack. MacDougall benefitted from some poor defensive work to put the Canaries ahead and Stringer added a second from Steele's corner before a mistake by Keelan gave them a late fright but again they held on to lift themselves off the foot of the table.

Hopes that Norwich could still pull clear of the relegation places were dealt a hefty blow when they suffered a defeat at home to Derby, which quickly sent them back to the bottom. City found themselves three goals down before Howard reduced the deficit. Then, after Derby had restored their three-goal advantage in the second half, the redoubtable Stringer struck a second consolation effort. The veteran defender had served six previous managers at Carrow Road, but since Bond's arrival he had been encouraged to get forward and join in the attack whenever possible. Bond wanted all his players to take the same attitude and as admirable as his philosophy may have been, it was on occasions fully exploited by the opposition. Bond's swashbuckling style of play was in sharp contrast to the more pragmatic approach of Saunders, as was his attitude to training but it quickly won over City's senior players, 'The impression I got was that the players had a lot of respect for Saunders but found his ways very regimented and everything was about running and stamina. They rarely saw more than one football at training but with John he always had sacks full of balls and his emphasis was always on ball work. He wanted us to attack more and become an attractive side to watch. The younger lads loved it and I think experienced guys like David Stringer and Duncan Forbes became better players and probably extended their careers as a result.'

After being beaten by a goal from their former striker David Cross at Coventry the side displayed plenty of character and determination to go undefeated throughout March, seemingly picking up new inspiration from Manchester United's plunge to the bottom. Boyer's first goal snatched a draw in the return derby at Portman Road, then against Chelsea at Carrow Road, they hit back after going two down early in the second half, with goals from Stringer and MacDougall, the latter meeting a Suggett corner with a firm header, much to the delight of the home supporters.

As the transfer deadline approached, Bond made unsuccessful attempts to sign Bobby Moore from West Ham and his former Bournemouth target Don Masson from Notts County. Meanwhile, Oxford United paid City a handy £35,000 for Max Briggs, a regular in midfield under Saunders, while Peter Silvester joined Southend after a loan spell at Colchester. With all business completed, a goalless draw at Tottenham provided another precious point but by now City's position demanded more than just a point a game if they were to have a realistic chance of avoiding relegation. They had to find a winning run and hopes were raised on what had been dubbed 'last-chance Wednesday', 20 March. No result other than beating fellow strugglers Birmingham would do and Norwich duly obliged, Boyer and Suggett scoring goals which were both set up by Howard in his 150th game for the club. Archie Styles hit back for the Blues but City hung on to grab the points, thanks to a late penalty save by the Calcutta-born 'India Rubber' goalkeeper, Kevin Keelan.

Still knowing that only a win would be good enough against Stoke the following Saturday, the thumping 4-0 victory gained that day was the Canaries' best in two seasons of First Division football and, just as they did the previous year, supporters began to believe that a 'Great Escape' might still be possible in the last few weeks of the season. All the goals came in the second half and after Sissons had opened the scoring, City's second was the result of a new tactical plan, literally dreamed up by Bond when he couldn't sleep in the lead-up to the game!

It was centred on making space in the penalty area by not sending any players inside it for a free kick on the edge of the box. The move worked perfectly as Stoke used up four players in a 'wall' and another four by marking two Norwich players positioned on each side of the penalty area. That left only two men to fill the gaps in the danger zone behind the wall. Two accurate passes by Benson and Suggett, plus quick running, switched the ball behind the wall and MacDougall raced through to send home a shot from the edge of the six-yard line, 'It was something different and that's what Bondy was always looking for. If defenders see men around the edge of the box they will step forward and mark them. By doing so on this occasion, Stoke left us space we could exploit because they had no idea what we were going to do. It was simple but very effective. It was the kind of originality that had made John so popular at Bournemouth. He was always breathing new ideas into the game, both on and off the field.'

A second goal from Sissons and another from Suggett completed a memorable afternoon for the Canaries and set up a crunch match with Tommy Docherty's Manchester United in early April, with the losers almost certain to be relegated. After MacDougall had tested Stepney early in the game, an hour of deadlock followed before United's Macari broke through City's offside trap and lifted the ball over Keelan to score. Twenty minutes later, Brian Greenhoff hit a second and at the final whistle, City were left seven points away from safety with just six games left, 'Docherty was fashioning a young side at Old Trafford but they were struggling against relegation like ourselves. We didn't play well on the day and the result was a real sickener. I think afterwards we all knew we had left ourselves too much to do and that relegation was probably on the cards. Mind you the result didn't do United much good in the end either!

'A young player called Paul Kent made his debut in this game. I used to pay him a fiver to wash my car, then at training one day when I was a bit grumpy, I caught him carelessly with my elbow as I challenged for the ball. So next time when I had the ball, Paul went right through me, took me out and Bondy sent him off. He thought he was finished at Norwich but John was so impressed with his bottle for kicking me that he made him substitute against United. Then when Mel Machin got injured, he came on and did okay.'

Spirits rose when Ted's far-post header gave City the lead at Goodison Park but Everton then struck four times in reply, before successive draws at home and away to Newcastle saw Norwich still rooted to the bottom of the table, but staved off relegation for a few more days. After a goalless draw on Tyneside, MacDougall headed in Benson's cross to rescue a point at Carrow Road, but ironically, relegation came despite a win against Burnley, which was settled by MacDougall from the penalty spot as early as the second minute. With closest rivals Southampton drawing elsewhere, City's fate was sealed. Defeat in their last two matches at Birmingham and Leicester meant they finally finished nine points from safety, although Birmingham's win ensured their own survival and helped to send Southampton and Manchester United into the Second Division with Norwich.

Relegation left a nasty taste, but supporters remained optimistic that better times may be just around the corner. For many, the club's fate had been sealed even before Bond had taken charge. Although he had been unable to halt the team's woeful away form, which had brought just 12 goals and one win all season, his style of football had certainly captured their imagination. MacDougall ended the season as the club's leading goalscorer with 13 goals from 26 appearances in all competitions, having gone some way towards answering his critics, and proving again that he didn't have to play in a successful side to score goals. Furthermore, he and Boyer had shown they could work well as a partnership in the First Division, 'Going down was an enormous disappointment. John was in the middle of building up a new side which would eventually be quite capable of making its mark in the First Division, but he ran out of time. Having to spend a spell in the Second Division did give him a bit of breathing space, but that was only a small consolation at the time. His vision was to manage a Norwich side the city would be proud of because of the exciting football we played and by the end of the season he now had many of the players he needed for the challenge ahead.

'Mel Machin had proved he was a First Division player. He moved forward into midfield and looked like he had been playing at that level all his life. John Benson was "Bondy's man" on the field, always encouraging others, while Duncan Forbes was the rock at the heart of the defence. Then there was goalkeeper Kevin Keelan, I don't think a lot of people realised how good Kevin was. He was always consistent and at times he could really be something special. Not forgetting "Charlie" Boyer of course, it was no surprise to me how well he settled into the First Division because he had so much ability.

'The boss did everything he could to ensure we were all looked after well at Norwich. For the first time since I left Bournemouth I was happy with my football again and felt settled. Now we all had to knuckle down and make sure City would come straight back up. I couldn't wait for the new season to start.'

12

A Licence to Entertain

MACDOUGALL and Bond may have arrived too late to halt Norwich City's slide out of the First Division, but both were equally determined to ensure its immediate return. The manager bolstered his resources during the summer, signing the tough-tackling 30-year-old Ipswich midfielder Peter Morris, attacking former England under-23 left-back Colin Sullivan from Plymouth, and uncompromising Bournemouth defender Tony Powell, who could also operate capably in midfield.

Powell, another of Bond's former Cherries players to follow him to Norfolk, did so much to the further displeasure of supporters on the south coast. Prior to signing him, City had also made an unsuccessful £80,000 bid for his fellow Bournemouth defender David Jones, then just before the season got under way, his Cherries team-mate Harry Redknapp was allowed to move to Carrow Road on a three-month loan, although a subsequent knee injury prevented him from playing. Meanwhile Trevor Howard, valued at £50,000, moved to Bournemouth in exchange for the want-away Powell and among the other players leaving the club were Terry Anderson, Billy Kellock, Neil O'Donnell and Les Wilson.

Behind MacDougall, there was now a unit capable of quickly and smoothly turning defence into attack. The centre of defence looked to be in good hands, with 29-year-old Stringer and 33-year-old club captain Forbes still a formidable partnership, so rather than initially playing Powell in defence, Bond looked to use him in midfield in his preferred 4-4-2 formation. Undaunted by the prospect of an extremely competitive league which included other former First Division clubs such as Aston Villa, Manchester United, Nottingham Forest, Sheffield Wednesday, Southampton, Sunderland and West Bromwich Albion, Bond told his players they had nothing to fear in the Second Division and promised supporters the team would continue to play with style.

After completing pre-season formalities with fixtures against Colchester, Lowestoft and Torquay, the Norwich side that started the first league game against Blackpool included all three new signings and only five players who had played for the club during Ron Saunders's reign – Forbes, Grapes, Keelan, Stringer and Suggett. Their first goal of the season was scored somewhat fortuitously by Powell, after a clearance struck his chest and rebounded into the net before MacDougall's header doubled City's lead as they opened proceedings with a 2-1 victory, watched by an attendance of 17,841 at Carrow Road, 'We made a great start to the season and I thought, "Here we go – we're off!" I was bossing it again and if the players didn't get the ball into me they got a right going over because I had made my run! I didn't care whether they wanted to take an extra touch, they had better get that ball in and the great thing was that John would be on my side and tell them to get on with it. I was never in a strong enough position to do that at West Ham or Manchester United and I wouldn't have got the backing from the manager.'

Winger Grapes popped up to score City's winning goal against Southampton, his first senior goal, before they faced Saunders's latest club, Aston Villa, in their first away fixture. Saunders's brief stay at Manchester City had come to an end when he was dismissed three weeks before the end of the previous season, with his team slipping dangerously down the First Division table. At Villa Park, Ray Graydon headed the home side ahead but Norwich equalised against the run of play when MacDougall and Stringer combined to set up Suggett who, from 30 yards out, thundered a shot past Villa goalkeeper Jim Cumbes.

It was enough for the Canaries to bring home a point and Suggett again struck City's equaliser in a bad-tempered return fixture at Southampton, which had also seen Forbes and Saints striker Peter Osgood engaged in a personal battle throughout. The fine form shown by the former England under-23 international had been a significant factor in the team's bright start to the season. Saunders had paid West

Bromwich Albion £80,000 for the winger's services during his spell in charge and though undoubtedly a gifted player, Suggett had sometimes shown an indifferent approach to the game and his performances had often been inconsistent. Bond had now converted him into an attacking midfield player of some class and in return, the player had showed an ability and application to work harder, and had become an integral part of the Norwich side, 'No manager could have asked for more from Colin. He was a very busy player who seemed to be involved in the game virtually all the time, making himself available for passes in defence, midfield and attack – in fact he became very much the general of the side. He often made the passes that mattered and he set up a number of goals for Charlie and myself.'

A sequence of five successive drawn league and cup matches in mid-September ended with a convincing 3-0 home win against Notts County, a game which saw Sullivan score his first goal for the Canaries, when he neatly tucked away a pass from Morris in the second minute. Later, MacDougall headed home from a Machin cross before Boyer was put through by Suggett to add a third. Three more goals followed in the League Cup replay against Bolton after the original tie had ended goalless at Carrow Road. Having initially fallen behind, Stringer brought the Canaries level from a Suggett corner on the half-hour, before another goal apiece from MacDougall and Boyer proved decisive in the last 20 minutes. Working together in tandem, the pair had by now served notice that they would be a highly dangerous combination in the Second Division and City looked set to reap the benefits.

Somewhat out of the blue, Norwich suffered their first and ultimately heaviest defeat of the season when they went down 4-0 at Fulham, a result that enabled the Cottagers to jump above City and take second place in the league table. The Canaries had been without the injured Machin and Keelan at Craven Cottage and both were sorely missed but fortunately the latter was able to return and help gain a point at Sunderland, where Bond also included an extra defender in full-back Geoff Butler. On this occasion the defence held firm and City regained their position, although they were grateful to Powell for a late goal-line clearance to keep the scoresheet blank.

Machin returned at Benson's expense for the visit of league leaders Manchester United at the end of September. A crowd of just over 25,000 packed themselves in and it was the Norwich supporters who were jubilant afterwards, as MacDougall sent his former club packing with a goal in each half, 'I always enjoyed playing against my former sides because I often used to score against them! Sadly there was an unpleasant element to the United support at the time and if I remember correctly there was a bit of trouble in the town before the game. We could hear the sirens and all that in the dressing room as we got changed. Anyway, we went for them straight from the start and put them under a lot of pressure.

'Charlie was covering a lot of ground and taking people on and after about 20 minutes, Sidebottom I think it was, took him down in the area and I had the chance to put us ahead from the penalty spot, which I did. Then in the second half Mel Machin played me in from a free kick and I volleyed the ball into the net. The crowd went mad, well most of them anyway! I don't imagine the United fans were too happy with me, but that's football.'

City's performances during September were duly recognised when Bond was named as Manager of the Month – an accolade not always welcomed in football circles, given the downturn in performances that often immediately follows it. But, on this occasion, the Canaries went from strength to strength, winning each of their four league matches in October, beginning with a 2-0 victory at home to Millwall in which Powell opened the scoring in the first half before MacDougall made things safe with a penalty after the break. The following week at Nottingham Forest, Machin scored his first goals since joining Norwich, completing a stunning second-half hat-trick before Stringer and a terrific solo goal from Boyer saw off Portsmouth at Carrow Road, the diminutive striker lobbing the ball over Pompey goalkeeper David Best after a magnificent run through the visitors' defence.

Despite the team's successful start to the season, Bond still wanted to improve the supply line to his twin strikers. John Sissons had not featured in his plans for some time and was eventually allowed to move on to Chelsea, while Grapes had not quite been able to provide the consistency the manager was looking for, so Bond paid Ipswich Town £45,000 for winger Johnny Miller. Miller was drafted in to the team at Orient and made an immediate impression in a convincing 3-0 victory. The scoring began when Boyer collected a pass from Morris to put City ahead after 25 minutes then, seconds later, MacDougall was brought down inside the penalty area and made no mistake in doubling the lead. The match was effectively settled before half-time, when Boyer netted again after Orient goalkeeper John Jackson failed to hold on to Miller's crisp volley.

Further success came in the League Cup, when after holding West Bromwich Albion to a 1-1 draw at The Hawthorns, City went through to the fourth round with a two-goal success in the replay. Boyer had the first and last word over the two matches; his header following a dipping cross from Morris had given the Canaries the lead at The Hawthorns and he eventually settled matters in the last minute of extra time at Carrow Road. Earlier, Albion had shown stubborn resistance in normal time before Machin's defence-splitting pass found MacDougall, who took the ball round goalkeeper Dave Latchford to net his eighth of the season.

Not to be outdone, Boyer's performances had already brought him seven goals in all competitions, quite apart from those he had set up for his colleagues, and had not gone unnoticed by new England manager Don Revie, who had described him as the most complete striker he had seen during his period in charge. Meanwhile, as press and television experts continued to sing the praises of Newcastle United's Malcolm Macdonald and John Tudor as the best goalscoring duo operating together in English football, there was an increasing belief in Norfolk that MacDougall and Boyer were every bit as good, 'Charlie was always a very quiet person, a fantastic person really. We just complemented each other perfectly but there was never any rivalry between us – as long as he kept playing me in and I scored more goals than him! He always took up such good positions to receive the ball and used it so well, his control and touch got better and better as he matured as a player and he began to do things that even I thought were beyond his capabilities.'

City's run of league victories came to an end at West Bromwich Albion at the beginning of November, where hesitancy in the Canaries' defence saw Don Howe's side take a first-half lead. In response, MacDougall struck following a corner soon after the break to bring the Canaries level and despite not being at their best, they then fought hard to come away with a point. However, when the *Match of the Day* cameras came to Carrow Road for the visit of Bristol Rovers, City missed their cue completely and slipped to a 1-0 defeat. Ted came close to a late equaliser when his shot struck a post but long before this a section of the Norwich supporters began venting their frustration at the side's poor performance by barracking stand-in right-back John

Benson, calling for him to be substituted. Bond was furious and refused to take Benson off, even though he may have wanted to make a change, 'Benno certainly didn't deserve that sort of treatment from the fans, bless him. He was a tremendously strong character in the dressing room and could play in a number of different positions. Wherever he played he gave nothing less than 100 per cent commitment. When the boss wanted to sign him from Bournemouth, Benno rang me and asked whether or not he should go as he wasn't sure whether he could play in the First Division. I told him he could and that while he might not have been the quickest of players, his knowledge would see him through.

'When fans look for a scapegoat to take out their frustration on, they don't seem to realise that it can sometimes shatter a player's confidence. I was on the receiving end plenty of times during my career but fortunately I managed to shut it out and never let it bother me too much. It was a typical reaction from Bondy though and was an example of the loyalty and support he gave to his players.'

The defeat was only City's second in 20 league and cup games since the start of the season and hardly cause for panic. Four days later they travelled to Sheffield United in the League Cup, where Butler replaced Benson and Machin, back again after another injury, returned to the bench. Norwich started strongly against a team lying sixth in the First Division. Indeed, poor marking allowed MacDougall to put City ahead on the half-hour before Woodward's powerful drive drew the Blades level immediately before the break. Ten minutes into the second half, Morris's deflected shot fell to MacDougall, who once again fired the ball home, but a penalty 20 minutes from time gave Keith Eddy the opportunity to save the home side's blushes, in a match which uncharacteristically saw Boyer sent off for fighting, together with United captain Eddie Colquhoun.

With Boyer ruled out of the replay two weeks later, it was his replacement, 20-year-old Steve Goodwin, who took centre stage after Billy Dearden had given the Blades a second-half lead. Five minutes from time MacDougall's downward header allowed Goodwin the opportunity to score his first senior goal and send the match into extra time. Then with just four minutes remaining, Suggett ran at the United defence before the ball eventually fell to Goodwin again, who guided the ball home to book the Canaries' place in the quarter-finals.

Before his absence, Boyer had twice been on target for City at Oldham, however the team fell away during the last half-hour and allowed the home side to rescue a point, slipping down to third place as a result. Miller's first City goals followed at home to Bolton but a below-par performance at York the following week condemned City to defeat, 'This was definitely one of the least memorable returns to one of my old clubs! Phil was still out but Steve Goodwin had come into the side and did very well in the League Cup, but nothing seemed to go right for us at York. We were awful and the boss made sure we knew it afterwards. Tom Johnston had somehow managed to get York into the Second Division, which was a heck of an achievement. They were somewhere around mid-table and had my old Bournemouth colleague Micky Cave in their team at the time.'

The draw for the League Cup quarter-finals gave Norwich a plumb home tie against Ipswich and four days after their dismal performance at Bootham Crescent, they faced Bobby Robson's First Division outfit in a highly-charged atmosphere at Carrow Road. The Suffolk side started the better, pinning City back in the early stages of the game, but against the run of play, Suggett broke and put Norwich ahead. The lead lasted around 20 minutes before a header from Trevor Whymark was adjudged to have crossed the line by World Cup Final referee Jack Taylor, despite Keelan's attempts to keep the ball out. Soon after a shot from Town's Bryan Hamilton struck a post but a goalless second half meant that for the fourth round in succession, City would be facing a replay.

They did however emerge with great credit for their performance against a side lying second in the First Division, in a game which attracted a gate of almost 35,000, 'Norwich and Ipswich was always a great rivalry and a battle on the pitch. They were a tough team under Bobby Robson, with players like Mick Mills, Trevor Whymark and Paul Mariner, who later became a friend of mine while he was coaching in the United States. When I saw Mick Mills shopping in Norwich one day while he was captain of Ipswich, I just blanked him! That's the kind of guy I was then and the way the rivalry was between the two clubs. But Norwich were always seen as the poor relations at the time because Ipswich were always near the top of the First Division and competing in Europe, so they were top dogs.'

Not surprisingly, Ipswich were strong favourites to win on their home ground and they went ahead after half an hour, striker David Johnson getting the final touch after the ball ran loose in the Norwich goalmouth. Four minutes later though City were level when Miller again profited from a MacDougall cross and then immediately after the interval, the winger collected a pass from Boyer and rounded goalkeeper Laurie Sivell to put the Canaries ahead against his former club. The home crowd was stunned and despite enormous pressure on the City goal thereafter, Ipswich could not find a way back. City were just two matches away from Wembley for the second time in three seasons and the fact they had reached the semi-finals thanks to two goals from a player who had only recently left Ipswich to join them, no doubt made their supporters feel even better.

While success in the League Cup was obviously good for the club's finances and its supporters, it had added a considerable amount to the players' workload at a crucial stage of the season. Already City had played eight matches in the competition, and there was a fear that their progress had begun to take its toll in the league. Before the replay at Portman Road, Norwich were held to a 1-1 draw by lowly Cardiff and defeat at Blackpool in mid-December meant City had managed just one win from their last seven league games. They remained in third place but by now they were seven points behind leaders and title favourites Manchester United and Bond began to look for reinforcements.

For the time being though, the team remained unchanged and against Bristol City shortly before Christmas, they received an early present when Suggett's wind-assisted corner was allowed to swing into the back of the visitors' net. Fortunately, another seasonal offering was to follow later, when after Norwich had allowed the West Country side to put themselves in front, Boyer struck two second-half goals in the space of a minute, the second coming after visiting goalkeeper Ray Cashley dropped a free kick at his feet.

On Boxing Day the Canaries were grateful to claim a precious, late point at Notts County when Boyer crossed for MacDougall to head a last-minute equaliser, before another anxious afternoon followed two days later, as a tentative looking City struggled to come to life against Oxford United at Carrow Road. Only after Boyer had scored the game's only goal shortly before half-time did they appear to play with any confidence.

It was perhaps a blessing in disguise that, for the seventh successive season City bowed out of the FA Cup at the third round stage, this time beaten 2-0 at First Division Coventry. Of more concern though, it proved to be the first of four defeats the Canaries suffered in January, as they failed to gain a single league point, yet still managed to hold on to third place in the table. The second reverse came at Ninian Park, where with the game against Cardiff just ten minutes old MacDougall somehow found himself in his own penalty area and tried to guide the ball safely back to Keelan. Unfortunately his header was so powerful that the goalkeeper could not hold on to the ball and Gil Reece stepped in to put the Welsh side in front. Tony Villars added a second before Ted broke free of the home defence in the second half to reduce the arrears but Norwich could not find an equaliser, 'Now you see why it wasn't a good idea to have me back helping out the defence!'

Bond's efforts to strengthen his midfield finally bore fruit with the signing of 22-year-old Mick McGuire from Coventry in a £60,000 deal. He went straight in to the side for the visit of York. He marked his debut by setting up a late goal for Stringer, but could not stop the visitors completing an unexpected double over the Canaries. Two goals inside the first two minutes of the game had stunned the home supporters and although Suggett's 30-yard shot halved the deficit after the interval, York added a third goal soon afterwards.

This embarrassing defeat was sandwiched between the two-legged League Cup semi-final against Manchester United. First there was a wonderful night at Old Trafford which attracted an attendance of over 56,000, where City held United in a 2-2 draw. Powell put Norwich ahead midway through the first half after skirting round home centre-half Steve James before shooting past Alex Stepney, but United hit back with two goals from Lou Macari soon after the interval. The diminutive Scotsman applied the finishing touch after the City defence had failed to deal with a United corner, then after receiving a pass from Stewart Houston, he proceeded to guide another shot past Keelan. Just as they began to believe their team would take a lead into the second leg though, United fans were left to agonise over a goal two minutes from time, when MacDougall capitalised on a back pass from Houston that became stuck on the muddy surface and brought City level, 'On the afternoon of the first leg at Old Trafford Phil and I were coming down in the hotel lift after a sleep and I remember asking him how he felt. "I feel absolutely fantastic," he said, and I said, "So do I," and I always remember that. I never worked that hard during a game but did I put some running in that night!

'We played a 4-4-2 on a heavy pitch and I can remember my goal vividly. The ball was going through to Stepney, and I didn't like him too much, so I decided I was going to go through and kick this ball as hard as I could, and if he gets in the way he's going into the back of the net as well. Anyway he dropped it and I stuck it into the net in front of the Stretford End.'

The second leg produced another tense encounter, the crucial goal eventually coming early in the second half after a corner from Powell caused a scramble in the United penalty area. Always ready to put his head in where it hurts, Suggett threw himself forward to send a brave header in to the back of the net. As United pressed hard for an equaliser, City were indebted to Keelan for two magnificent saves from Alex Forsyth and Sammy McIlroy as they booked a Wembley date with Aston Villa. City fans in the crowd of 31,672 celebrated loudly and long into the night as they dreamt of a cup and promotion double.

After playing a key part in both of the epic encounters with Manchester United, John Benson had decided to accept Bournemouth's offer to return to Dean Court as player-manager. The Cherries were struggling against relegation from the Third Division and wanted Benson to take over after the dismissal of Trevor Hartley, 'It was a great opportunity for Benno to step up to management at Bournemouth and I thought he was just what they needed at the time. Mind you, I hadn't realised quite how bad things were down there though, it certainly wasn't the club or the team it had been a year or so ago and times were hard for them.'

How Benson must have wished the Cherries still had players of the calibre of MacDougall and Boyer, the latter of whom now stood on the fringe of international recognition having been included in Don Revie's squad to play friendly matches against Arsenal and Spurs.

Just three days after the euphoria of reaching the League Cup Final, Norwich were brought down to earth with a defeat at Oxford United, prompting further suggestions that their efforts in the cup competition were now seriously distracting them from the major prize of promotion. However, February started brightly for City with a win at Bristol Rovers, where after setting up a goal for Suggett after half an hour, MacDougall was on hand to head home when the midfielder returned the compliment immediately after the break. A thrilling encounter against West Bromwich Albion at Carrow Road the following week drew a crowd of over 34,000 and after Joe Mayo had put the Baggies ahead, their lead lasted only until captain John Wile upended MacDougall, whose penalty then sent the teams in level at half-time.

Early in the second half, Lyndon Hughes fired Albion back in front but within a minute McGuire ended a fine solo run by bringing City back on terms. The match then became a real thriller as play swung from end to end, as both sides searched for a winning goal. Despite the Canaries being reduced to ten men after referee George Kew dismissed Machin for violent conduct, the decisive moment fell to MacDougall and he struck the ball home 20 minutes from time to give Norwich the points.

In Machin's absence, Morris stood in at right-back for the visit to Bolton as the home side looked to close the gap between themselves in eighth position and City, who were still lying third. While Morris managed to keep former England winger Peter Thompson in check, it was Keelan's splendid save from Peter Reid near the end that ensured the Canaries grabbed an important point. A late goal from Boyer, his first in nine games, then saw off relegation-threatened Oldham, who had earlier made City's life difficult. There were just six minutes remaining when he rose at the far post to head home a Morris cross to the relief of the Carrow Road faithful, who had seen their team go unbeaten during February, and with the promotion bid now very much back on track, they could look forward to the League Cup Final.

The competition had proved unusual as not one of the semi-finalists came from the First Division. Also, prior to reaching the semi-final stage City had needed replays to overcome their opponents in each round prior to the semi-final. Then, while they were overcoming Manchester United in one semi-final, Aston Villa saw off the challenge of Fourth Division Chester City in the other. Nonetheless, the all-Second Division final still attracted a crowd of 100,000 and record receipts for the competition at the time.

The Wembley line-ups on Saturday 1 March 1975 were as follows:

Norwich City: Keelan, Machin, Sullivan, Morris, Stringer, Forbes, Miller, MacDougall, Boyer, Suggett, Powell. Substitute: Steele.

Aston Villa: Cumbes, Robson, Aitken, Ross, Nicholl, McDonald, Graydon, Little, Leonard, Hamilton, Carrodus. Substitute: Evans.

For Villa boss Ron Saunders it was the third successive year he had guided a team to the final, having lost with Manchester City the previous year and Norwich in 1973. It proved to be third time lucky for Saunders, although the game turned out to be a disappointment and certainly a massive anti-climax for City and their supporters. Villa won by the only goal and thus condemned City to their second League Cup Final defeat in three years.

The only real excitement was limited to a brief flurry near the end. Villa's goal came ten minutes from time after right-winger Frank Carrodus had breezed past Powell and won a corner following a challenge by Forbes. Chico Hamilton crossed and as Keelan came out to clear the danger, Chris Nicholl beat him to the ball and sent a powerful header goalwards, at which point Machin, standing on the line, threw himself to his right and pushed it around the post. It was the kind of save any goalkeeper would have been proud of but coming from City's right-back, there was only going to be one outcome. Graydon came forward to take the resultant penalty and although Keelan guessed correctly, diving to his right to push the ball against the post, the Villa winger comfortably slotted home the rebound.

The match would prove to be MacDougall's only appearance in a Wembley final and this tense, scrappy affair gave him little opportunity to make an impression. Down in Bournemouth, as their team continued to struggle under new manager Benson, it did not go unnoticed that seven of their former players and management were included in the City party at Wembley – it may well have been eight of course had Benson not decided to re-join the Cherries a few weeks previously, 'The final was just one huge disappointment particularly after our two semi-final matches against Manchester United. Those games were immense and totally overshadowed the final which was a dreadful game. Both sides put in a dismal performance, we were as bad as each other but Villa got the break and went home with the cup. I've never bothered to look at a video of the game, just a few clips of the teams walking out and I look so arrogant, chewing gum and waving to everybody during the national anthem. Those clips were probably more interesting than the game!'

The following week Norwich returned to Second Division action in a bad-tempered match against promotion rivals Sunderland at Carrow Road. With the game heading towards a goalless draw, Boyer was sent off, receiving his marching orders for a second time after squaring up with the visitors' Ron Guthrie as things became heated in the latter stages. Bond later pulled a clever trick to avoid losing Boyer to another suspension, appealing to an FA tribunal and delaying the outcome and thus freeing him to play during the run-in.

With Manchester United and Aston Villa now looking likely to occupy the first two promotion spots, the remaining place seemed to be between Norwich and Sunderland, and Bond choose this moment to perform another masterstroke. Re-affirming his ambitious plans for the club, he paid Tottenham £50,000 for 1966 England World Cup winner Martin Peters. He and Peters had history of course, having been colleagues at West Ham in the 1960s and Bond knew he wasn't signing a 'has-been' lacking motivation. The 31-year-old Peters was the holder of 67 England caps, and despite possibly being in the twilight of his career, his signing still represented a great piece of transfer business. The first British footballer to have commanded a transfer fee of £200,000 when he left West Ham for Tottenham in 1970, Peters was as slim and fit as ever and remained a masterful player with an exemplary attitude. Although no longer part of new Spurs manager Terry Neill's long-term plans, Bond believed Peters's class and know-how would give Norwich the extra quality that would turn a decent team into a good one. Certainly his signing demonstrated that City meant business, 'Martin was wonderful, a true professional who always conducted himself well and I think his arrival at Norwich was a great coup for John. It gave us a bit of credibility and stamped Bondy's arrival as a top manager. Martin quickly settled into our style of play and brought extra class and imagination into the team. He was a very, very fine player and I liked playing with him. He just fitted in great and was known as "The Ghost" because he had this wonderful ability to arrive unnoticed in goalscoring positions.'

Peters added a new dimension, giving much-needed width to a Norwich attack previously built around the running of Boyer and the penalty area prowess of MacDougall. Fittingly his debut was in front of an Old Trafford crowd of 56,202, nothing he wasn't used to, and he helped City gain a 1-1 draw after they had initially fallen behind to a goal from Stuart Pearson. It was after a weak clearance by Stepney that Ted equalised soon afterwards, silencing the crowd's chants of 'United Reject' and adding to his growing record of scoring important goals against United, 'Of course I got plenty of stick whenever I visited any of my former clubs – except Bournemouth where they always loved me! It just fired me up and made me even more determined to score, and against United in particular, I had now established a pretty good record of doing so.'

Peters's arrival increased the competition for midfield places and just ahead of the transfer deadline, Doug Livermore became another to follow the road to Bournemouth, on loan for the remainder of the season. Machin was now unable to find a place in the side either in midfield or at right-back, where Butler had put together a run of consistent performances. Peters's home debut came in a grim battle against Hull, where after missing a number of chances, the Canaries were grateful for a MacDougall penalty three minutes from time to come out on top. Another narrow victory followed against Bristol City, Suggett firing home the only goal of the game at Ashton Gate, to dent the West Country club's own promotion hopes.

At the end of March, with just seven games remaining, Norwich suffered a home defeat against Fulham, who were also enjoying a fine run in the FA Cup which would eventually take them all the way to the final. Alec Stock's in-form side had lost only once in their previous nine away games before making it ten at Carrow Road. The defeat saw City drop to fifth in the table behind Manchester United, Aston Villa, Sunderland and Bristol City but Bond remained confident that with games in hand over their nearest rivals, his side could still finish in a promotion place, particularly as apart from the final fixture against Villa, their run-in to the end of the season included matches against five teams who were all in the bottom half of the table.

In the first of these, Boyer burst through Orient's offside trap on the stroke of half-time to put the Canaries ahead, but the game was not made safe until the last ten minutes when a shot from Boyer was handled and MacDougall completed the scoring from the penalty spot, much to the relief of the Carrow Road faithful. City's next opponents were bottom-of-the-table Sheffield Wednesday, who were destined for the Third Division and had failed to score in any of their previous seven home matches. To add to their misery, the only goal of the game came when Peters flicked on a cross for MacDougall to head in, but second-bottom Millwall proved a sterner test when Norwich visited the Den four days later. Barry Kitchener headed the Londoners in front and with City not at their best, they were eventually grateful to full-back Butler, who popped up to head home Sullivan's cross seconds from the end.

Now back up to fourth place and still with a game in hand on promotion rivals Sunderland immediately above them, City looked to hold their nerve for the visit of Brian Clough's Nottingham Forest. With Stringer suspended, Powell moved back to partner Forbes in defence while McGuire was restored to midfield having missed the match at Millwall. They started the game well but as half-time approached had nothing to show for all their first-half pressure until Peters ghosted in to the Forest penalty area to head them in front. After the break they really turned on the style and produced some excellent attacking football, with Boyer profiting from a Peters nod-down to double the lead and then hitting an unstoppable shot past visiting goalkeeper John Middleton five minutes from time.

Everything came down to the final Saturday of the season. Sunderland's last match was at second-placed Villa, while City entertained lowly Portsmouth and still had the cushion of a further game to come, also against Villa. A Norwich win and a Sunderland defeat would see the Canaries promoted. Almost 60,000 people packed into Villa Park, where two second-half goals condemned Sunderland to defeat. Over to Carrow Road, where a smaller but equally enthusiastic crowd of 18,977 greeted an unchanged City side eager to make the most of any opportunity that might arise to clinch promotion. To their supporters' delight they did just that, first when the impressive McGuire struck with a diving header after 25 minutes, then when Peters headed a second goal late in the game and finally after Player of the Year Suggett set up Boyer to run through the Portsmouth defence for a third two minutes from time. As news of Sunderland's defeat was broadcast over the tannoy, it was the signal for the celebrations to begin.

They were still in full flow four days later, but this time almost 36,000 people packed inside Carrow Road for the season's finale. With both City and Villa safely promoted but neither able to overhaul champions Manchester United, the result was somewhat academic for everyone except perhaps Ron Saunders, who undoubtedly savoured every minute of his side's 4-1 victory. Nonetheless the job was done and Norwich had regained their First Division status at the first attempt.

Although Wembley had been a big disappointment, overall it had been a wonderful season, Bond had reaped an immediate return on his investments and the club's success owed much to an impressive start and then the brilliantly astute signing of Peters just as they were showing signs of faltering. Never having dropped below fifth in the table at any stage, they were largely a settled side throughout the season, with nine players appearing in 35 or more league games. Undoubtedly the club would return to Division One the following season with a far better chance of staying there than they had had previously.

The partnership of MacDougall and Boyer had indeed proved more than a handful for Second Division defences and been responsible for a total of 41 goals in the Second Division and League Cup competitions during the season. MacDougall had struck on 22 occasions and Boyer, who was later named in the Professional Footballers' Association's divisional team of the season, added 19, 'Did Charlie get that many? The little bastard – some of those should have been mine! Seriously, I was lucky enough to have avoided injury and played in every game throughout the season, and the supporters were brilliant towards me and the team. Moving to Norwich and reuniting with John, and then Charlie was the best decision I ever made in my career, and I firmly believed then that there were still better times to come. Now I had another chance to prove I could score goals in the First Division and I knew this time I would be better equipped to take it.'

One person who had contributed to Norwich's success, but had little to cheer about at the season drew to a close, was John Benson. He had been unable to save Bournemouth from relegation and his club now found itself strapped of cash and dumped back in the Fourth Division, 'It was such a shame, a tragedy really and one the club took many years to recover from. I felt so disappointed for everyone there, especially the chairman who had ploughed so much money in and the supporters. Benno did his best and they had bad luck with injuries, but there had been such a turnover in players and the best of them had long gone. Even so they were only relegated on goal difference in the end after winning their last two games.'

At the end of the season Norwich took part in several benefit matches including one at Colchester for the Layer Road club's former Bournemouth striker Paul Aimson. The much-travelled Aimson had been signed by the Cherries from York in March 1973 in an attempt to help fill the void left by MacDougall, but had joined Colchester the following summer, where his career had been cut short by injury. City's own beneficiary, David Stringer, also had a well-earned testimonial match against West Ham, although the Hammers came close to pulling out of the game following comments Ted had inadvertently made, 'West Ham had reached the 1975 FA Cup Final and when Norwich visited Millwall, ITV presenter Brian Moore came along to interview some of the City players and staff who had previously turned out for the Hammers. They spoke to Bondy, then Kenny Brown and Martin Peters and I'm at the end of the line. John says how pleased he is for Ron Greenwood, Kenny says how great it was for the club, Martin's delighted for the fans and then when Brian came to me I told him my allegiance was with Norwich now and I was only happy for two people I knew from my time at West Ham – Bobby Moore and Frank Lampard – and I hoped Bobby would pull it off.

'Of course Bobby was now playing for Fulham – the Hammers' opponents at Wembley! Anyway, this was broadcast just ahead of the cup final and the following Monday West Ham were coming to Carrow Road for David, but as a result of my comments they refused to come unless I didn't play. I couldn't believe that! I told David it just about summed up Ron Greenwood but not to worry as I wouldn't be there and instead I went down to Bournemouth for a long weekend.'

In MacDougall's absence, West Ham turned out at Norwich, their appearance attracting a crowd of just over 13,000 in support of Stringer. Then, during May and June, City undertook a successful two-week tour to Kenya but by then Ted had other international plans on his mind.

13

International Duty

ALTHOUGH Tommy Docherty's arrival at Manchester United may have signalled the end of Ted's brief stay at Old Trafford, the Doc's simultaneous resignation as Scotland team manager opened the door for MacDougall to gain international recognition. Even while he was a Third Division player, there had been cries for Ted to be capped by his native country. However, Docherty had always resisted the temptation to make MacDougall the first player from this level of football to represent Scotland.

His successor as manager in 1973 was 46-year-old St Johnstone manager Willie Ormond, who steered Scotland to their first World Cup finals the following year where, despite emerging from the group stages of the competition unbeaten, they unfortunately failed to progress further and were eliminated on goal difference. Ormond's attention then turned to the qualifying competition for the 1976 European Championships where Scotland's most noticeable weakness, a glaring lack of goalscoring power, was endangering their hopes of reaching the final stages. Ormond, whose playing career had brought him 147 goals as a forward for Stenhousemuir, Hibernian and Falkirk, had watched MacDougall on several occasions during the early part of 1975 and had been among the crowd at Old Trafford to witness his goal there for Norwich in March. He had acknowledged that Ted had done much to restore his goalscoring reputation at Carrow Road, and now turned to him in an effort to solve his team's lack of firepower.

When the manager named his squad for the friendly international against Sweden in Gothenburg on 16 April 1975, MacDougall's name appeared for the first time and he made a successful debut, hitting the Scots' late equaliser in a 1-1 draw. Scotland's starting XI that evening was: Kennedy, Jardine (both Glasgow Rangers), McGrain (Glasgow Celtic), Munro (Wolves), Jackson (Rangers), Robinson (Dundee), Dalglish (Celtic), Souness (Middlesbrough), Parlane (Rangers), Macari (Manchester Utd) and MacDougall (Norwich), 'The first thing that struck me about playing for Scotland was when I got to the airport and saw all these officials getting on the plane. It was like a jamboree for all sorts of committee men from all over Scotland. It seemed the players were an afterthought. I was lucky enough to score against Sweden at Gothenburg in my first game and we did well. We had a good team, with the likes of Kenny Dalglish, Danny McGrain and Graham Souness – he was only 21 years old at the time and he became my room-mate in Gothenberg – it was a really good unit and I couldn't wait to get the shirt on, I was so proud.'

MacDougall won four more caps the following month, the first coming in a friendly against Portugal at Hampden Park, which the Scots were fortunate to win thanks to an own goal. Later in the month came the Home International Championship, and Scotland started by holding Wales to a 2-2 draw in Cardiff, goals from Bruce Rioch and Colin Jackson ensuring they returned north with a point. Three days later, back at Hampden they had little trouble in defeating Northern Ireland, with Kenny Dalglish and Derek Parlane joining Ted on the scoresheet in a comfortable 3-0 victory.

The tournament reached its climax with a match against the 'Auld Enemy' England at Wembley on 24 May. It would be fair to say that with Sir Alf Ramsey's England having failed to qualify for the 1974 World Cup and the team in the process of rebuilding under new manager Don Revie, the Scots fancied their chances of getting a result. From MacDougall's perspective, it was probably the most significant match in his brief international career but certainly not the most memorable, 'We had played Northern Ireland and I scored after a corner past Pat Jennings, then off we went to Wembley all cock a hoop. What a disaster that was, it was the worst experience of my career. It wasn't a match, it was a rout!

'Don Revie would have had dossiers on each of us but our team talk from Willie Ormond went like this, "Right lads, I want you to get bloody stuck into them. Get right up their bloody arses. These Scotland fans will have walked eight miles to get to the game because the Underground's on bloody strike. Give them something to bloody shout about!" He repeated it then asked if anyone had any questions, to which Sandy Jardine, our captain, replied, "Yes boss, the lads would like to know when we are getting our expense sheets?"

'We went into the game as favourites though and I remember standing in the tunnel alongside the England team as we waited for the dignitaries before we could go out. It was probably only seconds, but it felt like an eternity, the noise of the crowd was intense and I thought to myself, "What an occasion this is." And then I thought of my parents who were at the game, and all the great players who had been in this position standing where I was and I thought, "My God, this is too much." For the only time in my career I wanted to run away. Then by the time I got to the end of the tunnel and saw the thousands of drunken Scotsmen, I was blowing kisses to the crowd and thinking, "This is great!"

'Ten minutes later we were two goals down and that was it! We were by no means a bad side but it was one of those days when everything England did came off and we were dreadful. I never got a kick of the ball and was substituted by Lou Macari after 70 minutes, so once again Wembley had not been great for me. Our goalkeeper, Stewart Kennedy from Rangers, had an horrendous game. I believe the BBC commentator David Coleman remarked at one stage that Stewart had lost his geography – well he certainly appeared to have forgotten where his goalposts were! That just about summed it up – it was a nightmare because everyone in Scotland knows how big a game it is against England.'

England ran out 5-1 winners thanks to two goals from Gerry Francis and one apiece from Kevin Beattie, Colin Bell and David Johnson. In reply, all Scotland could muster was a penalty converted by Rioch. It was exactly the preparation the Scots didn't want with a European Championship qualifier in Romania just a week away. Their other opponents in the qualifying stage were Spain and Denmark, with only the group winners to progress to the finals in Yugoslavia the following summer. A home defeat against Spain early in the competition had left the Scots with ground to make up, although they had held the Spaniards to a draw in the return fixture. Romania were also strong contenders and had thrashed the Danes 6-1 in their previous qualifying match.

MacDougall was not selected for the match in Bucharest, Ormond preferring to go with Parlane and Macari up front. However, it was a goal from Leeds United centre-half Gordon McQueen that earned Scotland a hard-fought 1-1 draw, 'The Monday after the Scotland game we flew back up to Glasgow and then off to Romania. I was on the bench in Bucharest, but before the game we were all stood alongside the Romanians waiting to run out in front of about 100,000 people. The Romanian team was full of all these stubby, unshaven little guys and just before we started to walk out, Gordon McQueen, a giant of a man, gave out this enormous roar, "Come on!" and all these Romanians started to shit themselves, like he was something out of *Braveheart*! Sadly it didn't last for long though because we ended up drawing.'

Later that month MacDougall left for a spell in South Africa, having accepted a short-term offer to play for the Johannesburg club Jewish Guild. He was signed to play in three home games for Guild against Highlands Park, Cape Town City and Hellenic before returning to England in time to commence pre-season training at Norwich, 'I did it really to try and give me a head start for the following season. I always reckoned it took a couple of months back in training for me to get really fit. The club engineered a lot of publicity about my coming over there and when I arrived the local paper was full of it, "Ted MacDougall – sensational soccer star and current Scottish international – leading goalscorer in British soccer" and all that! I don't think I quite lived up to it because I hardly got a chance in any of the games and nobody seemed able to play me in, so I had to go looking for the ball all over the pitch. I remember Bobby Moore played against us for Hellenic in my last game and he was still different class. Not long after I left, the club got into financial difficulties and the owners sold out.'

MacDougall was omitted from Scotland's next European Championships game against Denmark in Copenhagen in September, where a goal from Hibernian striker Joe Harper gave them a victory. However, Spain's subsequent win over Denmark meant that despite having two games left to play in the qualifying group, Scotland could not catch them and were thus eliminated from the competition, much to the disappointment of everyone concerned, while leaving the future of manager Willie Ormond in some doubt.

The following month saw MacDougall restored to the attack for the return fixture against the Danes at Hampden Park, with the visitors also out of the competition and firmly entrenched at the bottom of the group. Playing up front with Dalglish and Leeds United's Peter Lorimer, Ted struck the Scots' third goal before being substituted by Parlane. With Dalglish and Rioch having earlier been on target, MacDougall's effort enabled the Scots to complete a comfortable 3-1 victory, 'It was just one of my usual goals from close in, nothing great, just another goal but it turned out to be my third and last for Scotland.'

Ted's last appearance for his country came on 17 December 1975 in the final group game against Romania, who had by then also been eliminated after failing to beat Spain in their previous match. Aston Villa's Andy Gray was preferred to MacDougall in the starting 11 but Ted appeared in the second half of the 1-1 draw as a substitute for Dalglish. However, it was a throwaway remark to a local newspaper reporter in Norwich later in the season, that led MacDougall into international exile, 'I had been playing all the previous year without really taking a break and I was talking to this local reporter in Norwich, who asked me if I was going to join up with the Scotland squad again in the spring. I said I didn't think so because I was really tired, which I was, but it was a bit of a joke really and then I said, "Well the press pick the team anyway!" It was an off-the-cuff remark but by the time I got home it was all out in print, and did I get some grief over that.

'The story soon travelled north, it was all over the Scottish papers the following day and I was branded a traitor. They were calling for the manager to get rid of all the Anglo-Scots in the team, I was absolutely slaughtered over it and I lost my place in the Scotland side because of it. Willie Ormond told me later it was why my international career ended – I wasn't left out because of poor performances.

'What I should have done was to deny it when the press came back to me but instead I tried to clarify what I had said. This reporter probably got a couple of hundred quid for the story and it cost me my international career. It was great playing for my country, Willie Ormond was a decent manager, there were some nice people there and some very good players. We called Willie "Donny Osmond" to fit in with a song we made up about the backroom staff which went, "There's Hughie and Ronnie and wee Doc and Donny!"

'To play for your country is the Everest of anything, but for me when it finally came about, I have to look back on it personally as a major disappointment. I shrugged it off at the time but as I've got older the honour of having represented Scotland means much more to me. It gave me a fabulous opportunity to play alongside a lot of much better players than me. I knew my own limitations as a player and that I would only have ever been selected when I was in prolific form, which is fair enough. I actually wrote in one of the newspapers at the time that if I was scoring goals I should be picked and if not, then I shouldn't be playing. I truly believed that, but I would have liked to have played more international football, although I never expected to be around long enough to feature in the 1978 World Cup squad.

'Football's changed a little bit in Scotland now, when you watch sides like Celtic, it's a case of spot the Scottish player! Also, when I was playing every English First Division club had four or five quality Scottish players in their squad. That's how players like Billy Bremner developed and the Scottish team was stronger for it. I'm not sure they will ever be as strong again.'

Without doubt, the competition for places in the Scotland side in the 1970s was a lot greater than in more recent times, and MacDougall was competing with players of the calibre of Dalglish, Jordan, Parlane and Macari for a place in the team. Even so, he had good cause to feel harshly treated in the way he was passed over and it is unlikely Scotland would so quickly discard a player of his ability today, particularly one who had scored three goals in his first seven international appearances. As the Scotland players only received one cap for every season in which they were selected, Ted was presented with just two, both of which he gave to his father, who later succumbed to Alzheimer's disease and sadly when he passed away the caps were never found.

14

The First Division's Leading Goalscorer

MACDOUGALL returned to Norwich for pre-season training fitter than ever after playing for Scotland and in South Africa during the summer. At 28 years of age and with over 150 goals to his name, he was back to his best. Seventeen league goals the previous season had re-established his scoring reputation, albeit still outside the First Division, 'I felt really fit and ready to go after the summer, my weight then would have been just under 12st so I didn't have the usual pre-season battle to get back in shape. I found as I got older I needed to be playing consistently throughout the year so although I didn't enjoy much success on the pitch in South Africa, I certainly benefitted from the experience when I came back to England. I desperately wanted another chance to prove myself in the First Division and this time I knew I had the people around me to help me make that happen.'

Having restored Norwich to the top level of English football, John Bond's next task was to make sure they were equipped to stay there. In the 15 months he had been at the club he had spent £600,000 on new players with only a minimal return from those who had moved on. Although only 12 of the 20 players who had featured in league games the previous season had any experience of First Division football, Bond was confident his squad was good enough to hold its own in the top tier. It was just as well that he had faith in the players' ability, as during the summer the club had spent a six-figure sum on much-needed improvements at Carrow Road and at the club's Trowse training ground, so there was little money available for new players anyway, 'John stood by us but we didn't start well and he may have had second thoughts after some disappointing pre-season performances. We lost in a competition called the Anglo Scottish Cup to Fulham and Bristol City, and then went down heavily at Manchester City in our first league game. Thankfully, things picked up a bit after that.'

City's team for their first game back in the top flight showed two changes to the one that had finished the previous season. Machin reverted to right-back replacing Butler and Grapes came in for the suspended Boyer. Boyer was forced to miss the first four league games as a result of his sending-off against Sunderland the previous March, which Bond had engineered to be carried over into the new season, rather than have the player miss the end of the promotion campaign. Suggett was pushed forward to partner MacDougall in Boyer's absence, though the pair had no joy on the season's opening day as the Canaries suffered a 3-0 defeat at Maine Road.

Undeterred, Bond kept an unchanged side for the visit of the previous season's European Cup finalists Leeds and his faith was rewarded as City picked up their first point of the season. That said, they were fortunate to take a second-half lead when Suggett's cross eluded MacDougall only to strike the visitors' Paul Madeley and find its way into the net, before Jimmy Armfield's side hit back through a shot from Trevor Cherry 20 minutes later.

Things really got under way, though, when Aston Villa made a swift return to Carrow Road and with City keen to gain some revenge for their defeat the previous April, the game turned out to be an eight-goal thriller. The scoring began when both teams were awarded penalties in quick succession; the first, after 24 minutes, came after Villa's Nicholl handled in the penalty area and MacDougall scored from the spot. Two minutes later, Forbes was adjudged to have pushed City's nemesis Graydon, who then duly levelled things up. Then, five minutes before half-time, Forbes broke his nose in a collision with the visitors' Keith Leonard, leaving the City captain covered in blood. Remarkably, moments later he bravely headed Norwich in front, and as the Canaries began to run riot, Grapes made it three after tapping home MacDougall's cross. He then repaid the compliment, enabling

Ted to head a fourth goal before half-time in front of an ecstatic home crowd, MacDougall's first for Norwich in open play since the previous March.

Ron Saunders's men fought back after the interval and were rewarded when first Charlie Aitken headed home on the hour and again when Graydon popped up to make it 4-3. But, just as the nerves were setting in, MacDougall put the seal on a great performance, completing his first hat-trick in the First Division with a marvellous goal. After beating three Villa defenders, he slotted the ball home eight minutes from time to restore City's two-goal lead. The match, watched by a crowd of 21,797 on a lovely sunny afternoon, was widely acclaimed as one of the finest seen at Carrow Road in years. Afterwards, Bond celebrated his first win in five attempts over Saunders and declared that 'football was the winner' while Saunders, not uncharacteristically, left the ground without saying very much at all.

Boyer returned to the side at Arsenal, where City looked like grabbing a point until Eddie Kelly popped up late to score for the Gunners with a shot from 35 yards, but the hard-working Norwich forward claimed his first goal of the season a few days later at White Hart Lane when, after John Pratt had given the home side an interval lead, he diverted in a shot from Sullivan. John Duncan restored Tottenham's advantage ten minutes later but Norwich were not to be denied a point this time, MacDougall stepping up to head home a cross from Grapes.

Ted was certainly reaping the benefit of his work during the summer and his impressive start to the season continued when he thundered home a brilliant first-half hat-trick in a 4-2 win against Everton the following weekend. His first goal came from a near-post header following a Peters cross and was followed by a crisp first-time shot from a pass by Boyer, while the third came after he had raced clear of the visitors' defence before applying a clinical finish to beat the on rushing goalkeeper, David Lawson. Three minutes into the second half, Suggett put Norwich further ahead before goals from Latchford and Pearson gave Billy Bingham's team some respectability, 'Things were going well and the press caught on, and they wanted to make a big story about the two hat-tricks, but I felt it was still early days and too soon to start talking about how many goals I was going to score that season. I had actually set myself a target of 20 goals from the start but I didn't want to put myself under unnecessary pressure by making a big thing out of it. I had learned from my experiences at Manchester United and West Ham and I knew there was always a chance I might go the next six games without scoring and then everybody would be screaming for me to be dropped. It wasn't really what the press wanted to hear though and probably not what people wanted to read!'

With the alternative 'Supermac', Malcolm Macdonald, always promising to score a hatful of goals to anyone who would listen, and Leicester's Frank Worthington telling the press he was the most skilful centre-forward in the game, MacDougall's cautious approach seemed wise, as Worthington had endured a woeful start to the season, and Macdonald now found himself looking up the scorers' chart at Ted's increasingly impressive tally.

Eight more goals followed by the end of September and set MacDougall well on the way to achieving his target. The first two came when the Canaries and Burnley shared eight goals at Turf Moor, although he was outscored on this occasion by the Clarets striker Peter Noble, who registered all four of his side's goals. He had already struck twice before Ted converted a penalty on the half-hour, only for City to fall further behind after Butler handled just before half-time. However, goals from MacDougall and Peters brought Norwich level with a quarter of an hour to go, only for Noble to strike again two minutes from time. The scoring did not end there though, and after Peters had broken forward his cross was finally put into the net by Boyer.

Bond was thrilled with the way City had fought back at Turf Moor and in doing so, had become the First Division's leading goalscorers, although the number of goals they had conceded suggested that defensively, there was room for improvement. Even so, rather than be accused of lack of enterprise by the press and public, Bond went so far as to put on record that he would rather City lost 5-4 than scramble a point in a no-score draw. When Leicester visited Carrow Road the following Saturday, his side wasted no time in adding to their goal tally, MacDougall coolly sending goalkeeper Mark Wallington the wrong way from the penalty spot in the fourth minute, after he had been impeded inside the box. Leicester then missed the opportunity to equalise from the spot themselves, Worthington's effort being brilliantly saved by Kevin Keelan before the Canaries went on to clinch victory when a poor clearance by Wallington fell kindly to MacDougall, who comfortably stroked the ball home and sent City up to tenth in the table.

Norwich drew a blank for the first time since the opening day of the season in the East Anglian derby, which attracted the second-biggest crowd seen at Portman Road, 34,825. This time, MacDougall and Boyer were well shackled by Ipswich defenders Hunter and Beattie, the latter even finding time to score the first goal in the Suffolk side's 2-0 victory. Fortunately, the Canaries bounced back quickly, returning to winning ways at bottom club Sheffield United, where MacDougall's second-half header proved enough to beat Ken Furphy's injury-hit Blades.

For a change, City did not progress beyond the early stages of the League Cup, but they did manage to stretch their second round encounter against Manchester City to three matches. Their first meeting at Carrow Road ended in a 1-1 draw, MacDougall taking advantage of some hesitation by Dave Watson to open the scoring late in the second half, only for the big England defender to make amends by forcing in an equaliser shortly afterwards. In the replay at Maine Road a week later, goals from MacDougall and Suggett saw the Canaries come back from two down to take the match into extra time, which still failed to produce a winner, so the two teams faced a farcical third match on a neutral ground.

The chosen venue was Chelsea's Stamford Bridge and for Norwich it turned into a nightmare. The game was played in pouring rain and watched by the lowest crowd to attend a senior match at the ground, 6,238, who saw the Canaries crash to a 6-1 defeat amid a calamity of defensive errors. Having been criticised by Bond for their defensive tactics earlier in the tie, Tony Book's side turned on the style this time and took complete control, with Dennis Tueart completing a hat-trick, to send Norwich crashing out of the competition with a severe beating.

The cup result aside, City had still made an encouraging start to the season, MacDougall had scored 13 goals already and his scoring feats in September earned him the impressive treble of club, *Evening Standard* and *Daily Mirror* Player of the Month awards. In addition to returning for pre-season fitter than ever before, Ted had also taken steps to sharpen his mind, 'While I was away playing for Scotland, the Chelsea player Charlie Cooke got me interested in the power of positive thinking and I read a couple of books on the subject by the American author, Robert Vincent Peale, which channelled your mind and thought processes into a positive outlook. For example, if you're lost in the desert, you don't think, "I need water." Instead you think,

"What a lovely suntan I'm getting." Anyway, it worked for me and I believe it had an impact on my game.'

He certainly looked razor-sharp, his predatory instincts ensuring he was ideally placed to seize the moment to strike. He was following Bond's instructions to the letter of course, and instead of spending time running up and down the pitch, chasing possession or putting opponents under pressure as others had tried to coax him into doing, he was there simply to score goals. Alongside him, as usual, Boyer was working tirelessly, full of running and covering an incredible amount of ground in creating opportunities for his strike partner. Opponents quickly took note of course, tightening their defences accordingly, and making goals slightly harder to come by, and as a result City struggled to maintain their early season league form into the autumn.

Stoke City were the first side to inflict a home defeat upon the Canaries, and after their single-goal victory at the beginning of October Bond criticised his players at length, finding it difficult to say anything positive about their display. They responded positively the following week against reigning champions Derby, who after being under intense pressure throughout, were fortunate to leave Carrow Road with a goalless draw.

The early season sale of midfielder Doug Livermore to Cardiff City for £20,000 had left Bond with money available to strengthen his defence and at this point he agreed a £55,000 fee with Nottingham Forest manager Brian Clough for centre-half David Jones. Bond had failed in a bid to bring the player to Norwich from Bournemouth the previous summer but Jones, now aged 23, became the eighth ex-Cherries player to come to Norfolk since Bond's arrival. Earlier in the season, 29-year-old John Sainty, who had made more than 130 appearances for the Cherries, had also arrived at Norwich via Aldershot to become youth team manager at Carrow Road, while to redress the balance slightly, coach Fred Davies had returned to the south coast club in the close season to become assistant manager to John Benson, 'The fact that so many former Bournemouth players went on to play in the First Division was testament to how good the team of the early 1970s was and no doubt hellish frustrating for Cherries fans. Bondy understandably took a lot of the heat for that.'

With defensive stalwarts Forbes and Stringer at the latter stages of their careers, Jones, a full Welsh international, looked a good signing but his debut was unfortunately not one to remember. It came against

Parents, Alexander and Kathleen. Ted never forgot the opportunity they gave him to become a professional footballer. (Author's collection).

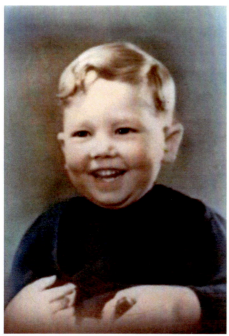

Early days. (Author's collection)

Ted first showed off the prowess of his right foot at a very young age! (Author's collection)

Ten years old, and always ready for a game! (Author's collection)

Substitute for Liverpool, that's Ted standing on the extreme right of the back row at Villa Park in 1966. (Unknown)

On parade for York City, August 1968. Ted is standing third from the right next to goalkeeper Mike Walker. Also included are Graham Carr (standing, third left) and Tommy Ross (seated, third left), whilst manager Joe Shaw and trainer Ron Spence are seated extreme left and right respectively. (Unknown)

In action for Bournemouth during the 1969/70 season. (Bournemouth Daily Echo)

When Ted was a trainee compositor at the Liverpool Weekly News, *he always ensured his own headlines were a little bit bigger and bolder! On a visit to the* Bournemouth Echo *offices in November 1970, he took the opportunity to reacquaint himself with printing techniques. (Bournemouth Daily Echo)*

Sam was a crazy border collie who travelled down when Ted signed for Bournemouth and became a well-known character at the club! (Bournemouth Daily Echo)

Anyone for tea? Ted and his first wife, Joan receive a silver tea-service from Bournemouth Chairman Harold Walker, after Ted had set a new goalscoring record for the club during the 1970/71 season. (Bournemouth Daily Echo)

'The Two Amigos' – MacDougall and Boyer at Bournemouth in 1971!
(Bournemouth Daily Echo)

A goalkeeper's view of Ted
scoring from the penalty spot for
Bournemouth against Chesterfield
in September 1971.
(Bournemouth Daily Echo)

'Record-Breaker' – Posing for the camera after his nine-
goal FA Cup haul against Margate in November 1971.
(Bournemouth Daily Echo)

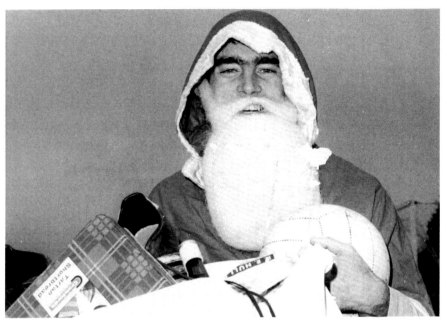

Ted dons a Santa suit to distribute presents to handicapped children in Bournemouth during December 1971. (Bournemouth Daily Echo)

Geoff (now Sir Geoff) Hurst joins Ted to sign autographs during a visit to his Boscombe sports shop in February 1972. (Bournemouth Daily Echo)

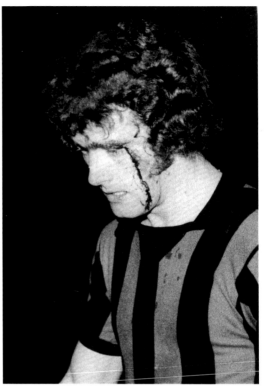

Celebrating a goal for Bournemouth against former club York City in March 1972. (Bournemouth Daily Echo)

Another battle wound! Ted picked up a number of facial injuries during his career including this one received whilst playing for Bournemouth against Tranmere Rovers in May 1972. (Bournemouth Daily Echo)

Bournemouth manager John Bond (suited, centre) opens Ted's new sports shop at Poole in July 1972. Amongst those joining in the celebrations are players Tommy Mitchinson, Trevor Hartley, Mickey Cave, David Jones, Phil Boyer and Bill Kitchener, whilst Mel Machin holds the baby! (Bournemouth Daily Echo)

A fond farewell – Ted runs out for his last appearance at Dean Court before joining Manchester United in September 1972. (Bournemouth Daily Echo)

"Joining the wrong club at the wrong time." – signing for Manchester United in September 1972, to the delight of manager Frank O'Farrell. (Press Association)

A man alone – leaving a United training session under new manager Tommy Docherty in January 1973. (Press Association)

What a relief! Ted had to wait until 8th October to score his first goal of the 1973/74 season for West Ham against Liverpool in the League Cup at Upton Park. (Press Association)

Take a good look at these 'Arabian' gentlemen! Ted (far right) is joined by fellow 'Arabian' Hammers, from left; Bobby Moore, Frank Lampard and Bobby Ferguson during West Ham's trip to Israel in May 1973. (Alamy)

After leaving Bournemouth, these former Cherries, together with manager John Bond, had climbed into the Second Division with Norwich City in 1975. From the top: John Benson, Ted, Mel Machin, Phil Boyer, assistant manager Ken Brown and coach Fred Davies. (Alamy)

Norwich and Manchester United both gained promotion from the Second Division at the end of the 1974/75 season. Here, Ted fends off a challenge from his former United team-mate, Martin Buchan. (Alamy)

England v Scotland, Wembley 1975 – "What a disaster!" In one of the better moments, Ted sends the ball goalwards under challenge from England's Colin Bell. (Alamy)

Upton Park, March 1976: Ted (left) beats Norwich team-mate Martin Peters (second right) and West Ham's Billy Bonds (second left) to head for goal as the Hammers' Keith Robson looks on. Having been pelted with eggs earlier in the game, Ted had the last laugh by scoring the winning goal. (Press Association)

On the attack for Southampton against Fulham in October 1976 and about to be challenged by friend and former team-mate, Bobby Moore. (Southern Daily Echo)

Lawrie McMenemy's Saints were all set to do battle with Manchester United in February 1977. Left to right: Peter Osgood, Ted, Alan Ball and Mick Channon. (Alamy)

Scoring for Southampton in the European Cup-Winners' Cup against Anderlecht in March 1977. (Southern Daily Echo)

Goal! Ted bags another for Saints and Peter Osgood is the first to offer his congratulations. Southampton v Plymouth Argyle, April 1977. (Southern Daily Echo)

MacDougall and Boyer (far left) in action together for Southampton against Luton Town in December 1977. (Southern Daily Echo)

Battling for a high ball with Notts County goalkeeper Eric McManus at The Dell in January 1978. (Southern Daily Echo)

Back with the Cherries! Running out to face Darlington after returning to Dean Court in November 1978. (Bournemouth Daily Echo)

Ted scores his 250th Football League goal for AFC Bournemouth against Rochdale in November 1979. (Unknown)

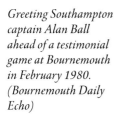

Greeting Southampton captain Alan Ball ahead of a testimonial game at Bournemouth in February 1980. (Bournemouth Daily Echo)

Meeting the press for the first time at Blackpool, together with Alan Ball in March 1980. (Press Association)

Skiing in Austria during 1983, with Lyne (far right), together with sports writer Malcolm Foley (left) and his wife Rachel. (Author's collection)

Ted and Lyne (far left) celebrate the re-opening of the Mill Arms at Dunbridge, near Romsey in December 1983. With them are Ted's parents Alex and Kath, Ted's daughter Alison and Lyne's son David. (Author's collection)

Sharing a joke with Alex Watson and the AFC Bournemouth players during a visit to training in November 1992.
(Bournemouth Daily Echo)

Another goalkeeper bows to the striking power of MacDougall! AFC Bournemouth Veterans v Hungerford Town, March 2000. (Bournemouth Daily Echo)

Coaching the young players at Atlanta Silverbacks in 2007. (Bournemouth Daily Echo)

Alongside a giant image of Ted's 'classic' goal against Aston Villa, whilst on a visit to AFC Bournemouth in 2007. (Author's collection)

With daughter Alison and grandchildren Harry and Jackson in 2008. (Author's collection)

Ted was inducted in to the Norwich City Hall of Fame in 2008, an occasion when Lyne and himself (far left) also enjoyed the company of (standing, left to right); John Bond, Kevin and Debbie Keelan and (front, left to right): Elaine and Ken Brown, Martin Peters and Janet Bond. (Norwich City)

A striking couple! Ted with his beautiful wife Lyne in 2011. (Author's collection)

With AFC Bournemouth chairman Jeff Mostyn at the opening of the 'Ted MacDougall Stand' in the summer of 2013. (Bournemouth Daily Echo)

Two Cherries legends – Ted with AFC Bournemouth manager Eddie Howe in March 2016. (Author's collection)

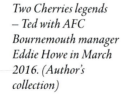

Newcastle at St James' Park in a match the press had billed as a shoot-out between the two 'Supermacs'. Both found their way on to the scoresheet, Macdonald first moving sharply on to a long free kick to put the Magpies ahead from close range after five minutes, only for City to equalise shortly before half-time when McGuire directed a crisp shot into the net following a goalmouth scramble. Unfortunately two second-half goals from Alan Gowling and another from Macdonald had already put the game well beyond City's reach before MacDougall reduced the arrears five minutes from time. Soon after, to complete a disappointing afternoon, Jones sliced the ball into his own net to give United a 5-2 victory.

City's first win in a month came thanks to Boyer, his goal bringing victory at home to Birmingham, and the same player came close to putting the Canaries ahead against Manchester United, when in a rare Norwich attack at Old Trafford, he hit the crossbar, shortly before Pearson scored what proved to be the winning goal for the new league leaders. MacDougall, back from international duty in midweek, had a quiet game on this occasion, with City confined to their own half for long periods of the game. Even so, they hardly deserved to be on the end of a disparaging post-match outburst from United manager Tommy Docherty, in which he implied they were a team of 'hangers-on' and capable of benefitting only from other teams' mistakes, 'Docherty was similar to Jose Mourinho today, always controversial, always making news with outrageous comments. I felt he was just trying to take the piss! He had a unique style of answering a question with another question and was very quick with his responses. If you were in his good books everything was terrific but unfortunately I only saw things from the other perspective.'

Certainly, the early season glut of goals had by now become a distant memory and consecutive 1-0 defeats, at home to Middlesbrough and away at Coventry started alarm bells ringing. Indeed, in torrential rain and on a mud-bath of a pitch they had provided the Sky Blues with their first home win in three months. Things then turned sour after a 2-1 home defeat against Newcastle during which strong claims for a late Norwich penalty had been turned down by the referee. It was enough to persuade a number of supporters to show their annoyance by throwing cushions on to the pitch at the final whistle and as the cushions rained down, with City dropping to 18th place in the table, Bond knew he needed to act quickly – but the team's next fixture was against Liverpool at Anfield, 'The strange thing was we weren't doing anything different to how we were early in the season, the ball just wasn't running or dropping for us but as a result we were beginning to lose confidence. John took us away for a few days and that seemed to lift the spirits a bit. He didn't chop and change the team much although David Jones had taken over from Mel Machin in defence and then Mel was restored to midfield for the Liverpool game.

'Oddly enough he played there for the reserves at Bournemouth while we were losing to Newcastle and scored the winning goal! I wasn't worried about going to Anfield because I always did well there and I had a feeling we would be OK. Bondy decided to play Martin Peters and I together up front and he wanted us to take up wide positions, just like Ron Greenwood had me doing when I first joined West Ham. It worked a treat on this occasion, Emlyn Hughes and Phil Thompson didn't know what to do as they had nobody to mark in the centre of the pitch and as a result they got pulled out of position.'

With Norfolk covered by a blanket of fog, many City supporters and a number of the club's directors were unable to get to Anfield, and were unfortunate to miss a superb performance. With Powell out through injury, Bond turned to long-serving defender Stringer, who had himself missed the start of the season through an ankle problem, to again partner Forbes in defence, and they were forced to soak up considerable pressure in the first half. After the interval though, the match turned on its head as City put in a brilliant display. The Kop had been subdued by a 25-yard blockbuster from Suggett which put Norwich ahead, before Peters made a perfectly timed run to tuck home Sullivan's pass. Liverpool eventually responded when Emlyn Hughes stabbed home three minutes from time but Bond was left beaming with delight after MacDougall sealed victory two minutes later, pouncing on a loose ball in the penalty area to score once more against his first club and register his 17th goal of the season.

The result at Liverpool was not down to luck, nor was it a freak result, it was the perfect execution of a pre-conceived plan, the effect of which would prove influential in establishing City as a team to be reckoned with in the First Division. The knock-on effect was felt by third-placed West Ham, who were defeated by a MacDougall goal to the delight of the home supporters in the crowd of 27,020 at Carrow Road. Looking far more confident after the victory at Liverpool, City controlled the game for long spells, and their efforts were rewarded 12 minutes from time, when Ted and fellow ex-Hammer Peters combined for the striker to head past Day in the Hammers' goal. But after fighting fans spilled on the pitch at the final whistle, MacDougall was criticised for the way he had reacted after his goal, 'No goal that season gave me greater pleasure than that one! I made one or two gestures towards the West Ham bench afterwards and I think it upset some people but after all the frustration I had experienced during my time at Upton Park, the goal and the build-up to it was perfect. Remember I'd had a lot of criticism, a lot of people just didn't believe in me and I just wanted to point that out to some of them. That's all it was.'

The Canaries' fortunes continued to fluctuate as 1975 drew to a close. Goals from MacDougall and Peters brought them a point on a bone-hard pitch at Villa Park before home draws against Manchester City and Wolves came either side of a defeat against Queens Park Rangers at Loftus Road. Things had again looked bleak against Tony Book's side after they had eased themselves into a two-goal lead, but two second-half goals from Boyer capped a fine fightback. After the diminutive striker converted a low drive into the penalty area from Morris, he netted again after MacDougall had helped on Sullivan's cross.

Boxing Day saw a lively display of attacking football at Loftus Road, in a game which saw both goalkeepers make a series of fine saves. Masson eventually put Rangers ahead on the half-hour, but the game remained in the balance until Bowles applied the finishing touch a minute from time. With no let-up in the holiday fixtures, City faced Wolves the following day and looking jaded, they fell behind midway through the first half and were eventually grateful for the athleticism of Peters, whose impressive overhead kick from Suggett's corner enabled them to pick up a point and end the year in 18th place.

The draw for the third round of the FA Cup appeared to have handed Norwich a straightforward enough passage, a home tie against Fourth Division Rochdale being more or less what City would have ordered. All seemed to be going to plan as early as the fourth minute when MacDougall stepped up to the penalty spot to score his 20th goal of the season, having been tripped moments earlier. With the floodgates seemingly open more goals were expected to follow but instead the only other one went to Rochdale. Try as they might to force a winner, City were unable to break down a resolute defence and they again drew a blank in the replay at Spotland, having been outfought for

163

long spells by the home side. Boyer had an effort ruled out for offside but City were fortunate to remain in the competition, with Rochdale striking the frame of the goal on three separate occasions.

As in the League Cup earlier in the season, the tie went to a third match, although this time Norwich secured home advantage through the toss of a coin. Despite another spirited performance, the Dale were finally seen off by a goal from Suggett with just two minutes remaining, despite their desperate pleas for offside. Earlier, just as he had in the first tie, MacDougall had put City ahead from the penalty spot before the visitors had equalised early in the second half.

Struggling Burnley were the first league visitors to Carrow Road in 1976, with manager Joe Brown faced with a host of injured players, one of whom was top scorer Noble. City inflicted even more pain on the Lancashire club as headers from Peters, Forbes and Boyer gave them a comfortable three-goal lead after an hour.

Having finally seen off Rochdale the Canaries headed north again, this time to face mid-table Everton, where pre-match preparations were upset when Bond's car was broken into at the team's hotel. City could not be accused of robbery at Goodison Park though, as they emerged from a scrappy game with a well-earned point. Martin Dobson had opened the scoring for the hosts early in the second half, his left-footed shot catching out an unsighted Keelan but Norwich hit back within ten minutes when Boyer headed in a cross by Jones.

Two days later, Bond took his side to Bournemouth for a testimonial match in aid of the former Cherries trainer and physiotherapist Arthur Cunliffe, who had worked behind the scenes during Bond's reign at Dean Court. In doing so, the City manager kept a promise he made to Cunliffe upon his departure to Norwich and the full City first-team squad participated, including former Cherries Boyer, Jones, Machin, Powell and MacDougall, 'I knew there was still a certain amount of bad feeling among the Bournemouth fans following the "exodus" to Norwich and towards John in particular so I wasn't quite sure what sort of welcome we would get. Mind you it was not all one-way traffic as Clive Payne and Trevor Howard had gone to Dean Court and since Benno returned to take charge he had persuaded John to loan him Billy Steele and Doug Livermore, then later in the season, signed Geoff Butler and took Steve Grapes on loan.

'Anyway, John was well aware of how the fans felt but he was not a man to break a promise. Those of us who knew Arthur all wanted to play for him and I think we all enjoyed going back, although it was sad to see the club in such a decline. We won the game comfortably and I like to think that perhaps by playing we helped ease some of the bitterness that had built up between the two clubs.'

Not many teams gained away victories at Liverpool and Leeds in the same season during the 1970s, but Norwich did so in some style when they defeated the Yorkshire club at the end of January. As early as the 11th minute Peters won possession before passing the ball to Suggett, who flicked it across the penalty area for MacDougall to strike home from close range. Leeds were thrown out of their stride for long periods of the game by a tenacious City performance but when they did break forward, Keelan and the defence dealt with things competently. Despite all Leeds's huffing and puffing, they were caught out again when McGuire's shot was deflected into the net just after the hour and then MacDougall put the game to bed three minutes from time, heading in Norwich's third and the 192nd league goal of his career, 'I told you I was always good for a goal at Liverpool and Leeds, although I sometimes left it late! Leeds were a great team, Billy Bremner, Johnny Giles, Norman Hunter, Jack Charlton…they had a reputation you know, "Dirty Leeds", but I never had any problems with them. Paul Reaney, or "Stan Laurel" as I think they called him, used to try and wind me up all the time, "Gaffer thinks you're really good, he wants to sign you!" He'd say all this sort of stuff to try and put me off! Leeds could play though, they would knock it about and put 20 or 30 passes together despite the fact the pitches were crap then, not like the lawns of today!'

City stretched their unbeaten run to five league games, their best spell of the season, with a 3-1 victory over Arsenal which lifted them back up to 14th place. Centre-half Terry Mancini left his mark on MacDougall in the second minute but his over-exuberant challenge only allowed Peters the opportunity to curl a free kick into the Arsenal net. The Gunners equalised just five minutes later, when Ball's cross was put away by Kidd, but went behind again when MacDougall slid the ball home after receiving a glorious through-pass from Machin. The game continued to swing from end to end into the second half and it was Peters who finally sealed a thrilling victory for Norwich, with a typical near-post header after 73 minutes.

Having played in excess of 300 league games, MacDougall was by now a senior figure in the dressing room and when a young City team entertained Red Star Belgrade in a friendly at Carrow Road, he was asked to captain the side. He had already skippered City the previous season when Forbes had been injured and was happy to oblige again in a game that the Yugoslavians won by a single goal. But despite being a strong, opinionated character, captaincy did not figure highly in MacDougall's priorities, 'I never really saw myself as a leader. I did it a few times during my career but I don't think I was great captaincy material because I was too wrapped up in my own game. People say football is a team game but it wasn't for me, it was about me really, my ego, my aspirations, my fans. I don't think that's what managers look for in a good captain!'

Typically, after the excitement of successive wins against Leeds and Arsenal came two successive home defeats, the first a thumping 3-0 reverse against Coventry and then a shock FA Cup fifth round exit at the hands of Fourth Division Bradford City. Norwich had made short work of Second Division Luton in the previous round, goals from Peters and Jones ensuring a comfortable home passage, before the match ended in a snowstorm. Much to the frustration, and at times anger, of those at Carrow Road, the tie against Bradford was then twice postponed at the Yorkshire club's request because of an outbreak of flu at Valley Parade, but when the game did take place, it was Norwich who felt under the weather after Billy McGinley's winner three minutes from time.

Earlier Don Hutchins had held off a challenge from Jones to fire the Bantams into a first-half lead, but Peters had equalised with another of his near-post headers. Despite not enjoying the best of luck in front of goal, both Forbes and McGuire having struck the woodwork, Norwich could reflect that they had already enjoyed a large helping of fortune in overcoming Rochdale earlier in the competition. Without doubt though, they had missed a glorious opportunity to reach the quarter-finals, while Bradford became only the third Fourth Division side to reach the last eight of the competition, where they were beaten by the eventual winners Southampton.

February came to a close with a visit to Birmingham, for which the Canaries recalled industrious midfielder Billy Steele from his loan at Bournemouth in place of the injured Machin, who would miss the rest of the season. They also welcomed the return of Powell after a long absence, and City's strong-tackling last line of defence duly marked his return from injury with an over-exuberant challenge on Trevor

Francis at St Andrew's. The referee had no hesitation in awarding a penalty and after the young Blues forward dusted himself down, he calmly beat Keelan from 12 yards. Powell's blushes were spared by Peters soon after the interval when his free kick found the back of the net after McGuire had been upended.

Having seen off Arsenal the previous month, Norwich handed Tottenham a dose of the same treatment at Carrow Road before continuing to bob along through March, rarely looking likely to drop into serious danger of relegation despite falling to 17th at one stage before rising to 12th by the end of the month. All the goals against Spurs came in the second half, after Martin Chivers had put the visitors ahead. Soon after, Suggett got the final touch in a goalmouth scramble to pull City level and they went ahead when defender Keith Osgood used his hand to clear an effort from Jones and MacDougall obliged from the penalty spot, before finally, with Spurs pressing for a late equaliser, Suggett broke away to set up Boyer, who buried the ball in the back of the Londoners' net.

At Derby, it was largely one-way traffic in the direction of the City goal before the Canaries scored with their first attack midway through the first half, Jones heading on a corner kick which eventually enabled Forbes to nod the ball home. Normal service was then resumed until finally the City defence cracked soon after the interval, Archie Gemmill's shot beating Keelan at full stretch. Once breached, they conceded again when Bruce Rioch rounded Keelan to complete a brilliant solo goal before Leighton James added a third to ensure Norwich went home empty-handed.

March was also a significant month for Boyer as a midweek fixture against Manchester United at Carrow Road saw him net his 100th career goal, which was followed by a call-up to the full England squad. Just to prove it wasn't always Boyer who did the running, his goal against United came after MacDougall had chased down a long ball more in hope than expectation, then having managed to keep it in play, he forced it across for his partner to hit home. Earlier, Gordon Hill had raced through to give United an early lead, but they were then forced back to defend for long periods and with Boyer also hitting a post near the end, a draw was the least City deserved for their efforts.

Boyer became the first Norwich player to be selected for England when he won what proved to be his only full cap against Wales at Wrexham later in the month, and although he was not on the scoresheet, he put in his usual high-tempo performance in England's 2-1 victory, 'Charlie had heard that Don Revie had been watching him but I'm not sure he really thought he would ever get selected. When the call came in to the club, Bondy went round his house to tell him and he was flabbergasted! I was delighted for him.'

Boyer was thwarted by the woodwork once again the following weekend against Liverpool, although he was also guilty of missing a couple of 'sitters' on an afternoon when England goalkeeper Ray Clemence was in outstanding form for the Reds. First he bravely thwarted MacDougall, rushing from his line to save before producing a world-class effort to turn aside a fierce drive from winger John Miller, who had been restored to the City side in place of Steele. Norwich again dominated the game for long periods but ultimately paid the penalty for a mistake by Jones, whose back-pass failed to reach Keelan, enabling David Fairclough to nip in and give the visitors some revenge for their defeat at the hands of the Canaries the previous November.

After the reaction to his goal celebration at Norwich earlier in the season, MacDougall was understandably expecting a lively reception when City travelled to Upton Park and, suffice to say, the West Ham crowd did not disappoint him. After their impressive start to the season, the Hammers were in the midst of a dreadful run of form, having won just once in 16 matches. Ted was certainly fired up and when he struck after just 16 minutes, volleying home his 26th goal of the season, his celebration afterwards only served to increase the tension. Later, following a fierce challenge on goalkeeper Day and another coming-together with his old mate Billy Bonds, the crowd responded by pelting him with missiles. Ted had the last laugh though, his goal being enough to give the Canaries a double over the out-of-touch Hammers, 'My "homecoming" to West Ham was certainly bitter-sweet! Martin Peters, who obviously knew a lot of Hammers fans, warned me that they were going to pelt me with eggs. I thought he was joking, but sure enough on came these eggs slap, slap – I even hit the ground at one point thinking it was more eggs and really looked silly when it turned out to be a flock of birds flying overhead!

'All goals were equally important to me, I used to say, arse or elbow, it doesn't matter, except THIS goal! A left-footed volley from outside the box, a feat for me anyway, rifled past Mervyn Day and into the top corner! My celebration consisted of running behind the West Ham goal, blowing kisses, and then running over to their bench with more blown kisses. At half-time though, somebody emptied a cup of tea over my head as I made my way down the tunnel and another person grabbed my hair. Ah, football life – it couldn't get any better!'

As the month drew to a close, Carrow Road braced itself for the visit of Ipswich and another eagerly awaited derby game with more than 31,000 people squeezed in to the ground. The visitors needed points to aid their bid for a UEFA Cup place the following season but it was Norwich who emerged triumphant. After MacDougall had tested Town goalkeeper Paul Cooper and Boyer again cracked a shot against the post, the decisive moment came shortly before half-time, when Peters dispossessed Ipswich defender John Peddelty and struck the game's only goal.

With six matches left Bond set his team a target of a top-ten finish, while MacDougall's sights were firmly set on ending the season as the division's leading scorer, although having scored only two goals from his last eight league appearances, he was now being increasingly closely pursued by Tottenham's John Duncan. The visit of Sheffield United seemed a good opportunity to strike a blow; with just three wins from 39 league and cup games, they were several points adrift at the bottom of the table and had dismissed manager Ken Furphy soon after City had defeated them in September. His successor, Bond's former Notts County adversary Jimmy Sirrel, had been unable to halt their side towards the Second Division, but amazingly, in a crazy first half, his side built up a three-goal advantage before Boyer managed to pull one back.

After the break, it was all Norwich, but United goalkeeper Jim Brown was in inspired form and kept out everything that the Canaries could muster. After a suitable blast from Bond, the team travelled north to face a Middlesbrough side comfortably placed in the top half of the table, and were grateful to see shots from David Armstrong and Graham Souness both hit the woodwork, then Keelan saved a Terry Cooper penalty, before the livewire Steele popped up to take advantage of hesitation in the home defence to win the game.

Still no more goals for MacDougall though, and when he looked set to increase his tally at Leicester, he was crudely hauled down by defender Jeff Blockley when clean through on goal. Happy to accept the referee's caution with a grin, Blockley had 'taken one for the team' and the game ended goalless, 'This sort of challenge would result in a sending-off today but back then the defender just used to receive a booking and laugh it off. If you were a forward you just accepted it and got on with things most of the time, but there were occasions when I took it personally. The game could go on while I had a personal fight with someone, even over the smallest thing!

'It also happened in training once, with me and Mel Machin at the Tottenham training ground. Bondy thought he had a chance of getting the Tottenham manager's job after Bill Nicholson had gone and we happened to go up there for a practice game against them, Peters, Chivers, Gilzean, all that lot were playing for Spurs at the time. Mel's played a ball short and he reckons I should have come off the defender to take it, the usual thing and he's had a pop at me and I've gone back at him, blah, blah, blah, and we're pushing and shoving and about to set about one another. I'd completely forgotten about the game.

'Anyway the referee stopped it and blew for half-time and John said, "That's nice isn't it, I'm trying to make a good impression and now they think I can't even control my own players." Mel and I made a point of walking off arm-in-arm but Bondy never heard any more about the job.'

At Filbert Street, Bond gave a first-team debut to his son, Kevin, the 18-year-old appearing as a substitute late in the game. Bond junior was another to go from Bournemouth to Norwich, having originally been an apprentice at Dean Court before joining City as an amateur in 1974, and had signed professional forms for the Canaries only the week before his debut, 'Kevin was a late developer and being John's son he had it twice as hard as anyone else. I first knew him when he was about 13 years old, when his Dad became boss at Bournemouth. He struggled as a youngster because he didn't start to develop physically until he was around 18. He started off as a right-back but John Benson convinced him he would make a good centre-half and he certainly did, enjoying a long career in the First Division and following his Dad around to Norwich and Manchester City.

'After he finished his playing career he became a very good coach and assistant manager to Harry Redknapp at Portsmouth, Southampton, Tottenham and Queens Park Rangers. Although he had a two-year spell in charge at Bournemouth a few years ago, I don't really see Kevin as a number one because his personality is not focussed in that way. He gets down too easily and sometimes finds it hard to pick himself up. As a manager you need to pep things up from time to time and I believe he finds that difficult.

'Kevin and I have had this discussion many times but I think he worked brilliantly alongside Harry. When you are a manager you don't need your own voice coming back at you, you need someone to offer you something different, you need to be a team and that's where he and Harry hit it off together.

'Kevin and his wife Trina became great friends, although he and I have had plenty of disagreements about football over the years. We often used to sit around the table at his Mum and Dad's just talking about football for hours, all of us! It was wonderful.'

Carrow Road's biggest gate of the season, 31,231, amassed for the visit of league leaders Queens Park Rangers, who themselves arrived with an 11,000-strong army of supporterss following a wonderful run of 11 wins and a draw which had seen them rise to the top of the table. Rangers led Liverpool by a single point and knew if they could win their final three games, they would clinch their first league title. Manager Dave Sexton had put together an exciting side with plenty of experience which included an England captain in Gerry Francis, a First Division and FA Cup Double-winner in Frank McLintock and a footballing maverick in Stan Bowles.

But it was City who revelled in the atmosphere and the presence of the *Match of the Day* cameras. Playing with the freedom of a side safely tucked in mid-table, they took the lead through a typical piece of opportunism from MacDougall. Suggett crossed from the left and as Boyer challenged, full-back Dave Clement tried to guide the loose ball back to goalkeeper Phil Parkes only to see Ted nip in between to grab his 22nd league goal of the season. The goal shook Rangers and brought more moments of panic in their defence before they gradually regained their composure and eventually produced a superb solo goal from winger Dave Thomas to bring them level a minute from half-time.

The visitors pressed forward strongly at the start of the second half only to fall behind again when midfielder Peter Morris reacted first after a corner was punched clear by Parkes, his shot on the half-volley nearly bursting the Rangers net. Things then became heated following an unpleasant exchange between Powell and Bowles, and got worse for the title-chasers when Boyer headed home a cross from Peters. Rangers eventually scored a second themselves when Powell, under pressure from Don Givens, looked to clear his lines but only succeeded in hooking the ball into his own net. Despite throwing everything at City, Rangers could not find an equaliser and at the final whistle, their miserable afternoon was completed when they discovered Liverpool had won to take over at the top after Rangers had led for six weeks.

In true Norwich style, after their magnificent effort against QPR, they fell quickly down to earth 48 hours later, suffering defeat to a John Richards goal at Molineux against a Wolves side battling to avoid relegation, 'These two results summed us up really, we were capable of beating anyone but also capable of losing to anyone! We blew a bit hot and cold but when we were hot, we were very hot, We always seemed to have this inconsistency about us though and it used to frustrate the hell out of Bondy.'

The season ended on a positive note with a 2-0 victory at Stoke, where a mistake by Potters defender Alan Dodd allowed MacDougall through to beat goalkeeper Peter Shilton, after which the Canaries' lead was doubled by a superb strike by Suggett. Meanwhile QPR bounced back to win their final two games, but Liverpool did likewise and captured the title. Bond and his players could take satisfaction that City's tenth-place finish was the best in the club's history and an excellent return in their first season back in the First Division, 'It was ironic that we should eventually put paid to Rangers' hopes of winning the championship, as John loved their stylish football and had been critical of Liverpool's more physical approach during the season. Apart from our early season defeats by Manchester City, the season went okay and we steered well clear of the relegation zone for most of the campaign. I think the chairman was also delighted because the club had established itself in the First Division.'

MacDougall ended the season with another ambition fulfilled – his 23 league goals meant he finished as the First Division's top scorer, the first and only time a Norwich player has achieved the accolade. He finished three ahead of his nearest rival, Tottenham's John Duncan, and in front of such notable strikers as Macdonald, Keegan, Toshack, Richards and Francis. Furthermore, his 28 goals in all competitions meant he was City's leading scorer for the third season in succession. The pattern in which Ted's goals were scored was certainly unusual – after an early burst in September, he scored just one league goal in virtually the next two months, went another five matches without scoring around the turn of the year and only scored twice in the last seven matches of the season.

Crucially though, he knew he was not playing badly during these periods and continued to make chances, which with better luck could have added three or four more goals to his final total, 'After I'd scored 12 in the league by the end of September, I was well away. Peter Noble of Burnley was my nearest rival early on and I can remember us both going all-out for it! Unfortunately, Peter picked up an injury midway through the season and missed a lot of games, so I went on to win the Golden Boot as top scorer in the First Division, not that I ever saw any trophy! I never got an award but the great thing about it all was that I had re-established myself. I was playing better than ever, I was strong, my touch was good and people were playing me in. My confidence levels were sky high and everything was great.

'From a playing point of view, Norwich was the best thing I ever did because by then I was older and more experienced, I was playing at a higher level and I was doing it in the First Division where people said I couldn't – and then I played for my country. That was the most important thing for me – having been branded a failure I had now done it. And nobody can take that away from me because it's there in black and white. It's not like a midfield player or a full-back who says, "I had a great season in 1973." How do you know? Being the leading goalscorer in 1975/76 and playing for my country are the two things I'm most proud of during my career.'

MacDougall's remarkable fitness and ability to steer clear of injury had enabled him to play in every game throughout the season and only once had he been substituted. His 23 league goals came in a Norwich total of 58, to which Boyer and Peters also contributed 11 and ten respectively. A fiery and unpredictable character on the pitch, MacDougall had this time been able to demand the service he expected from his team-mates and woe betide those who failed to deliver. There were occasions when his refusal to chase a lost cause was perceived as laziness by City supporters, though any comments in his direction were likely to be met with a large and sometimes prolonged V-sign. Despite his moods and gestures, Ted had proved at the highest domestic level that he was without doubt a natural goalscorer.

Even so, it was not enough to win him Norwich's Player of the Year award, which went to Peters, another ever-present who, in addition to chipping in with vital goals, was a marvellous influence on those around him and found his career revitalised. His performances throughout the season drew speculation of an England recall but his continued omission from manager Don Revie's squad did not seem to concern him unduly. Instead of touring North America with the England party for the USA Bicentennial Cup, Peters threw an end-of-season party of his own, entertaining the Norwich team and their wives at his new home. As Bond and MacDougall joined in the celebrations all seemed well, but it would soon become apparent that they each had very different things on their mind when it came to the new season ahead.

15

A Sad Farewell

DESPITE the success of the previous season, the long, hot summer of 1976 was a torrid one for MacDougall. He had been looking forward to a break after a long season and a chance to focus on his interests away from football, but instead found himself part of an unwelcome end-of-season tour. First Norwich flew on a 'goodwill' mission to Norway, where they played three low-key games, then moved on to Trinidad for two more before returning in mid-June. Unfortunately, Ted allowed his frustration to get the better of him against Norwegian sports club Larvik Turn and was sent off by a local referee.

The root of his problem was that living in Norfolk had made him feel increasingly cut off from his business interests on the south coast. He desperately wanted to return to that area and despite all the success he had enjoyed at Norwich, he had now reached breaking point and no longer could he keep it from John Bond, 'I told John I had reached the point where I was going to quit, and I meant it. The last two years at Norwich had been great for me on the field but hell off it. Sure, I continued to enjoy playing for City and strangely enough, my off-the-field problems didn't affect my game.

'But it became a miserable time for me and two years was a long time to feel unhappy. Now it had begun to affect my game and I knew the pretences were over – I had to leave and John had all sorts of problems with me. My general demeanour became poor and I let

175

what I was feeling in my head affect my body and influence what I was saying.

'My businesses were going on without me back in Bournemouth but I felt I needed to be there more, and had already arranged to have a new house built down there in Canford Cliffs. Norwich was a lovely place but it was in the middle of nowhere at the time, it took a couple of hours just to get to a motorway. So once training had finished I was sitting at home all the while just killing time. I was bored, I didn't have any hobbies and I rarely had anything to do. It became soul-destroying and I couldn't allow it to continue. I wanted to live in Bournemouth again, I guess that was at the back of much of the trouble and I wanted to get more involved in my businesses.'

Bond was stunned and his initial reaction was naturally to try and talk MacDougall round, desperately hoping that he could persuade him to change his mind. Norwich had relied on Ted's goals for more than two years and to replace him would be extremely difficult and no less expensive. The manager had already strengthened his squad with the acquisition of 29-year-old John Ryan, who joined City from Luton for £46,000. A tall and attacking full-back, Ryan was something of a modern version of Bond himself, but with the bonus of ferocious shooting power.

Meanwhile, striker Roger Gibbins arrived on a free transfer from Oxford United while Peter Morris left to manage his former club, Mansfield, and several fringe players also exited Carrow Road. Working on a relatively small budget, Bond found himself constantly juggling his options amid a succession of injuries, the worst of which had already ruled midfielder Mick McGuire out for the entire season. Now it looked as if he had to find a striker capable of scoring 20 to 30 goals a season, 'John had around £100,000 to spend on his team and he took issue with me because having had a good season back in the First Division, he had been given this money to improve the team and my leaving would mean he had to spend most of it trying to replace me. There was a bit of animosity between us and things were said and done as they are in football.'

Bond knew better than anyone that MacDougall was a complicated person and could be difficult to handle if he was less than happy with his game or the environment in which he found himself, so with much reluctance, he agreed to release him once a replacement had been found. He would have to do without MacDougall for the club's first two games of the season anyway, his dismissal in Norway during the summer counting against him under the FA's disciplinary totting-up procedure, which put him over the 20-point limit for the previous season. City's appeal was rejected and MacDougall was forced to serve a two-game suspension at the start of the new campaign.

The Canaries could not have begun against stronger opposition, travelling to Anfield to face the league champions and UEFA Cup holders Liverpool. Ryan made his debut, having taken over at right-back with Machin again operating in midfield, but a weak header from Powell led to Steve Heighway grabbing the points for Bob Paisley's side.

Four days later, City faced Arsenal in their first home fixture and despite adopting a more positive approach, they were beaten again. Gibbins made his debut in place of the suspended MacDougall but goals from Sammy Nelson, Malcolm Macdonald (his first following a summer move to the Gunners), and Frank Stapleton were met with just a solitary reply from Martin Peters.

MacDougall returned against West Bromwich Albion at the Hawthorns, and although he put in a decent performance, the spark seemed to be missing from his eyes, his mind seemingly elsewhere as City fell to a 2-0 defeat, 'I continued playing in the hope that something could be sorted out pretty quickly and I certainly still gave it my best, but I hadn't changed my mind about quitting Norwich.'

It was a desperate start to the campaign for Bond, with City anchored at the bottom of the league table and still, unbeknown to the vast majority of supporters, resigned to the fact that it was only a matter of time before they would lose the services of their major goalscorer. However, as August drew to a close, MacDougall netted his first goal of the season from the penalty spot in City's 3-1 League Cup victory at Exeter. Significantly, Ted's goal at St James Park would prove to be his last for the club.

Back in the league, Boyer struck again to beat Birmingham in a scrappy and occasionally bad-tempered match at Carrow Road, but the Canaries remained at the bottom after defeat against Coventry the following week. The game at Highfield Road proved to be a sad farewell for MacDougall, who finally left Norwich somewhat acrimoniously in favour of a return to the Second Division with FA Cup holders Southampton. With Ted intent on returning to the south coast, potential suitors were very limited but Southampton were able to offer the right deal to suit him, and reluctantly City allowed him to leave for just £50,000, a fraction of his true worth.

On the open market he would have been worth five times more but the move and the fee had been dictated by unusual circumstances. After three moves in just over a year for a combined fee of £505,000, 66 goals later Norwich had sold him for ten per cent of that amount.

The news came as a major shock to the club's supporters, none of whom would have wanted him to leave, although most shared the opinion that the club had been taken to the cleaners. However, few held it against MacDougall or Southampton – it wasn't as if he had gone somewhere for money or glory, he had in fact dropped down a division to be located where he could still play football but also be near his home and business interests, 'The supporters were pretty good to me at Norwich, as were the club and I had nothing against the place at all apart from it being so isolated. I will always be thankful that during my time at Carrow Road I had the opportunity to prove to people I could score goals regularly in the First Division. I believe that if I'd felt really happy living in the area I would have done even better. I hoped that everyone would come to appreciate the circumstances in which I found myself and that we could part on good terms. It took some time but I think that's how it turned out eventually.

'I always had the greatest respect for John Bond because he was the man who made me the player I was, and I think as much as he wanted me to stay at Carrow Road, he realised in the end that it would not have been in anybody's best interest to keep me because of the way I felt. It was fortunate that Bondy was a good friend of Saints manager Lawrie McMenemy, they did a deal and he managed to get £50,000 for me, which at least helped Norwich and, I like to think, also resulted in a good deal for Southampton.'

Even so, Ted's departure staggered the majority of the football press. Why would such a player want to leave a club where he was playing for a manager who understood him like no other and alongside a player who complemented him so perfectly? He had been the First Division's leading goalscorer only the previous season and had won seven Scotland caps while at Norwich. He was among the top ten Norwich goalscorers of all time, his goals coming in only 138 appearances. Imagine the sensation such a move would cause today. Critics argued that his drop into the Second Division could only have been outweighed by higher pay and the chance to play alongside Mick Channon and Peter Osgood,

'People said I'd made so much money out of all my moves, I was the luckiest bloke around. Well, I can't deny I made good money but my argument was simply that money wasn't everything. There's more to life, much more, than just money, big clubs and glamour. Happiness is far more important than those qualities. You've got to be happy in what you're doing and where you're doing it – and if you're not, it will eventually drag you down and it's the worst thing in the world. I wish I had been able to stay with one club throughout my career and really settle there. That would have been marvellous.

'Anyway, I felt I'd done enough travelling so I was delighted to get the chance to come back down to Hampshire and just wanted to settle down with Saints and never move again. I could live in Bournemouth and had my businesses to keep me occupied, although at 29 years of age I had no thoughts that I'd come to Southampton to play out my career quietly. I'd heard the rumours – "He's only going there because he's been put out to pasture" – that sort of stuff. Anyone who thought that was dead wrong. I still had a lot of pride – pride in myself and in my ability and I was proud to be joining the FA Cup holders. All I wanted to do was to settle down and score goals.

'I got something like a goal every other game in just over two and a half years at Norwich which was a ratio that made me very happy. I knew I could still get goals, I hadn't the slightest doubt about that and I was determined to prove it to people. I knew I would miss the First Division from the point of view of glamour and crowds but when I joined Saints, I felt as though a huge weight had been lifted from my shoulders.'

MacDougall travelled to The Dell to discuss terms with McMenemy and Saints' financial director Guy Askham, and once everything was agreed, Bond drove down to Southampton to hand over the paperwork personally and complete the deal. Soon after Bond and MacDougall had said their farewells, the City manager set off to replace the player he had likened to a 'son' and later the same day spent the £50,000 on the robust 27-year-old Fulham striker Viv Busby.

16

McMenemy Draws the Magnet Home!

FORTY-YEAR-OLD Lawrie McMenemy was known in the game as a strong personality with a warm smile, able to communicate with players and supporters alike. He was also a strong disciplinarian, a legacy of his days in the Guards. Having failed to make the grade as a player at Newcastle United, he joined his local club Gateshead in the late 1950s but his playing career was ended by injury in 1961. He stayed at the club as trainer/coach before becoming manager of Bishop Auckland three years later. Here he took the club to the Northern League championship and into the third round of the FA Cup before moving on to spend two years as coach at Sheffield Wednesday and then became manager of Doncaster Rovers. He took Rovers to the Fourth Division championship in 1970 but was sacked after they were relegated the following year. He was quickly offered the manager's post at Grimsby Town and the Mariners became Fourth Division champions at the end of his first season in charge.

In July 1973 McMenemy accepted an offer to become assistant manager under Ted Bates at The Dell. Bates planned to groom McMenemy as his successor but following his appointment as manager in December 1973, Southampton were relegated at the end of the season after eight successive campaigns in the top flight. He was heavily criticised when they did not go straight back up the following year but guided them to a shock FA Cup Final victory over Manchester United in 1976. One of his trademarks was to revitalise the careers of senior players, four of whom had featured in Saints' cup-winning side; Peter Osgood, Mel Blyth, Jim McCalliog and skipper Peter Rodrigues.

Despite enjoying the plaudits of cup success, McMenemy's priority was to return Southampton to the First Division. They had started the 1976/77 campaign as one of the favourites for promotion but when MacDougall joined them in mid-September, they were without a league win from their first five games, had been knocked out of the League Cup by Charlton and were beaten 1-0 by Liverpool in the Charity Shield at Wembley. The early signs were that the team that won them the cup was still not equipped to get them back in the top flight. Their first victory came the day after Ted arrived, a 4-0 thumping of the French side Olympique Marseille in the first round of the European Cup Winners' Cup at The Dell. Unfortunately, UEFA regulations meant he could take no part in this competition until the third round.

In fact, MacDougall's transfer was initially delayed when the Football League questioned his eligibility to receive a signing-on fee in the light of earlier press statements regarding his intention to quit football. These, they felt, could have amounted to him seeking a transfer and at the time, players were only entitled to five per cent of a transfer fee if they had not requested a move. Only after receiving assurances from both clubs was the transfer duly sanctioned before MacDougall's debut on Saturday 18 September against Nottingham Forest at The Dell. He wore the number ten shirt in a Southampton team which included eight members of the side that had won the FA Cup the previous May, the full line-up being: Boulton, Rodrigues, Peach, Stokes, Waldron, Blyth, Fisher, Channon, Osgood, MacDougall, Williams. Substitute: McCalliog.

Despite taking the lead through Bobby Stokes in the ninth minute, by half-time they were pegged back by a goal from Forest's Ian Bowyer, which proved enough to earn the visitors a point and send Saints to the foot of the league table. The closest MacDougall came to marking his first appearance with a goal came in the second half, when, after left-back David Peach pulled the ball back, his fierce header forced a full-length diving save from Forest goalkeeper John Middleton, 'I don't remember too much about what happened on the pitch that day but I do recall sitting in the dressing room 15 minutes before kick-off and wondering where most of my team-mates were. There were only three of us in there getting ready, so I asked Lawrie where the others were. "Oh, they'll be here in a minute, they're just watching the 2.45 race at Haydock!" After that, when people used to ask me if we warmed up before a game, I used to tell them, "Oh yeah, we put the heater on in the car on the way to the ground!"'

McMenemy had expected a tough start to the new season and knew that he needed to quickly make changes, as the FA Cup Final team had not been good enough to achieve promotion in the two years preceding the final. But nobody, least of all him, expected to see Southampton sitting at the bottom of the Second Division after the first month. Their problems seemed to stem from a series of injuries acquired in a glut of early-season fixtures which had included five friendly matches plus two more games in the Tennent Caledonian Cup tournament in Glasgow, as well as participation in the Charity Shield. They had been playing two games a week since the season started and unfortunately all the travelling and match action appeared to have taken its toll.

Prior to their next league fixture they took a 1-0 lead against Napoli at The Dell in the first leg of the rather superfluous Anglo-Italian Cup Winners' Cup competition, before three days later they travelled to The Valley to face Charlton, their 19th match since they returned to action in July.

Injuries ruled out cup-winning goalkeeper Ian Turner, defender Jim Steele, midfielder Nick Holmes and striker Peter Osgood and Saints soon found themselves three goals down. Peach reduced the arrears from the penalty spot after MacDougall had been fouled shortly before half-time but Charlton had restored their three-goal advantage before the break. Ted's first goal in Southampton colours came after 65 minutes, when he smashed the ball home from close range, but Saints' misery was compounded as they conceded two more goals in the last 15 minutes to give the home side an emphatic 6-2 victory. It was an awful performance by a Southampton side, lacking in strength and concentration, albeit the goals they conceded were superbly taken by their hosts.

For MacDougall, his first days at the club proved to be something of a rude awakening, 'When I arrived at Southampton they were still trailing the FA Cup around the town while we were bottom of the league and eventually it pissed me off and I said, "When are you going to put this cup away so we can do something in the league?" There were a lot of strong characters in the dressing room, senior players and we had a few words about things as you can imagine with my personality, but I wasn't putting up with it!'

Crowd trouble marred a bad-tempered second leg of the European Cup Winners' Cup in Marseille, where although defeated 2-1 on the night, Saints progressed to the second round with a comfortable aggregate victory despite having midfielder Hugh Fisher sent off late in the game. McMenemy was understandably delighted with the victory and believed that the reason his team could win in Europe while having made the club's worst start to a league season in 14 years, was because he had a number of players who seemed to do well against top-class opposition but who didn't get down to the basics against Second Division teams.

A further example of this came when Southampton finally secured their first league win of the season in a spectacular and controversial clash with a Fulham side which included Bobby Moore, George Best and Rodney Marsh. Saints made a wonderful start and in the second minute, Osgood pushed a pass up to Peach on the left who tore forward before sending over a well-hit cross which MacDougall met at the near post, glancing the ball wide of goalkeeper Peter Mellor with a perfectly timed, powerful header.

The rest of the action came in an exciting second half which saw Blyth head home twice from free kicks taken by Jim McCalliog. Immediately after the first, Best entered an argument with referee Lester Shapter about the initial award of the free kick, the outcome being a red card for the Irishman on the first day that red and yellow cards were used by referees in the Football League. Mitchell pulled a goal back for the visitors soon afterwards but the outcome was settled ten minutes from time, when MacDougall raced through the middle to latch on to Channon's pass and shoot past Mellor for Saints' fourth goal.

As well as taking some of the pressure off Channon and Osgood, three goals in his first three league games for Southampton was a good start for MacDougall and the side as a whole had shown a distinct improvement in their marksmanship since he arrived. Previously Saints had scored just two goals in five games and they emphasised their new-found confidence in front of goal by putting six past Wolves at The Dell. Channon and Holmes grabbed two apiece and Saints' scoring was completed by a goal each for McCalliog and fellow midfielder Pat Earles. As the home supporters left enthusing over a superb attacking performance, in front of the assembled press, McMenemy light-heartedly reflected upon the irony of having bought MacDougall to score goals, then when the team scored six he didn't get any.

Ted recalls, 'That was typical of Lawrie, he was an excellent man-manager who handled everyone very well. He would make these sort of remarks to try and fire us up! I don't think I ever enjoyed a game without getting a goal as much as this one. In fact, I can't remember being in another side which scored six without getting one myself! The match reports say I contributed in the build-up for all of the goals though, and fortunately Channon and the midfielders came through to finish them off! Lawrie realised I could be very short-tempered at times and a bit hasty but a lot of that stemmed from people telling me I couldn't play. He told me from the start he thought I could play and we got on well.'

Terry Paine, at the age of 37, received a warm ovation from the crowd when he returned to The Dell as player-coach of Hereford United the following weekend, the former Saints legend leading out his new side after having spent 18 seasons with the Hampshire club. However, Hereford had now replaced Southampton at the bottom of the league table and were first contained, then outplayed and finally beaten thanks to Holmes's chip over former Bournemouth goalkeeper Kevin Charlton from the edge of the penalty area shortly before half-time. The result pushed Saints up to 17th place.

While MacDougall moved into his new house in Canford Cliffs, his team-mates travelled to Ireland for a European Cup Winners' Cup date with part-timers Carrick Rangers, and returned with a comfortable 5-2 first leg advantage. Ted returned for the league game at Luton, where Southampton chalked up their fourth successive league victory. Late strikes from MacDougall and Holmes followed two first-half goals from Peach, although on-loan goalkeeper Jim Montgomery was powerless to keep out a header from the Hatters' Brian Chambers. Montgomery was already the fourth custodian to appear for Saints that season as, still without the injured Turner, McMenemy had drafted in the experienced 33-year-old from Sunderland to replace reserve goalkeeper Tony Middleton after Colin Boulton had returned following a loan from Derby.

Prior to the game at Luton, McMenemy pressed on with his rebuilding plans when to the surprise of many supporters, he made four members of his cup-winning side, Peter Osgood, Jim Steele, Bobby

Stokes and Paul Gilchrist, available for transfer, together with reserve Mike Berry. The particularly surprising name was that of Osgood, although he had not featured in any of Saints' last four away victories. There was no place for him again when Southampton travelled to his former manor to face league leaders Chelsea.

For the first time that season, McMenemy was able to field an unchanged team for the game at Stamford Bridge and until the last 15 minutes everything went right. They defended superbly against a young Chelsea side and had gone in front through MacDougall, but after Channon missed a chance to double their lead, they fell apart and conceded three late goals. Osgood was selected, however, for the return game against Carrick Rangers, where two goals from young striker Austin Hayes helped ease Southampton into the Cup Winners' Cup quarter-finals, with a comfortable 4-1 victory on the night and a 9-3 success on aggregate. With the next round not due to be played until the following March, McMenemy set his players a target of getting themselves into the top six in the league by Christmas. Unfortunately it was a challenge they were not able to even come close to achieving.

Without the injured Channon and Rodrigues for the visit of Orient in early November, a superb piece of opportunism by MacDougall saw Saints sweep into an early lead when, as Peach drove the ball hard through a crowded penalty area, Ted darted in at the far post to stab the ball home. However, as the game wore on, Orient were able to exploit shortcomings in the Southampton defence and had gone ahead just after the hour. Had Peter Bennett then not received his marching orders for a foul on Fisher, they may have gone on to win but Saints made the extra man count when Blyth moved forward to grab them a point, heading home ten minutes from time.

It proved to be the only point Southampton took in a bleak month which saw them drop to 19th after successive defeats against Cardiff, Bolton and Oldham in the league and against Napoli in the Anglo-Italian competition. A goal from Phil Dwyer was enough to give the Welsh side victory at Ninian Park, while in front of a crowd of 60,000 in Naples, Saints were unable to defend their single-goal advantage from the first leg of the Anglo Italian Cup Winners' Cup Final, going down 4-0. Blyth missed the game through injury but returned to lead the side in Rodrigues's absence on their return to league action however, they looked no more than a faint shadow of the side that had triumphed at Wembley. Despite taking the lead just before half-time against

Bolton, when MacDougall raced in to get on the end of a free kick from McCalliog, three second-half goals, the first after a poor piece of handling from goalkeeper Montgomery, ensured the Lancashire side went home with the points. At Oldham, Turner returned in goal after injury and was in the thick of the action for most of the game, but could not stop Saints from suffering a 2-1 defeat.

By now, McMenemy was coming under increasing pressure from supporters to enter the transfer market and strengthen the side. Injuries had allowed an opportunity to give a number of young reserve team players a chance, but with the exception of midfielder Steve Williams and defender Malcolm Waldron, the others had failed to make much impact in a struggling team. Despite the best efforts of Williams together with Holmes, Fisher and McCalliog, a strong-tackling midfield player appeared to be what Southampton were lacking, someone able to restore command in this area of the pitch. Meanwhile, Osgood, originally a £235,000 signing from Chelsea, was allowed to join Norwich on loan, with John Bond apparently keen to arrange a permanent move, 'I think Lawrie was at a loss to know quite what to do about our performances for a while. First there were injuries, then even when players came back things still didn't click into place. A manager is always looking for reasons, excuses even, for why something isn't working. Lawrie's relationship with the directors became a little strained because of poor results and falling gates, and of course he was under pressure from the press and supporters too.

'At the end of the day, whatever the manager may or may not do, he needs total commitment from the 11 players on the pitch. If they're not together running their legs off for each other and prepared to fight like hell to achieve success, then the team will get nowhere. The only way we looked like getting out of the Second Division at this time was by being relegated to the Third. It was frustrating the hell out of me so goodness knows what the manager and directors must have been feeling.'

As December dawned, Rodrigues returned to the side as Saints gained a morale-boosting victory against Notts County at The Dell. It was a thoroughly deserved win, and on the strength of the chances they created, it could have been by a far greater margin. Holmes's perfectly placed header put Southampton in front shortly before half-time and their lead was doubled before the break when Channon fired home two minutes later. Despite conceding a goal early in the second half, it failed to spoil a landmark Saints performance full of the kind of determination required to lead them out of trouble. A similar effort brought a 1-1 draw against league leaders Chelsea three days later, on a rain-soaked pitch. Despite the treacherous conditions, MacDougall wasted no time in volleying Saints ahead from McCalliog's second-minute free kick and although they succumbed to a second-half equaliser, the side's overall performance was again improved.

Peter Wells became Southampton's fifth goalkeeper of the season when he signed for £8,000 from Nottingham Forest and made his debut in a ding-dong affair against free-scoring Blackpool. It was a game which saw Saints fall behind, lead and finally draw 3-3, with Channon grabbing an impressive hat-trick. The match also saw Steele recalled to the side, the big Scotsman regaining his place after returning to Southampton from a loan spell with Glasgow Rangers, while Osgood was also reinstated upon the completion of his loan spell at Norwich, where although his performances had impressed John Bond, no permanent transfer deal had been agreed.

As Christmas approached, Saints and their supporters received an early present when McMenemy pulled off a major coup in signing Arsenal and former England captain Alan Ball. The manager signed the 1966 World Cup winner to specifically mould what remained of the FA Cup-winning team into a promotion side. Nobody disputed Ball's natural qualities of leadership nor his astute footballing mind, immaculate passing and visionary skills – the question was how, at 31 years of age, would he deal with stepping down to the Second Division? 'Lawrie got Bally for £60,000 and what a bargain that was. It was like a breath of fresh air when he arrived. He was a leader certainly but a grafter too who wouldn't stand any nonsense, which was exactly what we needed. For me personally, it was the start of a wonderful friendship with Alan and his wife, Lesley.'

With Rodrigues still injured, Ball captained the side on his debut at Plymouth two days after Christmas and immediately got the team ticking. MacDougall marked the occasion by unleashing a ferocious right-foot shot to give Saints the lead just before the interval. Often accused of scoring more than his share of tap-ins during his career, the goal was further evidence that Ted was also capable of striking some memorable goals. Unfortunately, Bruce Bannister spoilt the celebrations with a second-half equaliser but it did not diminish the optimistic mood that had begun to filter back into the club.

MacDouGOAL!

Two days later, Saints brought their cup-winning year to a close with a 2-1 victory against Bristol Rovers at The Dell, thanks to two late goals from Channon before bad weather meant Southampton's first action of 1977 came in their initial defence of the FA Cup. With bookmakers not expecting Saints to repeat their success of the previous year, the holders entered the competition as 100/1 outsiders this time around, and entertained Second Division leaders Chelsea in the third round. Seven members of the cup-winning side lined up for Southampton and saw the visitors take a first-half lead following a blistering shot from full-back Gary Locke.

Channon came to the rescue again soon after the break, sending the teams back to Stamford Bridge for a replay the following Wednesday evening, when despite very wintry conditions, 42,688 spectators turned out to witness two hours of football in which Saints' superior stamina surprisingly proved to be the key factor against a much younger Chelsea side.

After 90 minutes the deadlock remained unbroken in the heavy conditions but after just two minutes of extra time, Ball struck a splendid crossfield pass to Channon on the left, who avoided the challenges of two Chelsea defenders to play in MacDougall with a perfectly timed pass across the penalty area, which the Scot drove into the net past helpless goalkeeper John Phillips. Ball then set up Channon to double the lead and the scoring was completed by a penalty from Peach after MacDougall had been upended in the box. The result strengthened McMenemy's belief that despite the age of some of his players, they remained among the fittest teams in the country. Osgood, who seemed revitalised since his return from Norwich, Channon and MacDougall had grafted all night probing for openings which eventually came their way once they had gradually weakened Chelsea's defence.

Aching limbs appeared to catch up with them three days later though, when after wasting early scoring opportunities they were beaten at home by Millwall, who pounced on two uncharacteristic errors by full-back David Peach to grab the points. Despite the defeat, Saints continued to play with flair and imagination and they reaped a rich reward after making the long trip to lowly Carlisle United. At Brunton Park, Williams returned in midfield for the first time in a month replacing the newly transfer-listed McCalliog, who had borne the brunt of the crowd's displeasure the previous week, 'Saints fans always used to pick on the older players, they did it first with Jim

McCalliog, then Peter Rodrigues and after that it was my turn – more about that later!'

The 18-year-old Williams became part of a brilliant performance at the Football League's furthest outpost, which saw Southampton record a six-goal victory, their biggest winning margin in an away league match since before the Second World War. It could have been very different however, had young goalkeeper Wells not brought off a world-class save to keep out a header from Frank Clarke in the 14th minute. Seconds later Ball and Channon combined, before enabling MacDougall to chip over a cross for Holmes to head home. Williams's cross was then put away by Osgood and in the second half Peach added a third goal from the penalty spot, then played a long ball into the box for MacDougall to grab a fourth. Next it was Channon's turn to record his 150th league goal before Holmes ended the scoring by crashing home a 30-yard shot. It was a quite stunning show which lifted Saints up to 12th and sent a warning to those clubs involved in the promotion race higher up the table.

Meanwhile, FA Cup fourth round opponents Nottingham Forest also warmed up with a 6-0 win, their unfortunate victims being Bristol Rovers in a delayed third round replay, which set up an attractive tie at the City Ground. After early chances at both ends, Ball's over-exuberant tackle on John O'Hare left referee Jack Taylor with no option but to award Forest a penalty in the 34th minute, which John Robertson struck past Wells. The game threatened to boil over with a series of wild tackles early in the second half before Ball's first Southampton goal brought the sides level. Four more goals quickly followed – first Channon deflected in a shot from full-back Manny Andruszewski to put Saints ahead before Robertson replied again for Forest. Next it was the turn of Osgood to hit an unstoppable shot only for Tony Woodcock to squeeze home a drive from an acute angle to send the tie into a replay, 'This game was a real feisty affair! Bally got stuck in on Peter Withe early on, then there was a flare-up between Bally, Steeley and Forest's Martin O'Neill just after half-time. The referee let them get on with it and then booked me instead for a tap on Viv Anderson! Anyway, Martin caught up with Steeley just before the end, sent him sprawling and got himself booked as well! It would have probably ended seven-a-side if the game had been played today.

'Forest may have been Second Division at the time but remember this was the team that manager Brian Clough would take to the First

Division championship the following season. They were some side but we gave as good as we got in more ways than one. We were still a work in progress but Bally, Holmes and Stevie Williams were developing into a good midfield unit and we were coming together nicely as a side.'

With their team now unbeaten in 11 FA Cup games, a record for a Second Division side, the Saints supporters turned out in numbers for the replay, and the 'Ground Full' signs were put up at The Dell with 29,401 inside. Just as it had done at the City Ground, the game ebbed and flowed in exciting fashion and it took just ten minutes for the first goal to arrive. Williams, picking up a half-clearance from O'Neill, then hit a storming shot past goalkeeper John Middleton. Woodcock equalised soon after but the decisive goal came after 66 minutes when Ball controlled a loose ball before splitting the Forest defence and sending MacDougall clear. With Forest defenders appealing unsuccessfully for offside, Ted chipped Middleton to send Saints into the fifth round and to a home tie against Manchester United, the team they had beaten at Wembley the previous May.

MacDougall was again enjoying a good level of consistency in front of goal and it continued when he was on target in each of the three league games leading up to the United tie. However, in the first of these Saints fell into old habits, being brought down to earth by an unfashionable side after having given a champagne performance in midweek. Twice they had to come from behind to salvage a point against Hull at The Dell with young striker Trevor Hebberd, playing in place of the injured Osgood, involved in the build-up to each. First he beat two men before laying the ball off to Channon, whose centre was headed powerfully into the net by MacDougall, then after working hard for another opening, he enabled MacDougall to steal in and crack home a loose ball from five yards early in the second half.

Another 2-2 draw followed at Bramall Lane after Osgood had headed Southampton ahead, only for them to fall behind to Sheffield United shortly after half-time. But the equaliser came after a breathtaking run by Channon, which eventually allowed Ted to drive in the equaliser 15 minutes from time. Fog then brought Saints' midweek visit to Nottingham Forest to an abrupt end after 47 minutes, but nothing could stop them disposing of relegation-threatened visitors Burnley the following Saturday thanks to a penalty from Peach and another MacDougall trademark finish, taking an Andruszewski pass and firing home from six yards, 'The team was gradually being transformed. Bally never stopped coaxing and cajoling in midfield and it had begun to take effect, Channon's running suddenly had a greater air of urgency and Osgood was knocking passes about with the sides of his boots, the fronts of his boots and the back of his boots! We became very tight as a team and very tight in the dressing room. We had strong personalities who all came together at one particular time – Osgood, Channon, McCalliog, Rodrigues etc but they all settled down.

'Mick Channon was a larger-than-life character and he became a popular target for television producers who were keen to broadcast his opinions on the game. The only problem he had was that whenever he went on the box, he couldn't get any adjectives out without using the F-word! That was what he was like but as long as they had a good editor he would get away with it!

'Although I had a strong personality, I was about fourth in the pecking order but I loved strong characters in the dressing room, and they generally liked me. We all had an edge as did the manager, but he could handle us. He'd let us think we were getting away with things but handled it in such a way that we actually got away with nothing, we just thought we did! It must have been like walking a tightrope for him most of the time but Lawrie managed to carry it off.

'There were also a number of young lads with legs, like Stevie Williams and David Peach, who would do most of the running. Our biggest games were on the Fridays at training, when the old lads played the young lads in the gym. We'd knock the crap out of them, and Ossie would belt them one! So we'd pick up more injuries in that and Lawrie would go up the wall.'

With Steele suspended, Waldron returned to the side for his FA Cup debut against Manchester United in a match which saw four goals shared equally by the two sides in the first half. This time MacDougall was not among the scorers but though United twice led through Macari and Hill, each time Saints equalised, first through another penalty from Peach and then a drive from Holmes. Tommy Docherty's United, fielding nine of the players defeated at Wembley the previous year, had shown many of the attributes you would expect from a team the press were describing as a 'breath of spring' to English football, but Saints gave as good as they got and proved again that they could compete in the best of company.

A crowd of 29,137 had witnessed the Dell encounter but for the replay at Old Trafford the gate almost doubled. Steele returned for

Saints, who included six of their cup-winning side but quickly fell behind when Jimmy Greenhoff headed in for United. Immediately before half-time, referee Clive Thomas angered the home crowd by awarding Southampton a penalty following a clumsy challenge on Williams by Martin Buchan and Peach again stepped up to draw them level. As the tension grew in the second half, Steele and Greenhoff were involved in ongoing feud, but while the latter managed to deflect an effort past Wells for United's winner, Steele eventually received his marching orders for a series of infringements and Saints lost their first FA Cup tie after more than 21 hours of football.

Sandwiched in between the two games against Manchester United, Southampton travelled to Belgium for the first leg of their European Cup Winners' Cup third round tie. Sadly, Ted's first competitive game in European club football proved disappointing and left a sour taste. Peter Ressel and Robbie Rensenbrink gave the Belgian side a two-goal victory on the night after Channon had a goal disallowed following a very dubious offside decision. Ironically, when Anderlecht were involved in match-fixing allegations some years later, a story surfaced of bribery towards the officials prior to this match and suggested that the goal had been unfairly ruled out, 'I don't know if it was a conspiracy against us, but when we landed at Brussels Airport we were stuck on the plane for ages while staff tried to find a set of landing steps and then when we got to the hotel all the lights went out!'

A tremendous atmosphere prevailed at The Dell on the March evening when Anderlecht arrived for the second leg. The game looked to be going into extra time when MacDougall added to Peach's first-half penalty to bring the teams level on aggregate with 11 minutes to go, but then came a horrible moment for Steele, who failed to trap the ball under pressure from Francois Van Der Elst, allowing the Belgian international to run through and score the decisive goal, 'It was a shame our time in Europe ended as it did and of course the Anderlecht game was the end of Jim Steele. As well as scoring, I think I hit the post three times and Ossie hit the crossbar twice, but we'd just got back into the game at 2-2 and then Steeley tried to nutmeg Van Der Elst on the edge of his own box. That pissed us all off, Lawrie especially as he and Steeley had already fallen out after his sending-off at Old Trafford and they were at each other again in the dressing room afterwards.'

Steele's last appearance for Southampton came in a 2-1 defeat at Nottingham Forest the following week and the big Scotsman left the club at the end of the season, "'Six-foot-two, eyes of blue, Jimmy Steele is after you" – that's what the fans used to sing! Steeley went up to Rangers earlier in the season but couldn't come back quick enough after he kicked all the Celtic players and had a go at fighting everybody! To his credit though, he won back his place at Southampton before he and Lawrie fell out big time, so Steeley went over to play in America for three months and ended up staying there something like 18 years.'

Meanwhile, Saints had put in a dogged performance to gain some sort of revenge over Charlton for their heavy defeat earlier in the season, MacDougall having forced Channon's nod-down over the line before Andruszewski provided the winner with a long-range shot. It was Hebberd's turn against Fulham, heading home from Peach's cross to ensure Saints returned from Craven Cottage with a point before as April dawned, a goal from Alan Ball ended promotion-chasing Luton's 12-game unbeaten run at The Dell.

The Easter programme saw MacDougall on target four times in three games, all of which were played in the space of four days. Visitors Plymouth led briefly on Good Friday before Peach equalised ahead of a stunning overhead kick and a close-range tap-in from MacDougall, which was followed by a powerful shot from Channon on the run as Saints emerged as 4-1 winners. The match also marked the last Southampton appearance of Peter Rodrigues who, having been forced off through injury, would finally call time on his career due to a persistent knee injury the following summer.

John Sharpe replaced Rodrigues for the visit to Bristol Rovers the following day and Saints also gave a debut to 21-year-old Bournemouth-born centre-half Forbes Phillipson-Masters. Again they fell behind but a header from Osgood and second-half strikes from Hebberd and MacDougall brought about a 3-2 victory. Two days later, on Easter Monday, came a fourth successive win when Cardiff travelled to The Dell. On the half-hour Ted opened the scoring with a close-range header before crossing for Channon to double Southampton's lead. The England international nodded in a third ten minutes later and although two late goals for the Welsh club took some of the gloss off the victory, it was enough to move Saints up to a season's best ninth in the table.

Unfortunately the winning run came to an end with a poor performance at Bolton in which Saints were found wanting in all areas and crashed to a 3-0 defeat. As a result, McMenemy kept the team locked in the Burnden Park dressing room for 45 minutes after the final whistle and subjected them to a no-nonsense talking-to. The result all but killed off any lingering hopes that the team might sustain a late charge for promotion, 'We got beat so we were all pissed off and you could say, not for the first time, we had a frank exchange of views!'

Despite 'clearing the air', there was no immediate improvement in results when Saints returned to Lancashire a few days later and suffered another 3-0 defeat at Blackburn, which effectively booked their place in the Second Division for the following season. They returned to winning ways with a four-goal home victory against Oldham, MacDougall's looping header setting them on their way in the eighth minute. It was followed by a goal from Osgood and two more from Channon, the second, a penalty, breaking Terry Paine's previous Southampton league and cup scoring record of 190 goals. The game also saw the last appearance of another of the FA Cup Final team, Mel Blyth, who left the field with a hamstring injury and having been placed on the transfer list by McMenemy in the summer, the big defender eventually joined Millwall the following season. Another player to leave the club was Wembley goalscoring hero Bobby Stokes, who followed the same path as Steele and decided to continue his career in America.

Southampton completed the season with wins at Leyton Orient and at home to champions-elect Wolves and Blackburn, but suffered defeats at Notts County, bottom-of-the-table Hereford and in the last game, their 67th of the season, at Blackpool. MacDougall was twice on target in the 3-2 win against Orient at Brisbane Road before his final goal of the season put Saints in front against County in a match which later saw Peach sent off and Saints concede three goals in the last 12 minutes.

Why, after such a long season, Southampton would embark on an end-of-season tour to Norway is hard to understand, but thankfully this trip proved somewhat happier for MacDougall than the one he had endured with Norwich 12 months previously. Three-goal victories were recorded against Viking Stavanger and Vardo Haugesund, with Ted on target twice in each match. Once back in England, he also scored in a 4-2 win at Bradford City and again in Sweden a few days later, as Saints beat IFK Gothenburg 3-0, with Austin Hayes scoring the other two goals.

In reality Southampton's season had ended during the week in March when Manchester United and Anderlecht ended their cup

194

aspirations, the team simply not being consistent enough to graft a return to the First Division. As MacDougall and Ball arrived, many of the old guard departed during what had been a transitional season, as McMenemy laid the foundations of a 'new' team, one that he hoped would ultimately be capable of lifting the club out of the Second Division, 'We finished ninth in the league, which was disappointing because even with all the changes we should have done better really. Just like Norwich, we were capable of beating anyone on our day but equally capable of losing to anyone on a bad day! We were among the best in the country at going forward and scoring goals but our problem was defending.

'You could sense the supporters' frustration with us but the team was great fun to play in. Playing alongside Osgood and Channon – it was so easy. Ossie was such an enigmatic character, mind you he could be scary at times. He was 6ft 3in, must have weighed around 13st and looked even bigger than that! He was great on the ball and called me "The Magnet" because I always stuck so close to him, that way I knew I would get goals! I was the leading scorer and got 23 in the league that season, having joined in the October. Even more importantly to me, I was settled again and enjoying my football. I loved it really and it was just what I needed at that stage of my career.'

17

The Saints Go Marching In!

THERE was one very significant absentee when MacDougall returned to Southampton for pre-season training in June 1977 – 11 years after making his league bow with Saints, Mike Channon was missing. Channon had moved to Manchester City during the summer in a £300,000 deal, leaving Lawrie McMenemy with the unenviable task of replacing a player who had been the club's leading scorer on seven occasions. In Ted's opinion, there was only one player who would fit the bill – Phil Boyer, 'As soon as Mick went, I kept on to Lawrie about "Charlie", just like I did to Bondy when we were at Bournemouth. I knew he was set to leave Norwich and in fact he was about to join Queens Park Rangers when I phoned and told him, "No, you can't go there, you have to come here with me." Thank God he came!'

Having taken MacDougall's advice, McMenemy obtained the services of Boyer and was still £175,000 to the good, so took the opportunity to strengthen his defence, signing Aston Villa's Northern Ireland international Chris Nicholl and the comparatively unknown Mike Pickering from Barnsley. Also missing from the previous season's squad were the retired former captain Peter Rodrigues and goalkeeper Steve Middleton, who had been released, while full-back Steve Mills had finally been forced to give up his long fight to regain fitness after a car crash, 'Training was always great fun at Southampton, we didn't have a training ground or anything so we used to train on the common with the dogs or at Wide Lane, where it was windy and we would lose all of the three balls we had to play with. So we would go for a run up round the common and back or do laps at The Dell.

'Lawrie had his work cut out with us mind and although he was a great man-manager, he desperately wanted to be a coach as well, but he wasn't very good! We used to line up to take shots and it always used to piss me off because there would be a line of 15 people, ten of whom would never have a shot in a game, so I thought, "Why the hell am I waiting for these people? Get out the way and let me get on with it."

'Anyway, Ossie would often be the one who laid the ball off for each player in turn and when it was Lawrie's go, Ossie would belt this ball at him and it would hit him, or he wouldn't get it or the ball would bounce off him and Ossie would shout at him telling him his touch was crap! It was continual pisstake all the time! You had to be good at giving it and even better at taking it. Lawrie was a 6ft 4in ex-guardsman, a big man with a big personality and he would take the piss out of players like we took the piss out of him. Ossie was the best, we were driving past Big Ben one day and he said to me, "Look, there's Lawrie's watch!"

'Just before I joined Saints they had a player there called Brian O'Neill, and I'm told he used to come to training in his wellies, covered in crap and mud, dirty, stinking jeans and a smelly top. He would always be first off after training had finished and he'd go home wearing other players' clothes. So somebody had to go home wearing his!

'Lawrie used to boss the young lads, Stevie Williams and company, but with the likes of me, Ossie and Bally he was great. He treated us like responsible adults, used to give us plenty of days off and if we didn't fancy doing what he had planned for training, he'd ask us what we wanted to do instead. I would tell him, "I want to do some crosses and finishing," which was what I always wanted to do. "All right Bonny Lad, we'll do that then!" he'd say. He was brilliant and looking back I had such great, great times at Southampton. Driving through the New Forest on my way to training each morning, I considered myself very fortunate.'

A pre-season trip to Holland for the Astora Tournament in Alkmaar brought mixed fortunes, as Southampton first lost 3-2 to the Dutch club Haarlem before defeating German side Beerschot by the same score thanks to two goals from MacDougall and one from

Osgood. This was followed by another visit to Scotland for the Tennent Caledonian Cup, which brought a 3-1 defeat against Rangers and a 2-1 victory against St Mirren, with Osgood and Alan Ball on target for Saints. Ball was again the scorer in a 1-0 victory against Gateshead as the team made its way back to the south coast, where a goalless draw with First Division newcomers Wolves completed their preparations for the new campaign ahead.

The opening league game against Brighton attracted a gate of over 24,000 to The Dell as all three new signings made their debuts. All began well with Ball hammering home Southampton's first goal of the season before John Ruggiero netted a second-half equaliser for the Seagulls. This was followed by a disappointing 1-0 defeat at Stoke but a penalty from Peach gave Saints their first victory at home to newly promoted Mansfield.

The League Cup provided the season's first flashpoint, Boyer receiving his marching orders after clashing with Crystal Palace's Jim Cannon early on in an explosive second round tie at Selhurst Park. A penalty save by Turner kept the scoresheet blank and earned Southampton a replay but as a result of his actions, Boyer missed the league game at Notts County. McMenemy took the opportunity to draft in an extra central defender in his place, Waldron starting his first league game of the season alongside Nicholl and Pickering in a 5-3-2 formation.

County found it hard to break down Saints' big defensive barrier and fell behind shortly before half-time, when 20-year-old Tony Funnell, on his full league debut, finished impressively to put Southampton ahead. The home side responded shortly after the break though, when Pickering deflected a shot beyond the reach of Turner. However, when MacDougall was brought down, Peach once again fired home from the penalty spot, then six minutes later, the left-back rolled the ball into the path of Osgood, who struck a brilliant curling shot into the net. A late goal for County meant a tense finish, but Saints held on and continued to climb the table.

Boyer returned for Burnley's visit to The Dell and took the opportunity to score his first goals for Southampton, his sparkling two-goal performance capping a glittering Saints display. The inspired captaincy of Ball, accurate distribution of Osgood and the effectiveness of Boyer combined magnificently to give the supporters a treat. Another Peach penalty completed the scoring and things looked good for the season ahead, although MacDougall agonisingly found himself without a goal in six league and cup games, 'Like all strikers, when I wasn't scoring goals I became worried and bad-tempered. In fact I was a pretty unpleasant person during these times! I had young Tony Funnell breathing down my neck now, scoring regularly for the reserves, but fortunately Lawrie stuck with me.'

While Ted's goal drought continued, another penalty save by Turner played a large part in seeing Southampton safely through to the next round of the League Cup, beating Palace 2-1 in their replay at The Dell. Earlier Funnell, on as a substitute for Pickering, had snatched a very late equaliser to send the game into extra time, during which Boyer had put Saints in front before Turner sprang into action in the last minute. However, when the team succumbed to a three-goal first-half blitz in their next game at Millwall, McMenemy accused them of lapsing into old habits but despite a half-time blast from the manager, they were unable to reduce the arrears in the face of some superb tackling by the home defence, 'Lawrie was always clever enough not to storm straight into the dressing room immediately after the half-time whistle. He used to wait five minutes because he knew that with all the strong characters in the side, we wouldn't hold back on expressing our feelings towards each other and generally by the time he came in we had got things off our chests one way or another. Then he would give us a bollocking if he felt we needed one!'

Finally MacDougall got off the mark in the home game against Hull in late September, when exactly one year after scoring his first goal for Saints, he produced a typical piece of his old finishing power, striding into the penalty area to volley home the game's only goal from a cross from Osgood, 'While I was blowing kisses to the crowd, both Lawrie and I were breathing a huge sigh of relief!'

Ted was on the scoresheet again when Southampton travelled to Sheffield United, but only after they had again conceded three goals before half-time. Individual errors had presented the Blades with a comfortable lead, before MacDougall met a near-post cross from Waldron. They then dominated the second half during which Osgood pulled back another goal after a MacDougall shot was cleared off the line, but despite coming close to an equaliser in the later stages, Southampton were unable to rescue a point. Despite again working hard to try and get themselves back in the game, the team had still to show the level of consistency they would require if they were to make a successful promotion bid. McMenemy remained philosophical and his faith in the team proved justified as they went on to record successive wins against Orient, Sunderland and Crystal Palace respectively.

Osgood struck the only goal in a tight game against the O's, but the visit of Sunderland brought a much more open game, played at a furious pace after the pitch had soaked up several hours of torrential rain before kick-off. Gary Rowell put the visitors ahead with just five minutes played but almost immediately afterwards, Nicholl met Holmes's corner on the half-volley to bring Southampton level. Five minutes later Bob Lee headed Sunderland back in front but by half-time a close-range effort from Boyer and a scuffed shot from Williams had given Saints the advantage. The scoring was completed just after the hour, when Holmes cleverly chipped the ball over goalkeeper Barry Siddall and into the net.

Afterwards, Sunderland manager Jimmy Adamson told the press he thought the game was a wonderful spectacle for supporters but Palace manager Terry Venables was less gracious in defeat a few days later and after Southampton had emerged with a hard-fought 2-1 victory at Selhurst Park, Venables criticised what he felt was an over-physical Saints performance which had gone unpunished by the referee. A bullet header from Boyer and a forcing run and finish from Holmes had cancelled out Steve Perrin's opener for Palace in a game where Peach and Pickering received cautions from referee Brian Daniels. Pickering, though, ended the game with two black eyes, 'We had been giving away so many soft goals and had to tighten things up, so Lawrie brought back Peter Wells in goal and played Malcolm Waldron at right-back to form a back four with Chris Nicholl, Mike Pickering and Peachy. In front of them of course, there was Bally, Steve Williams and Nick Holmes plus Ossie could make a telling challenge! None of these players were the sort to pull out of a tackle, but I wouldn't agree that they were over-physical, not compared to a lot of sides I came up against. Anyway that's all part of the game!'

Southampton's response was to produce a golden hour of football against league leaders Bolton at The Dell, during which Holmes and Boyer were both on target again, only to spoil it by allowing the visitors to draw level in the last 30 minutes through goals from Frank Worthington and Willie Morgan. Despite dropping a point, Saints still moved up to third in the table and spirits were high as they travelled to Arsenal in the League Cup. Unfortunately, a mistake by Holmes spoilt a very creditable performance at Highbury, his handball giving Liam Brady the opportunity to put the Gunners in front from the penalty spot after 78 minutes and then as Southampton pressed forward in search of an equaliser, Frank Stapleton grabbed a second goal for the Londoners.

Arsenal's neighbours, Tottenham Hotspur, had been relegated from the First Division at the end of the previous season and were understandably among the favourites to regain their top-level status at the first attempt. They had already emphasised their promotion credentials by hammering Bristol Rovers 9-0 at White Hart Lane, so when Southampton went to Eastville seven days later, the Bristol club were desperately hoping to restore some lost pride. In Ball's absence, Osgood produced a stylish performance but was denied a winning goal by Rovers' 17-year-old goalkeeper Martin Thomas, who turned aside his stinging first-half drive. The home side were understandably happy just to avoid defeat and hung on for a goalless draw, while cautions for MacDougall, Nicholl and Williams added to Saints' increasing number of disciplinary points.

It was the following week's defeat at Blackburn which was to cause severe disciplinary problems for Saints though, as they finished with only nine men after Osgood and Williams were sent off within two minutes of each other at Ewood Park, in a game which also saw four other players booked. Before the commotion started, the home side had taken an early lead but then, following a handball by full-back John Bailey, Peach drew Saints level just before half-time, scoring from the spot for the 15th consecutive occasion.

Twenty minutes from time, Williams received his marching orders after chopping down Bailey as the Blackburn player raced forward. Then Osgood was alleged to have brought down the same player inside the Saints penalty area and was also ordered off by referee Tony Jenkins. As Osgood argued his case tempers ran high before he eventually left the field and after John Waddington had converted the penalty, Southampton managed to play out the last 18 minutes without further embarrassment.

After the game, McMenemy admitted that his players had contributed to their own downfall but also launched a furious attack on Bailey – who later in his career went on to become a First Division player with Everton – for his part in both dismissals and two more bookings. The Saints manager accused him of diving to get the penalty decision and also of taunting several of his players before and during the match, as Ted remembers, 'He was doing it big time, calling us "has-beens" and that sort of stuff. Both Ossie and Stevie had short fuses at times and they both let him have it. It wasn't the wisest thing to do but sometimes football gets you like that, anyway, this was Guy Fawkes Day and it certainly went with a bang.

'There was a bit of aggro afterwards and Ossie was livid. Before we left, he smacked the dressing room door down, he broke it right off its hinges!'

With Osgood and Williams suspended, McMenemy gave league debuts to midfielders Graham Baker and Steve Neville against third-placed Blackpool, and after scoring just twice in 14 league games, MacDougall was replaced by Trevor Hebberd. Baker could hardly have made a better start, crashing home a shot from the edge of the area in the first minute, and after a cross from Neville had been handled early in the second half, Peach stepped up again to make it 2-0 from the penalty spot, 'After the Blackburn game, Lawrie was livid and although he understood that we had received a lot of aggravation throughout, he was concerned about the bad image the club was getting. Ossie and Stevie were suspended automatically of course and also fined by the club, and as I had got myself booked towards the end of the game, Lawrie decided to leave me out of the next game as well.

'I couldn't really complain, he'd stuck with me earlier in the season but this was mid-November. I'd only scored two league goals and had added to the club's disciplinary problems. In fairness, I had become a bit unsettled and disillusioned with the game, but that was principally because I wasn't scoring.

'There was a bit of speculation going around at the time about me going back to Bournemouth but I wanted to prove to Lawrie that I was still worth my place in the Saints team.'

Whatever concerns there may have been about his club's disciplinary record, McMenemy's growing stature within the game had also not gone unnoticed by the Football Association. Indeed, as they searched for a successor to former England manager Don Revie, the FA asked Southampton's board of directors for permission to approach him and with Saints' blessing, McMenemy was interviewed by representatives in London, along with fellow candidates Brian Clough and Bobby Robson, but the job eventually went to another of MacDougall's former managers, Ron Greenwood.

Meanwhile, Hebberd took advantage of a goalkeeping error to grab Southampton a point at Oldham and could consider himself unfortunate to drop down to the substitutes' bench, when MacDougall was recalled for the visit of Fulham at the end of November, 'After we had been playing for about an hour and getting nowhere against a stubborn Fulham defence, I saw young Hebberd in his tracksuit doing his limbering-up in front of the West Stand and I thought, "That's it, I'll be off in a minute." Anyway with that Nick Holmes whipped in a perfect cross and Steve Neville headed it into the net. A couple of minutes later Holmes scored a second and I saw Hebberd zip up his tracksuit and return to the bench. As a forward you don't notice these things when you're scoring goals but you look out for them when you know you're having a bad run.'

The win moved Southampton back up to third, despite still being without the suspended Williams and Osgood, who were now joined on the sidelines by Peach, after the left-back had received a series of cautions. Injuries to defenders Nicholl and Andruszewski meant recalls for Sharpe and Phillipson-Masters at free-scoring Tottenham, but the reshuffled defence kept out the lively Spurs attack, earning Saints a valuable point in a goalless draw against their fellow promotion challengers. The only black spot was Ted's first-half booking for 'over-enthusiasm' administered by referee Jeff Sewell.

Throughout 1977, The Dell had become a fortress as Southampton put together an impressive run of 22 home league and cup games without defeat since losing to Millwall in January, but this came to an end in late November when Luton striker Ron Futcher headed the only goal in a game in which Saints played so poorly they were fortunate not to suffer more than a single-goal loss. McMenemy demanded an instant response in the next game at Blackpool and got it when Holmes pulled the ball across from the left for MacDougall to carefully net the only goal of the game. Osgood meanwhile had called time on his career in English football and decided to secure his financial future by accepting an offer to join Philadelphia Fury in America. Despite making efforts to change his mind, McMenemy did not insist the former England player should see out the rest of his contract and the two parted company on good terms, 'Ossie was a wonderful character whose company I enjoyed very much but once he had decided to do something it was always hard to get him to change his mind – a bit like me really! He'd joined Southampton after falling into dispute at Chelsea and although he never really regained the match fitness he had during his days at Stamford Bridge, he never lost his ability to play. His vision and passing ability was superb. I was very sorry to see him go and saddened to hear of his premature death at the age of just 59 in 2006.

'He was great company on the long journeys back to the south coast after games up north. I remember one occasion when we had to travel by train and it was late arriving at Euston for the connection at Waterloo. As a result there was a coach waiting for us at Euston instead. Of course, most of us had been drinking on the train coming down and a few of us stopped to get a bottle of wine before we left the train. Unfortunately, Ossie and I were at the back of the queue and when we got outside the station the coach had gone! Lawrie had told the driver to go. So we legged it across to Waterloo and just managed to catch a later train.

'Of course I travelled straight down to Bournemouth, so I didn't know what the hell was going on with Lawrie when I got in on the Monday morning. His assistant Jim Clunie told me that on Saturday night Channon and Bally apparently left half a bottle of red wine and a half-empty glass on the bonnet of Lawrie's Jaguar when they got back to The Dell, then cleared off home. Anyway, we all had to see the boss in his office and Lawrie starts steaming into us about drinking and larking about. Then Ossie says, "Hold on a minute, we went out of the goodness of our hearts to get a bottle of wine so you could have a drink on the journey home and you're giving us crap?" So Lawrie says, "Oh, sorry Bonny Lads, I didn't realise that!" That was Lawrie and Ossie to a tee!'

The year ended on a high note for Saints with three more consecutive victories which kept them in third place and closed the gap between themselves and the top two, Bolton and Tottenham. His confidence restored, MacDougall took just one minute to put Southampton ahead at home to Cardiff on Boxing Day morning, following up after Boyer's shot had been blocked. Further goals from Boyer and Ball gave them a comfortable lead before the Welsh club grabbed a late consolation. The following day's visit to The Valley brought more goals for the same trio and the same result to end Charlton's own 22-game undefeated home record. This time the scoring was started by Ball's clever lob after half an hour, only for the Addicks to equalise two minutes later. In the second half MacDougall paved the way for Boyer's shot to restore the visitors' lead before hitting home an angled effort himself from just inside the penalty area.

Stoke visited The Dell on New Year's Eve, having been relegated from the top flight at the end of the previous season, and their fate was sealed when Boyer finished off a cross by Holmes, his neat flick flying past City's former Bournemouth goalkeeper Roger Jones. While Saints were now benefitting from MacDougall's return to form, Boyer's willingness to go deep and create openings, as he had done so well in tandem with Ted at York, Bournemouth and Norwich, was also becoming an increasingly successful factor in Southampton's play.

Two days later, Saints returned with a vital point from fellow promotion chasers Brighton, where in front of the Goldstone Ground's biggest gate of the season, 33,097, Williams's goal just before the hour was cancelled out by Peter Ward's strike soon afterwards. With their push for promotion very much on course, the last thing Saints really needed was a strenuous encounter in the FA Cup, but that's exactly what followed after they were paired with the manager's former club, Grimsby Town, in the third round. The Mariners were now lying mid-table in the Fourth Division having lost the Third Division status they had gained under McMenemy, and the match also meant a return to Blundell Park for goalkeeper Turner, who was recalled for his first game in three months after Wells suffered a broken finger. Turner's appearance was marked by several fine saves to keep the home team at bay in a gripping and, at times, gruelling game. Southampton's best chances fell to MacDougall, who was foiled first at point-blank range by Grimsby goalkeeper Nigel Batch, and later when he had a shot cleared off the line. The goalless outcome was even more surprisingly repeated in the replay where, despite having home advantage, Saints were still unable to make the breakthrough even after extra time. It meant that with 210 minutes unable to provide a goal for either side, the two teams would meet for a third time at Leicester City's Filbert Street.

Before the FA Cup trilogy was concluded though, Saints picked up another useful league win on the road with a 2-1 success at Mansfield. MacDougall's former Norwich team-mate Peter Morris, now in charge at Field Mill, was facing a battle to keep his new club out of a relegation dog-fight in the second half of the season, so in his position, the last thing he needed to see was Alan Ball roll back the years to produce a world-class performance and dominate the game. Inevitably it was Ball who put Southampton ahead with a 36th-minute penalty following a hotly disputed collision between Holmes and home defender Colin Foster. There could be no complaints about Saints' second goal two minutes later though, MacDougall timing his run perfectly to beat goalkeeper Rod Arnold to a corner from Holmes and finding the net with a glancing header.

Mansfield hit back immediately, but in the second half it was easy to see who were the confident promotion challengers and who were the side desperately battling to stay up as Southampton chalked up a sixth away game without defeat to move within a point of second-placed Tottenham and remain just two points behind the leaders Bolton, 'We stayed up in the Midlands over the weekend as the second replay against Grimsby was scheduled for the Monday night. Of course by the Sunday afternoon we were getting a bit cheesed off, so Bally and I went for a sauna to help pass the time. To make it more enjoyable we took a bottle of champagne in with us, as you do, and were quite comfortable when suddenly Lawrie's face appeared at the door!

'I thought, "That's it, we're for it now," you know, two pros drinking the day before a game, but Bally invited him in for a drink! Lawrie had been out for a walk and was wearing a thick overcoat but he stepped inside and had a glass of champagne with us. The three of us were sat there chatting while Lawrie finished his drink with the sweat streaming off him! He could have thrown the book at us of course but instead he just smiled and shook his head, and we rewarded him the following evening!'

A horrid mixture of rain, sleet and snow greeted Saints at Filbert Street for the third encounter with Grimsby and this time, the 11,356 diehards who turned out to watch had only four minutes to wait for the first goal. On his 20th birthday, debutant right-back Tim Coak was released by Ball's free kick and crossed perfectly for Peach to head home. The lead was doubled before half-time when Boyer passed the ball to MacDougall 15 yards inside the Grimsby half, before setting off on a remarkable run to take a return pass as he outpaced the Mariners defence, before finishing with an unstoppable shot.

With snow falling throughout, Grimsby threw everything at Southampton in the second half but eventually ran out of steam and in the last quarter of an hour Ted took centre stage. First, after collecting a cross from Peach, he moved to his left before hooking an angled shot past Batch, then with three minutes to go, he set up a fourth goal, crossing for Holmes to head home. A minute later – nearly five hours after the start of the original tie – Joe Waters finally netted a consolation for Grimsby after Turner was unable to hold a shot from Malcolm Partridge.

There was no let-up in the battle for league points either and Boyer kept the promotion pot boiling with a virtuoso performance against Notts County at The Dell, Saints' ninth game in the space of three weeks. After 14 minutes he produced a terrific burst of speed, running 30 yards before placing a right-footed shot into the net, then midway through the second half, he rapped home an inch-perfect left-foot shot from Coak's low cross. Earlier, Southampton had struggled to break down County's defence after Mick Vinter had equalised, but as they continued to press, victory was sealed when Boyer set up a third goal for Williams in the dying minutes, 'Being a Nottingham lad, Charlie used to worship Notts County as a kid but whenever we came up against them he always seemed to come up with something special!'

Twelve days after their victory over Grimsby, Saints' interest in the FA Cup ended when they suffered a 2-0 defeat at Bristol Rovers. Struggling to control the ball on a muddy pitch, they were unable to play with any fluency and conceded late goals in each half, 'After that long battle against Fourth Division Grimsby, we went out to a team that was fighting to avoid relegation to the Third Division, but it was promotion we wanted and as the old saying goes, that's exactly what we were now free to concentrate on.'

In contrast to the game at Bristol, Southampton rallied to gain a precious point against mid-table Burnley after twice being two goals behind at Turf Moor. The home side got off to a dream start when, after five minutes, a long clearance fell to Steve Kindon, and his first-time shot nestled low into the net. They doubled their lead on the half-hour, Kindon's pace beating Saints' offside trap and allowing him to pull back a low cross for Terry Cochrane to fire into an empty net. Southampton emerged for the second half with greater determination though and were soon rewarded when MacDougall grabbed his eighth goal of the season with a low shot from close in. Kindon then restored Burley's two-goal advantage before, with time running out and Saints battling to save the game, Boyer ran on to MacDougall's header to shoot home with just three minutes left on the clock.

Then, in injury time, the Burnley defence failed to clear a free kick from Ball and Peach saved the day with a fierce low shot through a crowded penalty area. While understandably delighted with his team's fightback, McMenemy, still concerned about the club's disciplinary record, was less than happy about bookings for Ball, Peach and Williams on top of those received by Holmes and Coak the previous week. By today's standards this number of cautions would cause no great alarm, but back in 1978 referees issued far fewer yellow and red cards and Southampton were later fined £1,500 for their poor disciplinary record during the season.

Saints remained third despite receiving a jolt to their promotion hopes when relegation-battling Millwall completed the double over them with a 3-2 victory at a near-frozen Dell. The bone-hard pitch eliminated the gap between the promotion chasers and the-bottom-of the-table side, and instead of dominating the game against the division's lowest scorers, Saints were made to pay for their poor distribution of the ball throughout a game in which their big defenders, Nicholl, Pickering and Waldron, had trouble keeping their feet. The visitors had already taken a two-goal lead before centre-half Tony Hazell handled and Peach strode up once more to score from the spot to give Saints a lifeline.

As they pushed forward in search of an equaliser though, they were caught out when after two smart saves from Turner, the ball fell to Ian Pearson who gratefully slipped the ball into the net. Even so, Southampton hit back again to set up a grandstand finish when MacDougall headed home a last-minute cross from Ball. No further success came their way though, and Saints were made to pay for their poor distribution of the ball throughout the game.

Still concerned about the number of goals his team were conceding, McMenemy fought off competition from Middlesbrough and Ipswich for the signature of the highly rated Halifax Town goalkeeper Terry Gennoe, who was considered to be one of the best goalkeepers in the lower divisions and a fee of £35,000 brought the 25-year-old to The Dell. He would be forced to wait until the following season before establishing himself as first-choice though, the manager restoring Wells to the starting line-up for the home game against Sheffield United in place of Turner. The snow and ice of recent weeks had gone but rain and mud took over and a tense struggle against the Blades was finally settled by a glorious chip from Boyer, after he had spotted goalkeeper Jim Brown off his line three minutes from time. Earlier MacDougall had given Saints a first-half lead, applying the finishing touch to a low cross from Boyer, only for United to level immediately before the break.

Wells then took centre stage against Sunderland, another of the promotion challengers following their relegation from the First Division at the end of the previous season, their first in the top flight for six years. The former Nottingham Forest custodian produced a series of fine saves in a backs-to-the-wall performance at Roker Park which saw Southampton pick up a point in a hard-fought goalless draw, 'This game was billed as a battle of the two best attacking teams in the division, but in the end it turned out to be a dour struggle. Lawrie set the tone by replacing a forward [Tony Sealy, who had made his league debut against Sheffield United] with Manny Andruszewski to give him an extra defender and we toughed it out, much to the anger of the home crowd.'

A midweek friendly against Swedish side IFK Gothenburg brought goals for MacDougall and Funnell and it was the emerging youngster who was on target again when Crystal Palace visited the Dell on the second Saturday in March. He had entered the fray as early as the 15th minute, after the unfortunate Sealey had suffered a broken fibula, and soon afterwards provided the finishing touch to a sparkling move, with a crisp shot. His second was something of a gift, following a misplaced back-pass late in the second half, but there could have been more goals for Saints. MacDougall had a marvellous header pulled out from under the crossbar by goalkeeper Tony Burns in the second half and then in the final seconds, Boyer sent a close-range shot crashing against the woodwork. Having been so critical of Southampton's physical style of play earlier in the season, Palace manager Terry Venables conceded afterwards that on this form, they were very likely to get promoted.

After the struggle at Roker Park, another tense and fiercely competitive affair lay ahead when Saints travelled to face Bolton. With the two teams lying second and third in the league, it was no less than would have been expected and McMenemy was delighted to see his side take a point from Burnden Park in another goalless draw. In fact, they almost snatched a late winner when Funnell bustled into the penalty area but on this occasion the young forward shot narrowly wide. The result left Saints still occupying the third promotion place with ten games remaining, three points behind Bolton and four behind leaders Tottenham, who had played a game more. Importantly it also kept them two points ahead of fourth-placed Brighton, 'Tony Funnell, who ended up at Bournemouth later in his career of course, was a good lad who always seemed to do well when he came on as a substitute. So much so that when we left the dressing room, I used to tell the other lads there was no pressure on them and to enjoy the game but bear in mind this crowd out there want me off as quickly as possible! At five to three when we're kicking in to the goals and I've missed the target a couple of times, I'm getting told to "fuck off" by our supporters and to make way for Tony Funnell! I just laughed at them, I knew I'd missed a couple but we hadn't started the game yet – give me a break! There was no confrontation though or anything like that, it was all good-natured and Tony eventually earned a place in the side for the run-in alongside Charlie and myself.'

Funnell struck again on Easter Saturday when Saints gave a slick display of attacking football to see off Charlton at The Dell, after they had initially fallen behind. Williams brought them level shortly before the interval and soon afterwards MacDougall, lurking at the far post, scored from Andruszewski's cross. Funnell then increased the lead with a near-post header before finally, Williams added a fourth, gratefully accepting Ted's clever back-heel and finishing with a low shot.

The second of three games in five days brought Bristol Rovers to Hampshire and despite Ball missing a first-half penalty, the visitors still left empty-handed thanks to two goals from Boyer, and a late effort from MacDougall. In the 1970s, when fixtures came in quick succession, it was not common practice for managers to rotate their players in the manner they do today and McMenemy made just one change for the next game at Cardiff, Coak returning in place of Waldron. Tiredness may have played a part in Saints' lacklustre performance at Ninian Park though, as they suffered their first defeat in seven games, but whatever the reason, it would prove to be their last defeat of the season, as they set about closing in on promotion.

Undeterred by the setback in Wales, Southampton took full revenge for their unsavoury defeat at Ewood Park in November, sweeping Blackburn aside at The Dell as they romped home 5-0. Funnell was first to score, punishing an error in the Rovers defence, then in the 13th minute Ball carved out an opening for Williams, whose shot was pushed out only as far as MacDougall, who struck home the rebound. By half-time Holmes had added a third and two more goals followed from Boyer in the second half, the first after he had played a one-two with Ball before racing clear and the second a stab-in at the near post following a cross by Holmes.

With the supporters now firmly believing this could be their club's season for promotion, they got behind the team in good numbers for the final run-in. Almost half of Fulham's Craven Cottage ground was occupied by Saints fans among a crowd of almost 17,000, to see a goal from Funnell earn another vital point. With the best will in the world, nowhere near as many were ever likely to make it to Boothferry Park, Hull, the following Tuesday night, but those who could make the long journey to Humberside were rewarded with a performance that City caretaker manager Ken Knighton described as the best he had seen all season by any team in the division. MacDougall's early glancing header from Boyer's cross settled Southampton down and in the second half further goals from Boyer and Ball, both finishing off sweeping attacking movements, completed an impressive all-round performance which moved them up to second in the table.

Unable to move into the promotion places but safe from the threat of relegation, Oldham attempted to put a typically stubborn block on Saints' progress and twice went ahead at The Dell. In response, urged on by their highest league crowd of the season, 25,788, first Holmes brought Saints level from Andruszewski's cross before a piece of good fortune saw them grab a second equaliser. First, referee Eric Read correctly penalised Oldham goalkeeper John Platt for taking more than the permitted four steps with the ball in his hands and then, after Ball's free kick had flashed across the penalty area, Read allowed Funnell to knock the goalkeeper off balance and stab the ball home. As a result, Southampton remained second for another week but jumped to the top of the table the following Saturday after snatching victory at Luton. The finish could not have been more dramatic, with Peach crashing home a penalty three minutes from time.

Earlier, after a goalless first half, Ball sent over a free kick which MacDougall ran to meet with a diving header to put Saints ahead, only for Ricky Hill to equalise for Luton in a rough, tough game played in a raw atmosphere which saw Ball, Peach and goalkeeper Wells all cautioned, 'The fans were superb, they travelled in droves and it was a great time of the season for us to reach the top. Both teams ran their legs off but that penalty was one of the defining moments of the season. People were making comparisons with Southampton's previous promotion season of 1966, saying how similar a number of things were and we hoped they were right! This was the 18th consecutive penalty Peachy had scored by the way – think about that, it takes some doing!'

Just as they had done under the management of Ted Bates in 1966, Southampton faced a trip to Leyton Orient in their penultimate game of the season and exactly as before, they came from behind to pull level with a headed goal in a 1-1 draw to virtually clinch promotion. An estimated 12,000 travelling supporters saw Funnell head home from Peach's cross after Bobby Fisher had put the home side in front. Although their promotion could not yet be confirmed, the result meant that Saints' total of 56 points could not be overhauled by fourth-placed Brighton and their goal difference was seven better than their Sussex neighbours.

In the final fixtures of the season, Southampton were at home to third-placed Tottenham, where a point each would clinch promotion for both sides, while Brighton faced relegation candidates Blackpool. Those present at The Dell witnessed a game where Saints appeared happy to defend rather than take the game to their visitors, the nearest either side coming to a goal being when a shot by Funnell brushed the outside of a post. Had Southampton been able to secure a win, it would have given them the championship and elevated Brighton at Tottenham's expense. As it was, Bolton were champions, while Saints took second place – and in doing so sparked many a conspiracy theory on the Sussex coast. But, while the club celebrated its return to the First Division after an absence of four seasons, failing to win the league was in fact a major disappointment to many of the club's senior players, 'We wanted to win the league, make no mistake about that but we had Steve Williams in midfield trying to "nutmeg" people and just taking the piss. While we were having our tea at half-time, Lawrie steamed in to Steve and he responded by having a pop back at Lawrie, so I threw my tea at him and grabbed him round the neck. "Don't you have a go when you've never done a fucking thing in this game," I told him. Needless to say, that was the end of me and Steve. While all the other players went in to the directors' box to wave to the supporters after the game, I was in the bath! When Lawrie noticed I was missing he came and got me but it was all very disappointing.'

After a slow start, MacDougall had ended the season with 15 goals, 14 of which had been scored in the league, and once again he could look forward to starting the following season as a First Division player. Having re-established his partnership with Boyer, they contributed a total of 31 league goals between them and were an integral part of a team that had been rebuilt by McMenemy who, as he said he would, had replaced the cup final team with a squad capable of gaining promotion back to the top flight, 'It was great to get promotion for Lawrie, the supporters and everyone at the club. The team seemed to get better and better as the season progressed. Everyone played their part, Bally was an inspirational captain who at times played as if he would get us promoted single-handedly if he had to!

'Steve Williams learnt a lot from just being alongside him. Charlie got plenty of goals in the league and young Tony Funnell chipped in brilliantly at the end, which was great. Nicholl and Pickering became a strong partnership at the back and Peachy and Holmes made a lot of goals for us with their crossing from the flanks. Importantly though, we enjoyed each other's company and we became a strong unit. They were great times.'

18

Calling 'Time' at The Dell

THE death of club chairman George Reader and doubts over the future of Lawrie McMenemy cast a shadow over Southampton's preparations ahead of their return to the big time. The popular chairman, much admired by the manager, had passed away shortly before the players returned for pre-season training, while during the summer McMenemy had become the favourite to take over the vacant position at Leeds United following the departure of Jimmy Armfield. While the Saints board did their best to hang on to their manager, players and supporters waited anxiously for his decision. Meanwhile, assistant Jim Clunie had accepted an offer to become manager of his former club St Mirren and Alan Ball was still to return from America where, with McMenemy's permission, he was spending the summer as player-manager of Philadelphia Fury, 'Lawrie welcomed us back on the first day and we were all examined and weighed as usual. He had been concerned Peter Wells had been drinking too much the previous season, not alcohol but milk and orange, and when Peter got on the scales he'd put on another half a stone! Lawrie told him he had a week to lose the excess pounds so I suggested to Peter that he should get off milk and get on lager!'

A week into pre-season, McMenemy finally turned down the overtures from Yorkshire and announced that he had decided to stay on at The Dell. As successor to Clunie, he appointed former Saints player Lew Chatterley, who had also played under him at Doncaster and Grimsby, and got down to work, 'I had a chat with Lawrie about what he was going to do a couple of days earlier. I really thought he was going to take the Leeds job, and although I didn't want him to go, I wished him all the best. I was delighted when he brought a bottle of champagne in to training the next day and told us the bad news was that he had decided to stay!'

After a week and a half's training came the first friendly, not the usual gentle return to action but instead a game against Sunderland at Roker Park, which Saints won 1-0. Two days later came a renewal of acquaintance with Clunie, as the team travelled on to Paisley for a game against St Mirren. Among the crowd that witnessed a single-goal victory for the home side were Norwich manager John Bond and his assistant Ken Brown. With City due to meet Saints on the first day of the season, the pair had taken the opportunity to have an early look at their opponents, 'We had a few players missing that night and the game didn't go well but Bondy came back to the hotel with us afterwards and chatted with Charlie and I for a couple of hours in the bar. We had not parted on the best of terms at Norwich and I hadn't heard from John for some time, so I think we were both glad to have an opportunity to talk a few things through, which was good.'

When the organisers of the Tennent Caledonian Cup found themselves a team short, they turned again to Southampton, who made their third appearance in the four-team tournament in three years. The matches were again played at Ibrox Park and Saints went through to the final against Rangers after beating West Bromwich Albion on penalties, but suffered a 4-1 defeat to John Greig's side, having had three goals disallowed in front of a very partisan crowd.

With Ball now back from the States, he joined his Southampton team-mates for a trip to Belgium and a game against FC Malines, which they won 2-1. Yugoslavian international full-back Ivan Golac impressed in Belgium having joined the club for £50,000 from Partizan Belgrade, then upon the team's return to England, McMenemy concluded a £60,000 deal to bring Derby County's former Doncaster Rovers winger Terry Curran to The Dell, 'I had been on at Lawrie for some time to bring in a winger and I was delighted when Terry arrived. It gave us a boost just before the season got going, mind you I was pretty pumped up anyway at the prospect of returning to Norwich for the first game. On the bus up I told the lads that the whole city would be turning out to meet me!'

Norwich had finished the previous season 13th in the First Division, and despite not having the financial resources of some of the bigger clubs, Bond had succeeded in establishing them as a respectable mid-table side, a task that McMenemy now sought to replicate at Southampton. Unfortunately on a hot sunny afternoon, things did not start well. Golac still awaited a work permit so was forced to sit the game out but Curran did make his debut at Carrow Road. Kevin Reeves, a £50,000 signing from Bournemouth, gave City a first-half lead which was increased by John Ryan and former Saint Martin Chivers after the break. MacDougall did manage a goal upon his return to Norfolk, but it was merely a consolation when he chested down a Phil Boyer cross late in the game before lashing the ball home, 'Although I scored eventually, it was a case of too little, too late I'm afraid as I had already missed a couple of good chances that I would have normally put away. I remember feeling a yard slow during the game, which concerned me as I used to look for things like that. I apologised to Lawrie when I got back to the dressing room, though he told me not to worry about it.

'Norwich was a lovely club and I did get a decent reception on my return. The supporters clapped when I scored – mind you City were three up by then – and when Bondy came over afterwards, we walked off arm in arm.'

A couple of hours before Southampton's opening home game of the season, what had become a major wrangle over Golac's work permit had still not been resolved, but in the meantime the Yugoslav had at least been cleared to make his debut against fellow First Division newcomers Bolton as a non-contract player. The supporters turned out in strength, more than 21,000 being present to see 19-year-old Graham Baker head home following MacDougall's flick to put Saints in front. Their lead lasted until shortly before half-time, when Wanderers equalised from a Worthington free kick but early in the second half MacDougall restored Southampton's advantage after Boyer had dummied David Peach's low cross.

They led only briefly though, Worthington finding the net again from another free kick three minutes later, to earn the visitors a point. The following Saturday, a slip-up from Wells allowed a header from Middlesbrough's David Armstrong to go over his head and into the net before Saints hit back with second-half goals from Nicholl and Ball to register their first home win of the season.

MacDougall was twice on the scoresheet when Southampton made an impressive start to their League Cup campaign with a 5-2 success at Birmingham. His first goal came when he latched on to Ball's free kick which had landed conveniently in the penalty area before he went on to grab Saints' fifth, following up after the home defence had failed to clear a cross from Golac. By this time the majority of a rather hostile home crowd had left the ground, having already endured two more goals from Boyer and one from Peach.

An unchanged team returned to Birmingham a few days later and battled hard to take a point against City's neighbours Aston Villa. Despite falling behind midway through the first half, they drew level through former Villa captain Nicholl, who headed in from Ball's cross on the stroke of half-time. Putting aside the loss of the injured Andruszewski, the defence held firm after the interval and drew praise from the manager, who felt many of his team 'grew up' during the game and learnt what the First Division was all about. With five points from the first four league matches of the season, Southampton had made a reasonable start but were arguably still conceding too many goals. In the Second Division the previous season their defensive record had been outstanding, with only 39 goals conceded in 42 games. Since then, the inexperienced Waldron had taken over from Pickering and had coped reasonably well, but word had reached McMenemy that Derby's England international defender Colin Todd was available for transfer, and he set off in pursuit.

Meanwhile, Boyer put Southampton on the way to a 3-2 victory over struggling Wolves at The Dell, Waldron added a second, heading home Ball's free kick and MacDougall supplied a simple finish after Curran's run had left goalkeeper Paul Bradshaw stranded. Although Wolves twice replied, Saints dominated the game to such an extent that the margin of victory could have been much greater. Notably, Peach missed a penalty, Bradshaw pushing his shot away for a corner, the first time he had failed from the spot in 39 attempts with Gillingham and Southampton.

Todd had shaken hands on a £300,000 move but when his wife's family persuaded her that he would be better off by joining Everton, he pulled out of the deal and joined the Goodison Park club instead. To add to McMenemy's frustration, two goals in Saints' 3-1 defeat at Bristol City the next day came as a result of defensive errors. The game was not a memorable one for MacDougall either, as having already picked up a booking it was one of the few occasions when he failed to complete the 90 minutes through injury. Having pulled a muscle in his left thigh early in the game, he was eventually replaced by substitute Austin Hayes. The injury meant he missed Southampton's visit to Derby and a reunion with Tommy Docherty, who had taken over as manager in September 1977, having been sacked by Manchester United amid a blaze of publicity over his affair with the wife of club physiotherapist Laurie Brown. Gennoe made his long-awaited debut in goal though and Pickering returned as an extra defender, but unfortunately Saints ran out of luck at the Baseball Ground, with second-half goals from Steve Carter and Charlie George seeing the Rams home, despite Peach returning to normal service from the penalty spot.

The absence of the injured Nicholl proved crucial when Ipswich came to The Dell at the end of September, two goals from Paul Mariner inside the first 20 minutes leaving Southampton with too much work to do. They did their best to hit back though, only to see Ipswich goalkeeper Paul Cooper save a penalty from Peach and Williams hit the post with a rasping shot. After the break, Holmes became the next to strike the woodwork, while Boyer and Golac were denied by further saves by Cooper and their only success came when MacDougall pounced after Golac had set him up from a low cross.

Docherty's Derby side renewed acquaintance again in the third round of the League Cup, and the tie might well have included five or six goals but for some brilliant goalkeeping by Gennoe and John Middleton. In the end there was just one, but it was enough to send Saints in to the last 16 and was scored by Boyer against his first professional club, when he raced in to their penalty area to meet Holmes's cross and struck a shot into the net off the underside of the crossbar, 'I should have had a hat-trick but the goalkeeper stopped everything.

'I was in a foul mood after the game, hurling my boots around and cursing because I'd come off empty-handed. That was it with me, we had won the game but because I hadn't scored that was the big issue. Even at this stage of my career it was all about me scoring goals. I had a right go at Peachy because he had put over a cross which ended up by the far corner flag when I was unmarked in the middle. Lawrie told me off about it the next day but he understood it was just down to frustration. Bally and I told him we thought he should be buying players, as we were only getting results by running ourselves into the ground, and when we had burnt ourselves out, what would happen then?'

Knowing that the club had money available to spend, McMenemy continued to try and add to his squad but prior to the next game against second-placed Everton, two players made their way out of the club. Pickering had opted to join Sheffield Wednesday in a deal worth £50,000 while full-back John Sharpe, who had been on loan to Third Division Gillingham, joined them permanently for a fee of £30,000, 'Prior to the game at Goodison Park, Lawrie invited Bill Shankly into the dressing room to give us some encouragement and as he left he said to Terry Gennoe, "Son, when you go out there, throw your cap and gloves into the net and make sure that's all that goes in!" Thankfully, he followed Shanks's instructions to the letter!'

Everton fans gave Ball, their former captain, a rousing reception while Gennoe put in a heroic performance, which included saving a penalty as Saints stretched unbeaten Everton to the limit, taking a point in a goalless stalemate. Another draw came in front of the televison cameras at The Dell against Queens Park Rangers, when Southampton produced 45 minutes of superb attacking football and then threw it all away by going to pieces after the break. They took the lead in the 25th minute when Curran curled across a right-wing corner for Ted to score with a tremendous header. It was a trademark MacDougall finish for what would turn out to be his 44th and last goal for Saints. With their defence creaking throughout the second half, it became a question of whether Southampton would somehow manage to hang on to their lead. They came close but couldn't keep out Paul Goddard's header four minutes from time and the result left them 16th in the First Division table.

Following Jock Stein's brief tenure at Leeds the Yorkshire club were again on the lookout for a manager and not surprisingly, speculation was rife that the Southampton boss was still the man they wanted. He dismissed the newspaper reports as 'a typical Saturday morning story' ahead of Saints' visit to Arsenal, preferring to concentrate on the match itself. Having toyed with the idea of deploying three central defenders and four marking midfielders against the Gunners, McMenemy finally settled for his usual more attacking policy but to assign someone to stay close to influential midfielder Liam Brady. His decision appeared to be spot on, only for his team's failure to turn pressure into goals to prove costly in the dying minutes.

A weakened Arsenal team, which relied heavily on inexperienced reserves Kevin Stead, Steve Gatting, Mark Neeley and Steve Walford, appeared to be there for the taking. It was continuous Saints attacking from the start – and almost continuous disappointment. MacDougall and Boyer between them got five good scoring attempts on target but were foiled by a combination of good defending and the brilliance of goalkeeper Pat Jennings. In one frantic first-half scramble, Ted had two shots in succession blocked and a blistering drive by Boyer was headed away brilliantly by Walford. After the interval MacDougall got in a brilliant header but Jennings took off to make another superb save. Then Ball, back at another of his former clubs, beat two men only to see MacDougall hit his cross straight at Jennings.

In comparison, Arsenal created very little with Nicholl and Waldron dominating the Southampton penalty area until the last minute of the game, when Frank Stapleton broke on the right and saw his shot rebound off Gennoe into the path of Brady, who nipped in to score, having hardly had a kick otherwise. Ball immediately complained to referee Mike Taylor that Steve Williams had been fouled before the move had developed but it was to no avail. After the game the players were fuming in the dressing room having suffered what they considered to be an unjust result, 'The following Monday I asked to see Lawrie after training and told him I was worried about my performances. I told him I had felt lethargic against Arsenal, just not able to get anywhere and would have buried those chances I had at Highbury a few years ago. Arsenal were a young side who were quick in defence, maybe it was because they were so quick, but I wondered, "Is this the writing on the wall?" I felt that I could be costing the team points and that perhaps I should move on. I think Lawrie appreciated my honesty and told me to think carefully about what I was doing, but I think we both knew that one day I would end up back at Bournemouth anyway.

'I spoke to him again later in the week and told him I still felt the same way about leaving. He confirmed that Southampton would not stand in my way, which I appreciated. I think Lawrie felt that having only paid £50,000 for me two years before, the club had had its money's worth from me.

'My old Bournemouth and Norwich team-mate John Benson was still player-manager of Bournemouth. They were struggling on the pitch and financially but with all my business interests still based locally – I had sports shops in Bournemouth and Poole now as well as the original one in Boscombe – it was the one place where I really wanted to go. So, I spoke to John and told him how I felt, and he invited me down to Dean Court to try and sort something out.'

When MacDougall's desire to leave Southampton reached the attention of the media, it quickly became big news. Here was a player, still no more than 31 years of age, a first-team regular, who had scored seven goals in 12 appearances that season, who had suddenly announced he was going to jack it all in – and not for the first time. McMenemy now found himself with the same dilemma that had faced John Bond when MacDougall left Norwich City two years previously. He knew that finding an experienced striker to replace Ted was not going to be easy but like Bond, decided not to stand in the player's way. It was a surprise therefore, when he named MacDougall in his squad to face Manchester United at Old Trafford, although Ted did not travel with the party, 'Lawrie knew I had sold a story to the *Sunday Mirror* explaining my decision to quit Southampton but he didn't want anything more to be said ahead of the game. In return, he also didn't want to ruin the impact of the newspaper series which was due to start the following week. It was a nice gesture and typical of the man.'

Speculation grew among Bournemouth supporters that their former star was about to return to the club when, instead of being with the Southampton squad at Old Trafford, MacDougall turned up at Dean Court to watch the Cherries beat Torquay. Ted had also accepted Benson's invitation to come in to the home dressing room after the game and chat about the match and the team's performance, 'They played very well and I had no hesitation in telling them so! Benno and I later agreed financial terms and I left it to him to complete the arrangements with Lawrie.'

The following Monday, 6 November, Benson called McMenemy to quickly complete the transfer, grateful that Southampton had kept their word in not requesting a fee. His goalscoring record for Saints was 44 in 90 games, very respectable in any era, but he had given up his First Division career to cross the New Forest and return to the club closest to his heart, 'I had the best time of my professional career in the two years I spent at Southampton because it was so much fun. It was fantastic. I have nothing but fond memories. We got into the First Division and I scored close on a goal every two games – and I still got stick from some of the supporters!

'I wanted to score goals for the Cherries again and more important than that, to help get the club out of the Fourth Division. I believed I could help them and that I still had something to offer, but it was a mistake to leave Saints when I did really. Benno said he wanted to sign me for Bournemouth and I thought it was the right move, I felt I was coming home, I didn't return there to die though! I went there to try and do a job – then a few weeks later I had to put up with Alec Stock trying to teach me how to play the game.'

19

Return of the Prodigal Son

JOHN Benson was a likeable personality with a strong sense of humour off the field and a similar sense of duty on it. The 35-year-old Scot had been a hard worker throughout his playing career which had started at Manchester City in 1961, before a move to Torquay saw him play alongside John Bond. After making 240 appearances for the Gulls, Benson followed Bond to Bournemouth, and then to Norwich. Capable of playing as a defender or in midfield, he had initially surprised a lot of people with the quality of his displays in the First Division while at Carrow Road, but latterly became a target for criticism on the terraces after results took a dip.

When Trevor Hartley was dismissed in January 1975, Benson returned to Bournemouth as player-manager but had been unable to save the club from relegation to the Fourth Division. After the heavy spending days of Bond, which had seen the Cherries rival many a First Division club in respect of transfer fees and wages, the subsequent exodus of Bond and a number of senior players had left the club in a perilous position.

Relegation came as a cruel blow and Benson, himself of course one of the players who had initially left after Bond's departure, had been unable to regain the club's Third Division status the following season, resulting in drastic cost-saving measures which included the axing of the club's reserve team. Worse followed as the Cherries dropped to 13th and then 17th in the following two seasons, which had also seen the departure of several key players including future England international Kevin Reeves to Norwich. Benson had come under intense and often unfair criticism for the poor quality of the football played and the lack of results. Many supporters had become disillusioned and had lost interest in the club as gates fell dramatically from the heady days of the early 1970s to less than 3,000 on occasions.

Together with MacDougall, a crowd of 3,747 witnessed the win against Torquay, a result which moved the Cherries up to seventh in the Fourth Division table. The following week, proceedings commenced at Winchester Crown Court to settle a long-standing dispute between Bournemouth and Manchester United regarding the additional sum which Harold Walker believed was morally due to the Cherries as part of the transfer agreement when MacDougall left Dean Court in 1972. The sum, widely reported as £25,000 at the time but quoted as £27,777 in the club's records, was to have been paid when MacDougall scored 20 goals in league and cup football for United. The terms of the agreement stated that MacDougall should be given 'a reasonable opportunity' to score the 20 goals but Bournemouth claimed that he was never given that opportunity due to Frank O'Farrell's dismissal as manager shortly afterwards, 'United's defence was that I had asked for a move before they sold me to West Ham and as I had only scored five goals in 18 league games for them, the clause in the transfer agreement didn't apply. That was rich, as they were only too keen to get me out of Old Trafford and I had never formally requested a transfer! Mr Walker knew that and claimed that United were morally still liable and had been trying to get them to pay this money for a long time before finally taking them to court.

'Anyway, now United had all these top attorneys and barristers working for them, and they had this easel in the courtroom where they attached a photograph of my house in Manchester with a "For Sale" sign up outside. They told the court it was obvious I wanted to leave as I had put my house up for sale, so I took the witness stand and told them that, after several months of living with Joan's parents, we had finally bought a house six days after Frank O'Farrell had been sacked and the sign had been there since we moved in! We weren't there long enough to bother about taking it down. Tommy Docherty took the stand to explain why he got rid of me but Mr Justice Talbot eventually ruled in Bournemouth's favour, which was ironically on the day I agreed to re-join the club.'

The club was awarded £22,261 plus costs after the judge had taken into account the possibility that injury may have prevented MacDougall from reaching the 20-goal target. However, following an unsuccessful appeal by United, Bournemouth had to wait until August 1980 before the money was eventually received.

Benson desperately hoped to win over his critics with another bid for promotion, and it now centred on the arrival of his old mate MacDougall, whom he hoped would be capable of scoring between 15 and 20 goals during the remainder of the season and in doing so, bring the results he needed and entice more supporters through the turnstiles.

So, on 11 November 1978, instead of lining up for Southampton against his former Norwich team-mates at The Dell, MacDougall made his second debut for Bournemouth in a goalless draw at Victoria Park, Hartlepool, watched by a crowd of just 3,329. There was just one player in the Cherries team remaining from Ted's previous spell at the club, skipper Keith Miller, although he had played alongside experienced right-back Geoff Butler while at Norwich. The Bournemouth team was now a mixture of youngsters, players plucked from non-league clubs and one or two journeymen from the lower divisions. At Hartlepool they lined up as follows: Allen, Geoff Butler, Miller, Impey, Roger Brown, Barton, Borthwick, MacDougall, Mick Butler, Johnson, Kenny Brown. Substitute: Massey. Ted recalled, 'Ah, what sweet memories, my last game had been at Arsenal's glorious marble stadium at Highbury the previous week! We arrived up at Hartlepool on the coach some seven or eight hours after we left Bournemouth. It was a miserable day and going in to the dressing room I wanted to use the toilet, so I was directed back outside in the direction of an old door which was coming off its hinges.

'The game itself was pretty dour and with a couple of minutes remaining, I noticed most of the players were congregating near the tunnel as the game continued. Then, when the referee blew the final whistle, those players sprinted off the pitch and to my amazement, when I reached the dressing room muddied, soaking wet and freezing, they were all in the big bath with about three inches of reasonably warm water in it, which by now had turned in to a mud bath! When I had got changed, I was asked to do an interview for local television, and the first question they asked was what I found the biggest difference between the Fourth Division and the First!'

Although MacDougall and his new partner Mick Butler could not come up with a goal at Hartlepool, the Cherries' defence produced their fifth clean sheet in six matches to keep them within two points of the top four. When Ted made his first appearance back at Dean Court, just as Benson had predicted, a crowd of over 6,000 was there to see the return of the prodigal son. But it was Mick Butler, a £15,000 capture from Huddersfield the previous summer, who took the scoring honours. After a scrappy first half-hour a free kick from Gary Borthwick found Steve Massey, whose header beat Darlington goalkeeper Phil Owers only to strike the upright, but Butler was there to snap up the rebound. The visitors then stunned the Cherries with two second-half goals and Bournemouth had to fight hard to come back and grab a point.

MacDougall, after a quiet first half, became steadily more menacing as the game progressed, seeing one shot smothered by Owers, then sending a typical header just past the post before firing narrowly wide with a left-foot shot. However, it was the busy Butler who saved the day when he latched on to a through ball from centre-half John Impey, before going past two defenders and sweeping the ball under the diving Owers.

The Cherries progressed to the second round of the FA Cup for the first time in four seasons when they beat Isthmian League part-timers Hitchin Town 2-1 at Dean Court. Another better-than-average crowd of just over 5,000 may have been hoping to see a repeat of the last occasion MacDougall appeared in a first round tie, his scoring feat against Margate in 1971. But this time, the goals came from Massey and Butler and they enabled the Cherries to scrape through after the plucky visitors had taken an early lead.

Defeat at home to York proved to be the start of a desperately disappointing December in which Bournemouth failed to win a single game in league or cup and missed out on a potentially lucrative tie against Southampton. Benson was left shaking his head in disbelief as the slow and sluggish Cherries struggled to get a grip on the game after falling a goal behind and they were fortunate when Butler's cross and MacDougall's dummy enabled much-travelled midfielder Dave Lennard to fire a deflected shot into the net. The Cherries were left kicking themselves though, when York grabbed a winning goal deep into second-half injury time, 'We had a virus doing the rounds among the players the previous week and I think some of us were still feeling the effects. There wasn't any sort of service to Mick or myself up front and as a team we were simply awful I'm afraid. By Christmas I was beginning to have serious doubts about whether I had done the right thing in coming back to Bournemouth.'

MacDougall's first goal since his return to Cherries colours came in a well-earned draw against Wimbledon in the second round of the FA Cup. Bad weather meant the replay was postponed for ten days but in the meantime the Dons travelled to Dean Court the following Saturday for a league fixture. In only their second season as a Football League club, Wimbledon were now leading the way at the top of the Fourth Division and their well-organised side grabbed a two-goal lead in 32 minutes. Lennard chested a goal back before the interval and in the second half, Bournemouth pressed hard for an equaliser, but came up against an inspired performance from Dons goalkeeper Ray Goddard. Having been accidentally kicked in the groin by Mick Butler, the former Orient player hobbled on one leg for the rest of the game but still managed to pull off outstanding saves from MacDougall, Cunningham, Butler and Lennard, despite also being punched by a spectator as he went to retrieve a ball.

A dour Boxing Day defeat at Reading increased the pressure on Benson ahead of the cup replay at Dean Court, where the incentive for the winners was a home tie against Southampton in the next round. A bumper crowd of 7,192 turned up and the Cherries came agonisingly close to securing a money-spinning lifeline following a stupendous goal by MacDougall 20 minutes from time. It was a strike which must rate as one of the best among his vast collection and came after Butler, displaying pace and mobility in the calibre of Phil Boyer, switched the ball to Frank Barton on the edge of the penalty area. Barton then laid the ball off for Ted to strike a thunderous volley past the helpless Goddard.

With the prospect of a third round bonanza within touching distance, disaster struck when Alan Cork headed home for Wimbledon in the 88th minute to send the match into extra time. If conceding the last-gasp equaliser had left Bournemouth deflated, worse was to follow when in extra time, Cherries goalkeeper Kenny Allen failed to deal with a corner and the ball dropped into the net off the far post, 'Nobody wanted to win that game more than me and reaching the next round would have been a real money spinner for the club. Losing probably cost them around £20,000.'

After a 2-1 defeat at Bradford City two days later, the Cherries ended the year in eighth position, ten points behind leaders Wimbledon, but snow and ice brought a number of postponements during January and Bournemouth's only outing during the month saw a fifth successive league defeat at home against Crewe. Both sides tentatively picked their way around the bone hard Dean Court pitch but the visitors looked much more confident in doing so, especially after taking an early lead. The Cherries put in a terrible performance, not all of which could be put down to the conditions with only 17-year-old debutant Phil Ferns, playing out of position in defence, and centre-half Roger Brown emerging from the game with much credit.

MacDougall twice had good chances in the latter stages, but hit one shot wide and scooped the other over the bar with Crewe goalkeeper Kevin Rafferty lying on the ground. It was without doubt the Cherries' worst display of the season and was accompanied by repeated cries for Benson to be dismissed from the crowd of less than 3,000. For the manager it was the last straw. He had been subjected to verbal and written abuse from the club's 'supporters' for a considerable time and the pressure had now become too much for him. To save his family from further distress, Benson tendered his resignation as manager, which was eventually accepted with reluctance by the club's board of directors. Only a few weeks earlier they had awarded Benson a new four-year contract in an attempt to try and take some of the pressure off him, 'Benno was as honest and straight as the day was long and he had inherited a very bad situation when he came back as manager. He had kept it going by sheer hard graft and certainly hadn't had much luck. Some of the comments made about him were ridiculous or in many cases, just vicious. When actions and comments get personal in the way they did against John and his family, then it's time to get out. It became so bad that his daughters, Sara and Debbie, would come home from school in tears after hearing remarks made about their father.

'Bondy had stayed in touch with Benno since he took over at Dean Court and had been at the cup replay against Wimbledon. When Benno decided to call it a day, John took him back to Norwich as youth team coach. He was offered the manager's job at Carrow Road when Bondy left for Manchester City the following year but instead he went with him to Maine Road as assistant manager. Later in his career he carried out a number of different roles at Burnley, Wigan and Birmingham and also had a spell coaching in Dubai and Kuwait. Sadly he passed away, aged 67, in 2007.'

The search began for a new manager and among those names mentioned in the press were former England captain Bobby Moore and the flamboyant former Fulham, Queens Park Rangers and Manchester City forward Rodney Marsh. Both were apparently anxious to break into management but four days after the Bournemouth directors had accepted Benson's resignation, they appointed the experienced Alec Stock as his successor. The 61-year-old Stock had enjoyed a professional playing career at Charlton Athletic and Queens Park Rangers prior to becoming player-manager of Yeovil Town in 1946. He guided the Glovers to their famous FA Cup win over Sunderland in 1949 on their sloping Huish pitch, before having three separate spells as manager at Leyton Orient, leading them to promotion from the Third to the Second Division before taking charge of Queens Park Rangers. He guided the Loftus Road club from the Third to the First Division in successive seasons and to League Cup Final success in 1967 while still a Third Division side.

His next stop was Luton Town, where he similarly lifted the Hatters from the Third Division to the First before moving on to Fulham, whom he guided to the FA Cup Final in 1975. He also had brief and less successful spells as assistant manager at Arsenal, and as manager of Italian giants AS Roma. After leaving Fulham in December 1976, Stock had returned to Loftus Road to become a director and also acted as caretaker manager for a short period in July 1978. Clearly a man of vast experience, upon his appointment as Bournemouth manager his intention was to inject some pride and dignity back into the club.

Stock's first week in charge was marred by more bad weather and with ground conditions unfit for training, the manager barely had time to get to know the players' names let alone their capabilities before they faced Doncaster Rovers at Dean Court on Saturday 3 February. He could hardly have expected the performance that followed, which saw the Cherries display the sort of goal-getting aggression they had not shown since MacDougall's first spell at the club. The final 35 minutes saw Bournemouth score five times to complete a 7-1 victory over Billy Bremner's side, the club's biggest winning margin in a league match for over 22 years.

The destruction of Doncaster was even more remarkable considering it was achieved without the two leading marksmen, Butler and Massey, who were both out injured. With former Welsh international striker Derek Showers having joined Portsmouth in a £12,000 deal, Joey Scott, a summer signing from Western League Falmouth Town, was promoted from the reserves to start only his second league game. Partnered by MacDougall up front, Scott opened the scoring ten minutes before the break, when his shot from close in was only half-parried by Rovers goalkeeper Dennis Peacock and eventually spun into the net.

After the interval, Scott soon doubled Bournemouth's lead with a left-footed shot high into the net from eight yards, before Rovers captain Joe Laidlaw clawed a goal back. As he did so, he could hardly have expected his team to completely fall apart thereafter. Three minutes later, Cherries winger Peter Johnson scored a fine solo goal before MacDougall, who had gone seven league matches without a goal since re-joining the club, got off the mark in the 61st minute, following up a shot from Lennard which Peacock could only parry. It was just the touch Ted needed and soon afterwards he scored again, firing in a left-footed shot from a centre by Johnson, who was enjoying what was probably his best game for the Cherries.

Lennard volleyed home Bournemouth's sixth goal in the 80th minute before Barton completed the rout with a shot on the run two minutes from time. Incredibly, in their first game under Stock's guidance the Cherries had scored one more goal than they had in all of their previous eight matches. Stock, having told his players to simply go out and impress him, was no doubt thrilled with the goals but probably hoped they hadn't scored them all at once, 'This was just one of those occasions when the ball seemed to run or drop for us in all the right places really, especially in the second half! As the goals went in I felt a bit sorry for Benno, if we had played like this against Crewe two weeks previously, he wouldn't have quit, but I was obviously pleased to get a couple of goals myself. I think all the players felt a bit sheepish afterwards.

'Poor Billy Bremner was getting angrier and angrier on the Doncaster bench and I could hear him tearing into his team in the dressing room afterwards. He felt they had thrown in the towel and that was something that went against the grain for him, and boy did he let them know!'

Four days later, MacDougall and Scott were on target again at Dean Court, as Port Vale were beaten more convincingly than the 3-1 scoreline suggested. A prolific goalscorer at Western League level, Scott was now intent on making his mark in the Football League and struck after just two minutes with a perfectly timed header from Ted's perfect cross. Centre-half Roger Brown doubled the Cherries' lead on the half-hour, heading home from a cross by Lennard, but two minutes after the break Brown turned villain, putting the ball into his own net following a defensive mix-up.

Nonetheless, 20 minutes from time Bournemouth sealed their win, despite heavy rain which had made the conditions difficult. Johnson made light of the greasy pitch, scampering along the left wing and enabled Lennard to put over a cross which just eluded Scott but found MacDougall, who turned to hit home a low shot from the edge of the penalty area.

With interest growing, supporters travelled in good numbers to promotion-chasing Portsmouth the following Saturday. An attendance of more than 12,000 at Fratton Park witnessed a fighting Cherries performance and when the side returned with a point thanks to a goal from Johnson, it seemed for a moment that the glory days may have returned. Sadly, it was not to be and despite MacDougall scoring winning goals against Halifax and Torquay during March, these proved to be the only victories in a run of 16 league games, until he scored the winner at home to Bradford City in late April.

After their ten-goal flourish against Doncaster and Port Vale, the team had in fact gone back to square one, scoring just eight goals in those 16 games and dropping alarmingly down the table. To try and halt the slide, Stock had signed the diminutive 25-year-old former England youth international midfielder Phil Holder from Crystal Palace, initially on loan, to replace Barton, who had joined Seattle Sounders in America. Then in the prolonged absence of Butler through a foot injury, Stock tried almost every permutation up front alongside MacDougall, yet somehow the team failed to score the goals their performances often deserved. In several matches it was a question of simply not taking chances but on other occasions the side scarcely created any chances at all. Defensively, they had performed well for much of the season and it was not until their 2-0 defeat against Barnsley in early April, their 17th loss of the season, that they had been beaten by a margin of more than one goal. Things got worse later in the month though, as in the space of six days the Cherries suffered successive four-goal away defeats at Wimbledon and Northampton, 'I remember an occasion when we had played up north somewhere and on the way back, the club had arranged a meal for us at a hotel. I went to order a drink at the bar and had the pleasure of bumping in to the late comedian, Les Dawson, who was buying a round of drinks – which he had listed on the back of a fag packet! He asked me who I was now playing for, and when I told him I had returned to play for Bournemouth, his response was, "Bournemouth…the only team to lose on Fantasy Island!"'

Attendances fell away again and only 2,285 people turned out for the game against Stockport at the end of April, Dean Court's lowest gate of the season. Those who were there saw MacDougall on the mark again and together with two goals from former Barnsley midfielder Kenny Brown, the Cherries were able to register a much-needed win. Defeats at York and Newport followed, before goals from Massey and Johnson enabled Bournemouth to complete their season with a 2-1 home success over league newcomers Wigan. Victories in their final three home games had enabled the club to escape the ignominy of having to apply for re-election to the league for the first time since 1933/34. However, a final placing of 18th, one position lower than that of the previous season, was, to say the least, a great disappointment.

Like the supporters, Stock was pleased to put the season behind him, and promised a summer of hard work for everyone at the club. He took solace in the performances of the club's reserve team which had won Western League Division One and scored over 100 goals in doing so. Even so, it was asking a lot to expect these players to take the huge step up to the Football League, and Stock knew that to have any chance of improvement the following season, the club had to strengthen its playing resources as a matter of urgency, 'When I came back to Bournemouth the players were poor and so unprofessional, and it soon crossed my mind that after everything I had come through, I was now back to this. Once again, it was the wrong move for me really at the wrong time. Benno tempted me back but he was gone after a few weeks! I wouldn't have come back but for him.

'I was 32 by the end of the season, not particularly old and I respected Alec Stock for what he had done, but he was not what I needed at this stage of my career. I got fed up when he tried to teach me how to play! I told him that I knew what I could do and what I couldn't by now, and unless the team could make use of me, then I was wasting my time. Fred Davies and John Kirk did their best as coaches but the players weren't good enough to see what I was doing or to give me the ball when I wanted it.

'I was still the same player but I still needed the players around me to help me play, and they were just not good enough to enable me to do that. I didn't have the ability to beat people and create things – I never was that type of player – but I could get on the end of things if they could be created.

'Alec was the typical English gentleman and did his best to try and encourage the supporters to get back behind the club, but he didn't have anything new to offer tactically and he didn't capture the imagination of most of the players. It didn't help when he used to turn up on the training pitch wearing a lounge suit! Then he would put us into two lines to carry out different exercises. Needless to say, that wasn't for me!

'Of course the club had no money to bring in better players, so everything just fell flat. Alec was very strong on commitment and effort, which was fine, but it just wasn't enough. I was so disappointed and basically this was the start of the end of my career. I thought where can we go as a team from here?'

20

American Express

WITH Bournemouth's agreement, MacDougall spent the summer of 1979 in America on loan to Detroit Express playing in the now-defunct North American Super League. The NASL was in its 12th season and had maintained its extraordinary ability to attract a number of world-famous stars from overseas with lucrative financial deals, as well as a number of other ex-professionals from across Europe and a splattering of home-grown American and Canadian talent. The teams operated on a franchise basis and were located across the United States, in towns and cities where their backers believed there would be sufficient support to sustain them. The competition enjoyed a good level of media coverage and attendances were still rising, with almost 75,000 people attending the previous season's grand final, or 'Soccer Bowl' as it was known, at the Giants Stadium, New Jersey, in which defending champions New York Cosmos beat Tampa Bay Rowdies.

For the 1979 season, Los Angeles Aztecs had tempted Dutch superstar Johan Cruyff out of retirement for a reported $700,000-a-year deal, while Franz Beckenbauer and Gerd Muller, both members of West Germany's 1974 World Cup-winning team, signed up for New York Cosmos and Fort Lauderdale Strikers respectively. The strongly fancied Cosmos no longer included Pele in their squad but instead boasted the Dutch pairing of Johan Neeskens and Wim Rijsbergen, former Brazil captain Carlos Alberto and England international Dennis

Tueart. Among the other British players engaged were Rodney Marsh (Tampa Bay Rowdies), Alan Ball, Kevin Hector, Willie Johnston, Phil Parkes and Trevor Whymark (Vancouver Whitecaps), Kevin Keelan (New England Tea Men), Alex Stepney (Dallas Tornado), Clyde Best (Portland Timbers) and Alan Hudson (Seattle Sounders), where MacDougall's former Bournemouth colleague Jimmy Gabriel was coach.

Detroit Express were co-owned by American sports broadcaster and promoter Roger Faulkner and England's own former player, manager and chairman turned television pundit, Jimmy Hill. The team, which had been founded the previous year, was coached by former Watford and Sheffield United manager Ken Furphy, and had won the Central Division of the American Conference in 1978 but just missed out on a place in the Soccer Bowl, losing to Fort Lauderdale Strikers in the conference semi-finals, 'Bally and Ossie had played for Philadelphia Fury the previous year and had told me what a good time they had, so I thought, "I fancy a bit of that!" Detroit was a good set-up and football had really taken off in the States. Trevor Francis played a big part in their first season and there was great excitement about him returning, especially as he had since become the first £1m player following his transfer to Nottingham Forest.'

Before Ted made his way across the pond, a player strike had threatened to disrupt the season but after this had been quickly resolved, the 24 teams got under way. There were two conferences, the American Conference and the National Conference, each having three divisions of four teams. The top 16 teams would qualify for the play-offs later in the season, and these would determine which two would eventually contest the Soccer Bowl.

Detroit again competed in the Central Division of the American Conference and were in direct competition with Houston Hurricanes, Chicago Sting and Memphis Rogues. In addition to Trevor Francis, their squad list, or 'roster' as it was known in the States, included some other familiar British players such as former Sheffield United captain Eddie Colquhoun and goalkeeper Jim Brown, ex-Manchester United and Bolton Wanderers full-back Tony Dunne, Steve Seargeant – formerly of Everton, Ipswich Town's Roger Osborne and Mick Coop from Coventry City, 'We drew crowds of around 20,000 and played our home games at the Pontiac Silverdome. That was only about a quarter of the capacity though, as the stadium held around 80,000. Trevor was the big name in the side and I enjoyed playing alongside him, and of course there were plenty of other guys I had come across before in the Football League playing with and against me. Unfortunately one of them, Terry Hennessey, the former Nottingham Forest and Derby County defender, caught me during a game in Tulsa, Oklahoma, and I suffered ligament damage as a result, which ended my season. Nonetheless, it was a good experience on the whole but unfortunately we didn't progress beyond the first round of the play-offs.'

MacDougall made 19 appearances for the Express, scored nine goals and was credited with 11 'goal assists' in a season which saw Detroit finish third in the Central Division, having won 14 of their 30 games played. In doing so they qualified as a 'wild card' for the first round of the two-legged play-offs, where their opponents were Tampa Bay Rowdies. Detroit crashed 3-0 in the first game at the Silverdome in front of a crowd of 21,539 and duly exited the competition following a 3-1 defeat in the return leg in Florida. Francis and the coach's son Keith Furphy, who had arrived at Detroit from non-league Wealdstone, had been the team's top scorers with 14 goals each.

Tampa went on to beat Philadelphia Fury and San Diego Sockers to reach the Soccer Bowl where they faced Vancouver Whitecaps, who were managed by former Blackpool and England goalkeeper Tony Waiters. The Whitecaps had beaten the star-studded favourites, New York Cosmos, in the semi-final following a shootout, 'The shootout was used regularly to decide games in the NASL as the Americans never really bought in to the concept of a draw. There had to be a winner – hence the shootout. It differed from today's penalty shootout in that the player started 35 yards out from goal and had four seconds to beat the goalkeeper and score.'

A row over players' bonuses on the eve of the Soccer Bowl threatened to split the Vancouver camp, but it was resolved in time for them to triumph at Giants Stadium. More than 50,000 spectators saw the Rowdies fall at the final hurdle for the second season running, in a game which also marked the last appearance in the career of their talisman Rodney Marsh, the former England player having decided to call time on his colourful career. The goalscoring plaudits went to former Ipswich striker Trevor Whymark, who scored both the Whitecaps' goals in their 2-1 victory. The star of the play-offs however had been Alan Ball, who scored seven goals for Vancouver during the knockout stages and was named as the NASL's Most Valuable Player,

'Bally told me the Whitecaps fans loved him and that thousands of them lined the streets to welcome the team home after they had beaten the Rowdies! I guess my spell with Detroit whetted my appetite for the American way of life. We had quite a bit of time off so I had the chance to explore a bit and it was quite an adventure really. I knew it was a country I would want to return to someday.'

21

Joining the 250 Club

BACK in Bournemouth, Alec Stock's priority was to increase competition for first-team places ahead of the new season, but to do so he needed to come up with the cash that would enable him to strengthen his squad. This duly came with the sale of popular 26-year-old centre-half Roger Brown, who became yet another player to leave the club for Norwich City in an £85,000 deal. Brown had cost the club just £10,000 when John Benson signed him from non-league AP Leamington in February 1978, so the transfer did in fact prove to be good business for the club.

As he looked around for new players, Stock was aghast at the extortionate transfer fees he was faced with. These, together with players having difficulty in finding affordable accommodation in the Bournemouth area, meant that not only was the club faced with paying a large transfer fee, it then had to subsidise the player's domestic arrangements.

Stock eventually brought in three experienced players; 29-year-old former Northampton Town and Southend United defender Neil Townsend, who arrived for £15,000 from Weymouth, plus midfielders Brian Chambers (29) from Millwall, and John Evanson (32) from Fulham for fees of £12,000 and £20,000 respectively. In addition, defenders Jeff Bryant and Jon Moore arrived on free transfers from Wimbledon and Millwall, together with former Tottenham reserve team captain Tommy Heffernan and former Orient goalkeeper John

Smeulders, while ex-Swansea striker Barrie Thomas linked up with the Cherries on a three-month trial. Meanwhile full-back Geoff Butler joined the club's coaching staff and other departures from Dean Court included winger Peter Johnson and midfielder Dave Lennard. Stock was also mindful of the need for the club to produce its own players for the future and took the first steps towards re-instating a youth policy after a three-year absence, by entering a side in the Dorset County Youth League, 'Roger Brown had done well the previous season and attracted some interest, so it was only a matter of time before Bournemouth would sell him. Alec brought in a number of experienced players but some of them were past their best I'm afraid. I came back with an open mind as to how things would go in the new season but my main aim was still to try and get the club promoted.'

Stock had a reputation throughout his long managerial career of being one of the most thoughtful and kindly of men, but he could also be a hard taskmaster when necessary and his keyword for the new season was 'enthusiasm', which he demanded from his players and urged incessantly from the supporters. By the time MacDougall had returned from the States and been cleared again to play in England, the Cherries had kicked off their season with a 4-1 aggregate defeat to John Toshack's emerging Swansea side in the first round of the League Cup, but had won their opening league game 2-0 at Rochdale thanks to goals from right-back Ian Cunningham and a penalty from Chambers. This was followed by a 1-1 draw at home to Walsall, where Heffernan scored his first goal for the club in front of a crowd of just under 5,000.

MacDougall's first game of the season, against Newport County at Dean Court on 25 August, was also his 500th appearance in the Football League and it produced a highly entertaining game from which the Cherries eventually emerged as 3-2 winners, despite having to play with ten men for almost the entire second half. Before kick-off Ted was presented with a silver salver to mark the occasion by Bournemouth vice-chairman Peter Hayward and once the game got under way Steve Massey gave the Cherries a perfect start, putting them ahead after just four minutes. Massey coolly accepted his chance following a neat one-two with Chambers but Bournemouth's lead was cancelled out when Keith Oakes equalised for County. The home side were awarded a penalty just 20 seconds into the second half which Chambers duly despatched, before being sent off after clashing with County's Dave Bruton.

It was a former Cherries player, Howard Goddard, whose near-post header brought the visitors level again but the depleted home side fought back commendably and the winning goal came from Townsend, who looped in a shot from the corner of the penalty area.

Ted's next two appearances saw successive 2-1 defeats, first at Scunthorpe and then at home to Wigan. As a result, Bournemouth's encouraging start of five points out of six suddenly became a less impressive five out of ten. Stock had made changes to his team for each game as he continued to experiment with different players and formations. As he did so, nobody could be sure of a first-team place, not even MacDougall, who found himself out of the side for six weeks, and instead made three appearances for the reserve team in the Western League, scoring four goals including a hat-trick against Dawlish at Dean Court.

While Ted waited for a recall, the team's results went from one extreme to the other. A dismal defeat at home to Halifax, played out to the accompaniment of slow hand-clapping from frustrated supporters, was followed by a remarkable performance against Tranmere, which saw the Cherries record a 5-0 victory at Prenton Park with two goals apiece from Butler and Borthwick and another from Bryant. The game would also be remembered by Kenny Allen, the 6ft 4in goalkeeper, being the victim of an attack from an elderly Rovers fan who ran on to the pitch and struck him across the backside with a walking stick.

There were two defeats against Portsmouth, a four-goal hiding at Fratton Park and an unfortunate 1-0 reverse after a much improved performance at Dean Court in front of an attendance of almost 14,000 – around 11,000 more than were present to witness goals from Butler and skipper Holder ensure victory over Hartlepool in Bournemouth's next home game – before the team gained creditable draws on the road at Walsall and York.

MacDougall returned to first-team action for the visit of Huddersfield in late October, when he came off the bench to replace Heffernan in a disappointing 3-1 defeat. The following Saturday though, Ted was restored to his regular number eight shirt against managerless Hereford, a match in which the Cherries took a two-goal lead within the first ten minutes through Chambers and Butler, but then instead of hammering home their advantage, they allowed their visitors to draw level inside half an hour and go on to claim a point.

Chambers was also on target when MacDougall scored his first goal of the season in another 2-2 draw, this time against Bradford City at Valley Parade. Now requiring just one league goal to reach the coveted 250 mark, Ted fittingly claimed it at Dean Court, completing the scoring in a convincing 4-0 victory over Rochdale. Earlier, Holder and Chambers both found the target with long-range shots and two minutes after half-time, Butler raced clear of the visitors' defence to hammer home a third goal. Then, at last, the goal the crowd had been waiting for came in the 51st minute, 'Phil Holder made a break from defence with a long ball and Gary Borthwick picked it up on the wing, clipped over a low cross and I hit it on the volley with my left foot. I was obviously delighted to get the goal and I was especially pleased it was at Dean Court. I always enjoyed them more when I knocked them in with my left foot too, as it was never my best side! I remember there was a mini pitch invasion afterwards, as some of the younger supporters ran on to congratulate me! It was a special moment and it was good that it happened in a game when the team had played so well.'

MacDougall's tally of 250 league goals, 113 of which were scored for Bournemouth, had been accomplished in 506 appearances. At the time he joined a band of 15 post-Second World War strikers who had reached the magic figure of 250, men like Arthur Rowley – still the leading hotshot of all time with 434 goals for West Bromwich Albion, Fulham, Leicester and Shrewsbury before his retirement in 1965 – Jimmy Greaves, Brian Clough and Nat Lofthouse. A measure of MacDougall's striking consistency was that his goals came at a rate of virtually one every two games, which was an excellent achievement considering he played in an era when defensive tactics were commonplace. In more modern times other strikers to reach and pass the 250 goal mark have included Alan Shearer (283 goals in 559 games), Teddy Sheringham (276 in 734) and Steve Bull (252 in 478).

Ted's landmark goal helped lift the team into the top ten and after all the chopping and changing earlier in the season, the team had now settled down with Allen in goal, Cunningham, Impey, Townsend and Ferns as the back four; Chambers, Holder, Evanson and Miller in midfield, the latter having lost his place at left-back to the emerging Ferns; and Mick Butler partnering MacDougall up front, 'The performance against Rochdale proved we could play, mind you they were second-bottom of the league at the time! Alec was trying to turn the club around and stabilise things, and when the experienced players like myself and Dusty Miller, Chambers, Evanson and Holder etc, were on song, and the younger players like Borthwick and Ferns responded, then we were a half-decent side but unfortunately it didn't always happen. That was the nature of the beast I'm afraid.'

MacDougall's third goal in successive games came in a 2-1 defeat at Hereford, where, after the Cherries had given away two more soft goals, they subsequently bombarded the home side's penalty area throughout the second half without being able to find an equaliser. It was another significant goal for MacDougall however, being his 300th in league and cup competitions.

The Cherries then embarked upon an unbeaten run of seven games, although five of these ended in draws. A goal from Holder earned them a point at Lincoln ahead of goalless stalemates against Doncaster and Peterborough at home and away at Crewe. It was with some relief therefore that Butler and MacDougall found the net against Northampton at Dean Court but the visitors still returned home with a share of the spoils. Butler was on target in both games over the Christmas period, scoring winners against Aldershot and Darlington to maintain the club's mid-table position.

Apart from the thumping at Portsmouth, away form had been good with three wins and six draws from 12 games, but disappointingly, home performances had mustered only one more point than had been gained on the road and gave the Cherries a total of 29 points from 25 games. Only league leaders Walsall had lost fewer matches away but only the bottom two clubs, Crewe and Rochdale, had been less successful at home – a fact which pretty much summed up the first half of Bournemouth's season.

The new year of 1980 was ushered in by a 5,000-plus crowd at Dean Court for the visit of promotion hopefuls Torquay, but it failed to produce the start to the new year that Stock had hoped for, as despite MacDougall scoring the Cherries' first goal of the new decade, Torquay hit back twice to take home the points, 'At least I could now say that I scored league goals in three different decades!'

A goal from Evanson secured a point at lowly Port Vale before two weeks of freezing weather brought football to a standstill. When conditions relented at the end of January, Smeulders took over in goal from the injured Allen, who had seemed likely to join Cardiff for £50,000 but, during protracted transfer negotiations, he suffered an untimely training injury. Smeulders kept a clean sheet on his debut to help earn Bournemouth a draw at Newport before producing an outstanding penalty save as Stockport were beaten 2-0 at Dean Court, the Cherries' goals coming from Butler and MacDougall. Butler had also been the subject of transfer speculation, Aldershot having bid £20,000 for his services – which the club were prepared to accept – but the player turned down the move.

The club were still losing money and while that continued they would always be open to offers for players as the directors sought to try and make ends meet. It was frustrating for the supporters but there was little alternative and although Stock had begun to resurrect the club's youth policy, it was likely to take several seasons before the club could hope to see some of these players forming the nucleus of the first team. The present team had just one locally produced young player with promise in full-back Ferns, the only other 'home-grown' player was Glasgow-born right-back Ian Cunningham, a Scottish youth international and the sole survivor of the previous Cherries youth side.

The reserve team also needed to provide a better stepping stone to the first team and with this in mind Stock switched the side from the Western League to the London Midweek League for the following season. Behind the scenes there was plenty of hard work going on to try and provide the club with a financial lifeline, with valuable additional revenue beings created through sponsorship and lottery ticket sales. In addition, the club had collected 4,824 empty cigarette packets from supporters over the previous year, enough to earn them £500 commission from Rothmans of Pall Mall – a line in fundraising that is unlikely to be repeated today.

When January's bad weather relented, it left the Cherries facing two long trips to the north of England in the space of four days, first when they visited Wigan in a re-arranged fixture on a Wednesday night where although MacDougall was again on target, they were unable to snatch a point. Then the following Saturday, perhaps not surprisingly, a rather weary looking performance saw them beaten 2-0 at mid-table Halifax. In mid-February, Lawrie McMenemy brought his Southampton side to Dean Court in in a testimonial match for long-serving former Bournemouth club secretary Harry Stace. The game went some way to compensate for the FA Cup disappointment of the previous season and it gave the Cherries fans a chance to see Phil Boyer in action again, together with England stars Alan Ball, Charlie

George, Dave Watson and Mick Channon, who had re-joined the club the previous September.

The previous day, McMenemy had pulled off an amazing transfer scoop when he announced the signing of England captain Kevin Keegan for what McMenemy described as a 'giveaway' fee of £425,000 from Hamburg SV. To the disappointment of those present at Dean Court however, Keegan did not make an appearance.

In the absence of Holder, MacDougall captained the Cherries in a memorable match against his former club, which was played in front of a crowd of well over 7,000. Saints took the lead in the tenth minute when Holmes drilled the ball past Smeulders following Ball's pass, but Bournemouth stuck at their task and broke up the visitors' rhythm before equalising in the 29th minute thanks to a shot from young winger Mark Elliott. Elliott, on trial from Cardiff, also played a key role when the Cherries took the lead ten minutes later. Massey's corner was only half-cleared and the winger's shot from the edge of the penalty area was deflected past Wells by Bryant. The second half saw Ball, Holmes and Baker take charge of midfield and it was another trialist, 22-year-old Andy Rogers, whose cross led to George scrambling a shot past Smeulders to level the score before Holmes struck the winning goal with a shot from 20 yards, 'For a testimonial match, this was quite a competitive game with local bragging rights at stake! It was good to see Lawrie and to be in the company of the Saints lads again, we chatted afterwards and Bally mentioned to me that Blackpool had sounded him out with a view to appointing him as manager. He was keen to give management a try in the near future and he asked me if I would fancy joining him as coach should the opportunity arise. At the time the idea appealed to me because I wanted to get into coaching and I wasn't all that happy with things at Bournemouth.'

MacDougall's goal in a comfortable 2-0 win over Tranmere a few days later eventually turned out to be his last not only in a Bournemouth shirt, but also the last he would score in the Football League. Events about to unfold at Blackpool meant Ted's final game for the Cherries was on 23 February, an uninspiring goalless draw against York, during which he was substituted in the second half. His request to be released from his contract four days later followed Ball's appointment as Blackpool player-manager, and he was granted a free transfer by Bournemouth which enabled him to link up with his former Saints team-mate at Bloomfield Road.

MacDougall's second spell at Bournemouth had seen him make a further 52 league appearances and score another 16 goals. He left the club having scored 119 goals in 198 league appearances in his two spells at Dean Court. With a further 25 goals in cup ties, he had smashed every post-war scoring record for the Cherries, 'Bally got the player-manager's job at Blackpool and he asked me to go along with him as player-coach, and to be honest I just needed to get out. Unfortunately, Bournemouth was a very different club to the one I had left in 1972. All the financial problems made things difficult and despite Alec's efforts to restore some dignity and pride, there were some poor players there – on and off the pitch – not what I call pros. They took things just because they were there to be taken and a few of them had chips on their shoulders. The team were heading for a mid-table finish, which was at least an improvement on the previous year I suppose. I was grateful that the club were good enough to let me go without asking for a fee – but then when I got to Blackpool everything went south for me.'

22

Holding the Fort

THERE has been a football club in Blackpool since 1887 but it remains best remembered for the exciting team assembled at Bloomfield Road during the late 1940s and early 1950s. Under the captaincy of Harry Johnston and blessed with the attacking flair of Stanley (later Sir Stanley) Matthews and Stan Mortensen, Blackpool reached three FA Cup finals during this period, winning the trophy in the famous 1953 'Matthews Final' against Bolton Wanderers. The 'Pool also provided four players, Matthews, Mortensen, Johnston and debutant Ernie Taylor, for the full England international side in the same year.

Having come close to winning the First Division championship on several occasions, Blackpool achieved their highest league placing when they finished as runners-up to champions Manchester United in 1955/56. The 'Tangerines', as they were nicknamed locally in recognition of the colour of their playing shirts, typified in their spirit and through their play the new exciting era that the country was heading in to. When ill health finally persuaded manager Joe Smith to hand over the reins to former Blackpool player Ron Suart in 1958, he could look back on 23 years in charge at Bloomfield Road during which time he had transformed the club into one of the great forces in English football.

From pretty much that moment onwards though, Blackpool began to fall into a decline which eventually led to the loss of their

First Division status under Mortensen's management at the end of the 1966/67 season. His eventual successor, the former Arsenal assistant manager Les Shannon, brought them back to the top flight in 1970 but their stay was to last only one season, during which Shannon resigned and was replaced by Bob Stokoe. Stokoe had played 261 games for Newcastle United before trying his hand at management, with Blackpool being his fourth role. Unable to restore the club to its former glories, Stokoe himself resigned during the 1972/73 season and was succeeded by ex-Burnley player and manager Harry Potts.

Former Tangerines favourite and Scottish international forward Allan Brown took over the reins in 1976, but less than two years later with the club in a mid-table position in the Second Division, Brown was sacked after an argument with club chairman Bill Cartmell which spilled over into the newspapers. Coach Jimmy Meadows was placed in temporary charge of the team but only one win in their last 15 matches saw Blackpool tumble into football's third tier for the first time in their history. Stokoe returned and guided the team to 12th in the Third Divison in 1978/79 before walking out the following summer, leaving his former coach Stan Ternent to take charge but after just five months, he was dismissed to make way for Alan Ball as player-manager.

New chairman Peter Lawson had pursued the 34-year-old Ball for some weeks before his appointment in March 1980. Ball was handed a three-year contract, which was greeted ecstatically by the club's supporters who took it as an indication that the glory days were about to return. Born in Farnworth, Lancashire, Ball had made 126 league appearances for the Tangerines between 1962 and 1966, scoring 45 goals, and had been one of the most exciting players ever seen at Bloomfield Road. A tireless midfielder, he was transferred to Everton in 1966 for £112,000 then five years later went to Arsenal for another record fee, this time £220,000. Ball played 76 times for England, including the 1966 World Cup Final when he was only 21 years of age. His England days had ended dramatically when he was axed by Don Revie in 1975 shortly after he had been appointed as team captain. More recently he had of course helped Southampton gain promotion back to the First Division and enjoyed spells playing abroad in America and Canada, 'Alan was certainly one of the most popular and exciting players during his time at Blackpool, but he could be an extremely fiery character at times. When he was taking his first steps in league football, Sir Stanley Matthews, one of England's finest players, was still in the side and part of Bally's job as an inside-forward was to feed the ball out to him. Well, Alan kept playing the ball inside the full-back expecting Sir Stan to run on to it but unfortunately he wanted every ball at his feet. When he confronted Bally and demanded this, Alan, despite only being a teenager, turned to him and shouted, "When I play these balls, you get on the fucking end of them!" Matthews turned to the bench and said, "You need to get this man off!"'

The first suggestion that Ball's tenure as manager of Blackpool would not be destined to run smoothly came immediately after he was appointed. Ball was prevented from officially taking over straight away as he was contracted to return to Vancouver Whitecaps for the 1980 NASL season, where he was to assume the role of player-coach. A short-term transfer had been agreed with Southampton to enable him to do so but although Saints had agreed to release him to play and coach overseas, they were not prepared to release him in order that he could play for or manage another club in England, 'Not very much went smoothly really, right from the start! When Alan and I had to go up and meet the press at Blackpool, we travelled up the night before but stopped off at the popular Tramp club in Jermyn Street, London. We had a bottle of champagne and before long it's 2am. So Alan asks me, "What are we going to do now?" I said, "Don't worry, I'll drive," so we head off up the M1 and after a while I got a feeling we were heading up the wrong side of the country. We needed to be on the west side of course and were heading up the east. Anyway I headed across country and eventually the two of us ended up together in a double bed at Alan's father's house, sleeping it off!

'Anyway, we made it for the press conference in the end, and were pictured wearing floppy hats and holding a scarf! We were greeted by some of the coaching staff who had stayed on for a few days to show us around and hand over the keys. Of course Bally now had to fire them, so that wasn't a great start! Bally was in the crazy situation of being the first person to manage one league club while still under contract to play for another. Lawrie told Alan's wife Lesley that if he was still in the country on 22 March he would be playing for Saints against Forest, so he couldn't delay his departure any longer than that.'

Ball duly left for Canada on 21 March and Southampton duly relinquished his contract once he had joined Vancouver, while Blackpool paid them £25,000 in compensation for allowing Ball to take over at the club upon his return, 'I just wanted to get into coaching but Bally couldn't get out of the second year of a two-year contract with Tony Waiters at Vancouver. The Whitecaps just would not budge, so I was left to take charge of the team! They had lost seven of their previous ten games and my job was to somehow avoid relegation. Phew! There were some players at the wrong end of their careers, two or three old pros there who had done it all and were on big money, and it was difficult. Fred Davies joined me from Bournemouth to help with the coaching and we were left to run the side with the help of the club's general manager, Freddie Scott. It was a big responsibility after being a player.'

Ternent had initially managed to stabilise the club but his hopes of building on the budding striking partnership between Northern Ireland international Derek Spence and former Exeter striker Tony Kellow had taken a blow when Spence suffered an injury in August which kept him out of the side for six weeks. Then, at the end of December, Spence joined Southend in a £125,000 part-exchange deal which brought 26-year-old midfielder Colin Morris to Bloomfield Road. It was Ball's decision however to allow Kellow, a £105,000 signing in November 1978, to re-join Exeter for £65,000 at the beginning of March, following the signing of experienced striker Paul Fletcher from Burnley the previous month. The move enabled Fletcher to link up again with his former Burnley colleague Peter Noble, who had moved to the 'Pool for a £20,000 fee in January, but the sale of Kellow was unpopular with the club's supporters and not quickly forgotten.

Blackpool found themselves just four places off the bottom of the Third Division when MacDougall donned the tangerine shirt for the first time against mid-table Exeter on 15 March. The side that day included club record signing Jackie Ashurst, who Ternent had signed from Sunderland for £132,400 the previous October, while another former Sunderland midfielder, 1973 FA Cup-winning captain, Bobby Kerr, was named as substitute, his first appearance in three months, having been sidelined through injury. Ted was partnered up front by 29-year-old Fletcher, the scorer of 71 goals in 293 games for Burnley before making his 'Pool debut in February. The full line-up was: Hesford, Gardner, Pashley, Ashurst, McEwan, Doyle, Morris, Fletcher, MacDougall, Drummy, Harrison. Substitute: Kerr. The game proved to be one of few chances, a single goal from Fletcher being enough to give the Seasiders victory in front of a crowd of 4,155, 'It was a good start really, the sort of thing that often happens in football after a change of manager, although it doesn't always last!

'My first training confrontation as coach involved a really good professional, Peter "Nobby" Noble. A few seasons ago we had been competing for the honour of leading goalscorer in the First Division. Now we were playing five-a-side at Blackpool and I was acting as referee! I gave a wrong decision, so Nobby just booted the ball away and came over to confront me. He was a Geordie and he just kept talking, going on and on, I kept saying, "Peter, Peter, Peter," three times I said his name but Nobby wouldn't stop talking. In the end I said to him, "Peter, chill out, I'm under pressure, you're under pressure, we are all under pressure – so go and get the ball." And thankfully he did!'

Hopes of continuing this upturn in form were quickly dashed after away defeats at Carlisle and promotion-chasing Sheffield Wednesday which saw Blackpool drop down to 23rd in the table. Having left himself out of the side that lost at Hillsborough, MacDougall returned to the starting 11 for the home game against Millwall at the end of March together with Noble, who had recovered after injury, but Kerr was missing again and would be out for the rest of the season. By half-time the 'Pool were two goals down but a second-half recovery, which brought goals from Noble and Fletcher, proved enough to salvage a point. A goal from Morris earned a draw at home to Barnsley on Good Friday, but a 3-1 defeat at Hull the following day left the Tangerines in need of something special in their last six games if the club was to avoid relegation.

Having failed to score in his five appearances, MacDougall decided to leave himself out of the side once again, this time in favour of the 6ft 3in 20-year-old striker Dave Bamber, 'In the previous six games we had won one, drawn two and lost three. We had been competitive each time – in fact the team had never really got thrashed all season. Our defensive record had been good but we didn't score enough goals, and that had been the problem since the turn of the year really. I hadn't been able to change that and I thought big Dave Bamber deserved a chance.

'We now had six games left and unless our performances improved, the writing was on the wall for us. I couldn't make too many changes, we didn't have a big squad to work with anyway. Dermot Drummy had come on loan from Arsenal but after he had returned to Highbury, I brought Jimmy Weston back into the side in midfield. Bobby Kerr played two games then got injured again but had been out for a large part of the season anyway. I think some of the experienced lads like Peter Noble and Paul Fletcher were a bit unsure about me to begin with but after a while they responded, and then we beat Carlisle and were on a roll.'

Bamber's first senior goal, together with another from Stan McEwan, gave Blackpool a 2-1 win at Bloomfield Road, which was followed by a 2-0 victory at Oxford United, where Fletcher and Wayne Harrison were this time on target. A vital relegation battle against fellow strugglers Mansfield saw Fletcher net his fifth goal for the 'Pool to give them a first-half lead and although the visitors fought back to grab a draw, the point gained was enough to lift Blackpool out of the relegation zone and into 20th place.

A McEwan penalty secured a crucial victory against Reading at Elm Park before a goalless draw at home to Chester ensured that a win in their final game at mid-table Rotherham would be enough to guarantee survival. MacDougall had restored himself to the side in place of Bamber for the previous two games but had still failed to find the net, and while he drew another blank at Millmoor, first-half goals from Morris and Fletcher proved enough to win the game and steer the Tangerines to safety, 'To win that game and avoid relegation was a fantastic feeling! We finished 18th in the end, two points clear of the drop. Of course it was nothing more than a start, that's all, but I was delighted to have helped prevent the club being relegated for a second time in three years. It had been tough holding the fort while Bally was in Vancouver but in the end I liked it, especially the coaching side. Just as well because it was the worst part of my playing career – I was awful! Fortunately the team did superbly under a lot of pressure in those last six games. Home attendances picked up a little, though they were still less than 6,000, but the supporters got behind the team especially towards the end.

'So now I thought, "That's great," I'd held the fort, it was just a question of waiting for Bally to come back in July and everything would take off from there. Little did I know that the following season I would lose my career, my wife, my family, my home, just about everything really in a very short space of time.'

23

On the Rocks

HAVING fulfilled his obligations at Vancouver Whitecaps, Alan Ball finally took full charge at Blackpool in time for the start of pre-season training in July 1980. By this time he had already been restored to celebrity status in the town and was as much in demand for personal appearances that summer as any of the club's current players, as MacDougall recalls, 'Blackpool was a place where a player could get himself in to all sorts of bother. There were so many beauty queens about it was unbelievable! Me and Bally were among the judges for the Miss Blackpool competition, along with all the stars of the summer shows. It was a big beauty pageant, only one step down from Miss United Kingdom I think, and when we saw the girls they were all saying, "All right Ted, okay Alan?" because they all knew us! The other judges were staring at us and we thought, "This is not looking good!"'

Soon after training had commenced, Ball described his players as the most unfit group he had ever seen. He knew he had to make changes to the side that had only just managed to avoid relegation at the end of the previous season and was anxious to lower the age of his squad. There were a few players who were at the wrong end of their careers, some of whom were also among the highest paid, and Ball was very conscious of the need to reduce the club's wage bill. He had already released two of Stokoe's expensive signings from Sunderland, Bobby Kerr and Dick Malone, the previous May and now began to trawl the country for promising young players, 'Bally had set himself high standards throughout his career and left the players in no doubt that he expected them to do the same. The problem was they were just not good enough to do many of the things that came naturally to him and he couldn't really understand why.'

For long periods during pre-season training Ball could be seen on the verge of exasperation as he barked out orders to less talented and totally bemused players. By the time he made his re-appearance for the 'Pool against Blackburn in the Anglo-Scottish Cup at the end of July, his efforts seemed to have had some effect as the side put in an impressive display and ran out 2-0 winners through goals from Bamber and McEwan. This was followed by a 2-1 success at Carlisle and a single-goal victory at Preston, as Ball used the pre-season competition to try out a number of his younger players. Eighteen-year-old midfielder Andy Brockbank was employed as an emergency full-back, while Ormskirk-born midfielder John Deary (17), and emerging winger Andy Welsh were also handed an opportunity to shine as the team went on to qualify for the quarter-finals of the competition later in the season.

However, perhaps understandably, during the course of these games, Ball had noticed a tendency for the players to look for him as soon as they got the ball and to play through him at any opportunity rather than to play their own game, 'In the beginning many of the younger lads were a bit in awe of Ball, but they soon got over it and by the time the league season got under way, morale was good and we all looked forward to starting afresh.'

Before the league fixtures began, Blackpool beat Walsall in a two-legged first-round tie in the League Cup. MacDougall started the first game at Fellowes Park but was still unable to break his scoring duck for the Tangerines but two goals from McEwan, one a penalty, and another strike from Morris gave them a 3-2 advantage. In the return leg at Bloomfield Road, Fletcher replaced MacDougall and netted in a comfortable 3-1 win, with Morris and Ashurst also on target to give the 'Pool a 6-3 aggregate victory.

Despite Ball's intention to build a new young side, the Blackpool team that took to the field for the club's first league game of the 1980/81 season showed only four changes from the one that had finished the previous campaign. Ball made his league comeback for the club in place of the departed Weston, Gary Williams, a £40,000 summer signing from Swedish club Djurgaarden made his debut at left-back in place of Terry Pashley, while Bobby Doyle and Dave Hockaday came in for Noble and MacDougall respectively. Hockaday and Fletcher were the scorers in the 2-1 opening-day victory over Swindon at Bloomfield Road, although Ball's outstanding performance grabbed the headline in that evening's local paper – 'Bally saves 'Pool's bacon'. Next came away draws at Rotherham and newly promoted Huddersfield, while there was speculation linking Ball with the manager's job at another of his previous clubs, Everton. The player-manager finally ended it all by stating publicly that he had signed a contract with Blackpool which he intended to honour, while the hard-working Gordon Lee remained under pressure in the hot seat at the Merseyside club.

MacDougall had returned to the team in the 1-1 draw at Leeds Road, where he came on as substitute for Fletcher in a game which also marked the debut of central defender Colin Greenall. At the age of 16 years and 237 days, Greenall became Blackpool's youngest player at senior level and replaced the injured Ashurst. The Tangerines' first defeat of the season came in the second round of the League Cup, in which they were ironically drawn to play Everton. Ted did not feature in the first leg at Goodison Park, where as Ball continued to shuffle his pack, Lee's First Division side emerged as 3-0 winners. MacDougall appeared again as substitute during Portsmouth's visit at the end of August, but made little impression, as Pompey, another newly promoted club, inflicted a first home defeat on the 'Pool with a 2-0 victory.

A McEwan penalty and another goal from Morris earned Blackpool a creditable 2-2 draw in the return leg against Everton, although the visitors' aggregate lead was never threatened at any stage. By now, Ball had paid Walsall £35,000 for their 24-year-old defender Ricky Spragia and after making his first appearance against the Merseysiders, he made his league debut against Fulham at Craven Cottage. Spragia replaced Greenall in defence and also scored the Tangerines' first goal in an impressive 2-1 victory. The ever-reliable Morris added a second in a game which saw MacDougall plough a lone furrow up front following Ball's decision to replace Noble with midfielder Deary. The following Wednesday though, Ted finally scored in Blackpool's 2-1 victory over Kilmarnock in the first leg of the Anglo-Scottish Cup quarter-final at Bloomfield Road, 'How could I forget it? I think that was the only goal I ever scored for Blackpool! I remember there was a very small crowd, around 4,000 and I believe Wayne Harrison scored our other goal. It was a poor time for me as a player though.'

Another goal apiece from Morris and Harrison ensured the 'Pool took a point from a home draw against Hull, but it was a match that was watched by another disappointing attendance of just over 6,000. The Tangerines then travelled to face Sheffield United on Tuesday 16 September, 'I was no longer making much impact on the field and my last game as a pro turned out to be this one against Sheffield United at Bramall Lane, although I didn't realise it at the time. In the end I quit because my marriage went sour. I never forget my Dad telling me, "Son, you've lost it," and I said to him, "You bet your life I have."

'I had been at Blackpool for about six months and I was still enjoying the coaching but results on the pitch had not really been anything special. The supporters had been expecting big things pretty much as soon as Bally returned and I could see that wasn't going to happen. The club had been in decline for some time and it was going to take a while to change everything around. Then the chairman, Peter Lawson, who had been instrumental in taking Alan back to Blackpool, was voted off the board at the club's AGM and one or two directors started to question his actions. I liked the players and I gave it a good crack, in fact I got letters from Peter Noble and Paul Fletcher afterwards saying that although they thought I was a bit arrogant from a distance, they had discovered by working with me that I was a great lad, which was nice.

'My routine was that I'd go home at weekends. I was flying up regularly from Bournemouth and Manchester and used to get picked up and driven to Blackpool at the other end. The day before the Sheffield game I phoned home to check everything was all right and my wife said, "I don't want you to come home anymore."

'We never had a row or anything like that. I was shattered and Bally took me off at half-time. I flew back to Bournemouth the next day and Alan told me to take as long as I needed. It came as a complete shock, I lost my family, lost my house, lost my way, lost my profession so yes, I certainly did lose it. There are no winners in separation or divorce. Thankfully Joan and I get on great now though, no problem – which is fantastic, very nice.'

24

Time to Re-Build

'I DID all I could to put my marriage right but it didn't work and Joan and I ended up getting a divorce. I had a lovely house in Meyrick Park, Bournemouth overlooking the English Channel and backing on to the golf course, everything I needed really but life sometimes has a way of coming back and kicking you in the teeth. Although I still had my shops and everything, I left the house in the spring of 1981 and moved in to The Mill Arms at Dunbridge, near Romsey in Hampshire. The pub was a free house which I had originally bought for my parents, so I lived upstairs and threw myself into the business.

'It was a listed building in the countryside, about 180 years old, and a bit off the beaten track. Between us, Dad and I refurbished the lounge bar, he did a lot of the electrical work and some of the brick-work and tiling while I did the demolition and painting. One lunch-time, we were knocking through a wall when I looked up and saw a big coach pulling into the car park. It was Bally and the Blackpool side! They were playing at Plymouth that day and had dropped in to see me. My former Manchester United team-mate Willie Morgan had come back from America to help Alan out at Bloomfield Road and it was great to see them both. All the guys were trying to get me to go with them on the bus. It was fantastic, absolutely fantastic! I missed all this, but I had decided to follow the typical ex-footballer's way and get into the pub.

'Early the following year though, I went away to Barbados for a few weeks on my own but while there my life changed direction again, as I met my second and present wife, Lyne St-Amand, who I've now been married to for over 30 years – so I wasn't on my own for long! We met at a jazz club, having been introduced by her cousin but when I first asked Lyne to dance, she refused and left soon afterwards. Not a good start, but a couple of days later I saw her again at the Sandy Beach Club Hotel and this time we made a better connection. Later in our relationship, Lyne admitted that she initially thought I was far too arrogant for her taste and that was why she had refused to dance!

'Unfortunately, while I was enjoying myself in Barbados, things were not going so well for Bally on the football front and by the time I flew back to England, he had left Blackpool and the club was heading for the Fourth Division.'

A run of just two wins in 23 league games culminated in Ball's dismissal after a defeat at Brentford in February 1981. He had by this time lost the backing of the club's supporters and had not helped his cause when he bitterly attacked them after an FA Cup victory over neighbours Fleetwood in November, complaining that the majority of the 10,000 crowd had not wanted Blackpool to win as much as he had. Ball stubbornly refused to acknowledge calls for a change in the team's style of play and was eventually replaced by former manager Allan Brown, although he could not prevent the club from being relegated at the end of the season. Meanwhile, Ball resumed his playing career back at Southampton, 'Blackpool was a disaster really. Bally wanted to build this new young side and he unearthed one or two good players – Colin Greenall and Eamonn Collins eventually made the club £1.5m – but time was against him. The supporters expected instant success and the club had financial problems as well.

'I didn't remain in England for long, I was keen to see more of Lyne, who was French-Canadian from Montreal, so I went over to Canada to join her in May, then we fell in love and the usual stuff!'

MacDougall was tempted out of retirement by Salisbury City manager Dave Verity upon his return to England the following August. After returning to action with the Southern League club, Ted then had further spells in non-league football with Poole Town, Gosport Borough and Totton during 1981 and 1982. Ted also coached Andover briefly the following year but spent the summer of 1982 playing in Australia, 'My fall from the First Division into retirement had been extremely quick. I played for these teams but my head wasn't in it really. I don't know why I did it, I guess it was to help out old friends, things like that. I had a big row with Graham Dexter, the owner at Poole and he asked me to leave, so I told him that was fine by me. I don't remember playing for Gosport but you're probably right! I only played a few games for any of them though and even played for my pub's Sunday morning side in the local Commercial Houses League.

'The former Southampton winger, John Sydenham, invited me over to Australia to play for a team he was running in Perth. By this time I needed some time away from the pub, my beautiful Lyne and I had got engaged, so I left my Mum and Dad to run things and the two of us set off down under. To be honest I had bought the pub for them in the first place, not for me.

'John's team was called Floreat Athena and the club had its roots in the local Greek community. What a nightmare they turned out to be! Let's just say they weren't very good. In fact I called Bally and asked him to come over and help, which he did. The first game we played together I scored two goals. I just made the runs and Bally picked me out with a pass. Eventually I left and moved to Melbourne, where I tried to play for South Melbourne, who were managed by Tommy Docherty. Would you believe it!

'Ironically he wanted to sign me then, which just showed how bad the other players must have been, but the club already had its quota of four overseas players so he couldn't. He had this foreign lad playing in the reserves that he didn't even know about. It meant I had ten days to either find a club or go home and I ended up playing for a largely Hungarian side in Sydney called St George Saints. They were managed by a guy called Frank Arok, who went on to manage Australia's national team, and we won the league. I had a fantastic time out there in the end, the goulash was good and Lyne and I were enjoying life together.

'When we came back we made a big effort to really get the pub going and increase the turnover. It was doing okay but I felt it could do better, so I closed it down for a short while, and spent about £40,000 refurbishing the place. We lived above the pub and installed a carvery and brought in chefs and extra staff, and as a result it began to make double or triple what it did before. A number of the Saints players became regular customers, Bally and Kevin Keegan lived close by and they would come in along with Mick Channon and we used to have some laughs. Mind you, Channon was still struggling with his adjectives, "Get them fucking drinks on the bar you fucker!" normally being his first words upon arrival!

'But I soon found that pub work was hard work, Mondays were the same as Fridays, Tuesdays were the same as Sundays, just different levels of business, but each day was tough. Running the pub did wonders for my personality though and I lost the "attitude" that I had as a player. As I became more "human", the better I did, and the more I enjoyed it. It wasn't all about me any longer, it was about me remembering which beer a person had to drink and what type of glass he liked to drink it from. People used to come in to see me and I became more outgoing and I gradually became a different person really.

'Before I left Australia, Frank Arok invited me back for another year but some weeks later he called me to say the club couldn't offer me a further contract after all. I cried the blues and told Frank I had a car and furniture to dispose of over there, so they paid for me to go across and deal with it. On the way, Lyne and I stayed for a week in Hong Kong with Bobby Moore, who was manager of a team out there. Funnily enough the movie on the flight out was *Escape to Victory*, the film about Allied POWs during World War Two, who play a game of football against a German team. The film starred Michael Caine and Sylvester Stallone of course, but received more attention because it also featured a number of professional footballers including Bobby and Pele.

'When Bobby picked us up at the airport I told him that I had just been watching him in the film! I remarked that they looked pretty healthy for POWs, all of them seemed to have red, rosy cheeks and Bobby laughed. Apparently they spent six weeks filming in Hungary, and each night they would all go to a restaurant and drink red wine and have a party. Bobby had a high regard for Michael Caine but less so for Sylvester Stallone, who he described as a "typical Hollywood type". Everyone else was good as gold and one day, Pele had to take some penalties against Stallone and was so fed up with him, he nearly belted his head off!

'Bobby was going through a divorce at this time which was all over the tabloids, the paparazzi were up trees near his home and all sorts of stuff was going on. Having not long been through a divorce myself, I was amazed at the way Bobby handled things. I will never forget, one evening he took Lyne and I out for a meal at a restaurant overlooking the South China Sea. He bought a bottle of 1966 vintage Taylor port and we sat there drinking it together in temperatures of 80 degrees. Absolute quality, one of the most wonderful evenings of my life, really.

'As we chatted, Bobby asked me if I could still play and if I would be interested in turning out for his team. I went along and watched a game but it looked more like kung fu than football with plenty of high tackling. I tried to strike up a conversation with Micky Horswill, who had enjoyed a good career in England with Sunderland and Manchester City but his jaw was wired up – yes he had been kung fu'd during a game out there!

'Bob was a great, great man, I loved him and I was so upset when he passed away. He was special, he looked after me at West Ham and he was just a great pro.

'Then we went to Sydney, sorted out my belongings and returned to the pub. Eventually the hard work took its toll and we decided to cash in, sold everything, including my shops, where my business partner George Webb bought me out, and Lyne and I took a holiday in Portugal. So here I was, in my mid-30s with a whole life ahead of me. I thought I had finished with football and I had no idea what I was going to do next. Eventually, Lyne and I decided to move to Colorado and while I was there I learned to ski. We went skiing every weekend and really got into it.

'This was something I was never allowed to do while I played football of course and I found I really enjoyed it. I also started coaching again at the Air Force Academy, where they had superb facilities. I loved the lads there, they were the future officers. Then after about six months I thought about going to Vancouver and I asked Lyne what it was like there? She said it rained a lot so I thought, "Great (not)!" I phoned Bally, who had played there of course, and we ended up going anyway! We drove there, got married in 1985 and stayed for about 12 years.

'Unfortunately I couldn't work in Canada for the first six months until I received my full immigration status. It became a bit depressing really, our dog came over from England and was welcomed with open arms, while I was hauled into a room and interrogated! Once I was able to re-join the working ranks, I spent seven years in women's clothes. This was because Lyne was a fashion designer and she started manufacturing ladies' garments in a factory of about 6,000 square feet. So I had gone from a men's environment to a women's environment. Instead of blokes coming up to me and asking me what the problem was, I had to deal with women who would sometimes just burst into tears!

'Lyne fired me more than once for saying the wrong things to them. She took me back on each time but I had to remember to tell the ladies how much I loved their hair, their shoes etc. "Ooh, how lovely!" It was okay for a while but eventually drove me daft and then Lyne fired me again, so I decided to go into property development, which I did well in.

'I felt happier in the building trade where I was dealing with about 60 different tradesmen who were all basically liars! We had some people build a place for ourselves and I thought, "I can make a mess of doing that just as well as these guys!" They'd tell me they would be there to do a job the following day and I used to say, "Yeah, and the cheque will be in the post." But there was terrific banter going on and I liked that. We built five or six houses and tried to design them like show homes. Lyne was very good at matching colours together, if it had been left to me it would have looked crap! We had a super lifestyle and I made good money, more than I did in the whole of my playing career, but I wanted to get back into football. It was the banter I missed, the dressing room and all that kind of stuff.

'I should have stayed in property development really, but I had a call from a British guy called Alan Churchard who was the director of coaching for the British Columbia Soccer Association. He needed someone to look after an under-12 squad and he asked me if I would like to come and do some coaching. Now I hadn't done any coaching since the early 1980s and my initial reaction was that I've had my own daughter and Lyne's son David was in his early teens, so if this guy thinks I'm going to look after somebody else's kids he's got another think coming.

'Anyway, a bit reluctantly, I went along and it was great, I really loved it. So I started my own academy and all these lads came and joined me. I signed them all up for a year and took them through. Among them was Terry Dunfield, who later signed for Manchester City and played for them in the Premier League. I had been bitten by the football bug once again!'

25

Cherries in the Red

DESPITE being based on the opposite side of the Atlantic, MacDougall continued to follow the fortunes of his former clubs in England, and those of AFC Bournemouth in particular. Since Ted left in 1980, the club had first appointed David Webb to succeed Alec Stock as manager and the former Southampton, Chelsea and Derby County defender guided the Cherries to promotion back to the Third Division at the conclusion of the 1981/82 campaign after six seasons in the league's basement. The following season, the League Cup, or 'Milk Cup' as it had become known, brought a two-legged tie against Manchester United and despite exiting the competition 4-2 on aggregate, the club had the compensation of a healthy boost to its finances before Webb was sensationally dismissed in December, following several controversial moves behind the scenes. Coach Harry Redknapp took caretaker charge but started his managerial career in disastrous fashion, with a record 9-0 defeat against Lincoln City on an icy pitch at Sincil Bank.

Early in 1983, chairman Harold Walker bowed to mounting pressure and sold his majority shareholding in the club to a Guernsey-based company called Wigbourne Holdings, the club's financial affairs being put in the control of former Rotherham United and Aston Villa defender Brian Tiler. Former Sheffield Wednesday captain Don Megson became the club's new manager but soon afterwards it was discovered that the sale of the club had breached Football League rules because of the involvement of entrepreneur Anton Johnson. Johnson, the wealthy 'Mr Fixit' of Football, also known as 'The King of Clubs', had been involved in similar takeovers at Rotherham and Southend, however his ownership of more than one club was in contravention of League regulations. Nonetheless, before a remarkable season came to an end, Johnson managed to secure George Best's signature for Bournemouth and the wayward genius made five appearances for the Cherries but failed to show up for two others.

Nearly a year was to elapse before in January 1984, Rodney Barton, a local builder, was able to bring ownership of the club back to the town. By then Redknapp had taken over again as manager, this time on a permanent basis following the dismissal of Megson. The team continued to struggle badly in the league but became celebrities overnight when they beat holders Manchester United 2-0 in the third round of the FA Cup at Dean Court. Despite exiting the competition in the next round at Middlesbrough, the club managed not only to avoid relegation but went on to enjoy more cup success when they became the first winners of the Associate Members Cup by beating Hull City 2-1 in the final at Boothferry Park.

The signing of Colin Clarke from Tranmere Rovers in the summer of 1985 proved to be a masterstroke by Redknapp, the Irishman scoring 26 goals in the league the following season before starring for Northern Ireland in the 1986 World Cup. Upon his return, he was the subject of a £400,000 transfer to Southampton, which provided the Cherries boss with the cash to transform what had been a mid-table side into one that would gain promotion to the second tier of English football for the first time in the club's history. Victory at home to Rotherham in their final game of the 1986/87 season brought unprecedented scenes as players and supporters celebrated together upon the Cherries' promotion as Third Division champions.

The club went on to spend three seasons in the Second Division under Redknapp's tutelage but survival at the higher level proved a great challenge both on and off the field. Barton was forced to resign as chairman in the wake of his company's financial difficulties and the team just managed to keep clear of relegation in a difficult first season. The second, however, saw the £60,000 arrival of former England international forward Luther Blissett from Watford, together with the gifted young midfielder Ian Bishop, a £35,000 signing from Carlisle, and the pair provided the team with a cutting edge. The Cherries went on to finish the 1988/89 season in 12th position, with Blissett scoring 19 league goals, and they were unlucky to again exit the FA Cup at the hands of Manchester United after earning a replay at Old Trafford.

Safety requirements meant that the ground capacity was cut to just 11,000 at Dean Court the following summer and as the club continued to try and find a site for a new stadium, they also continued to spend heavily in a bid to consolidate their position in the Second Division. To help balance the books, Bishop moved to First Division Manchester City in a player-plus-cash deal worth £725,000. However, the new season brought a series of injuries to key players, particularly after Christmas and the situation was made worse by the forced sale of popular striker Paul Moulden due to financial pressures, (Moulden was valued at £260,000 in the deal that took Bishop to Maine Road), and as results went against them, the team dropped from a comfortable mid-table position and eventually fell into the bottom three.

Everything rested on the final game against Leeds, who needed to win to clinch the league title, while Bournemouth required the points to avoid relegation. Leeds won 1-0 to send the Cherries down but the appalling behaviour of the Yorkshire club's followers, many having travelled to the game on the May Bank Holiday weekend without tickets, brought scenes of running battles with riot police and damage to many properties throughout the town. A number of Bournemouth supporters turning up for the game choose to return home in fear of their lives, amid scenes that would scar the town and the image of football for many years to come.

Tiler resigned as managing director at the end of the season and was sadly killed in a road accident in Italy a few weeks later. Redknapp was travelling in the minibus with him when tragedy struck as the pair returned to their hotel after watching a match in the 1990 World Cup. The manager suffered serious injuries and by the time he was able to return to work the following October he found the club £600,000 in debt and losing around £10,000 a week, with many players remaining on high wages. He spent the next two seasons trying to win back the club's Second Division spot without success before resigning in 1992 in rather acrimonious circumstances, and subsequently became coach at West Ham the following season. Former Cherries player and coach Tony Pulis took over, but with the club's financial position worsening all the time he was forced to offload his best players and the quality of football declined, as the team remained rooted in the bottom half of the table.

Purbeck-based scrap metal dealer Norman Hayward stepped forward to take a controlling interest in the club in 1991 but his exhaustive efforts to keep it afloat eventually took its toll on his health and three years later he announced that he was no longer prepared to continue and put the club up for sale. Despite all of Hayward's efforts the club were now burdened by a £2.1m overdraft and its future was in serious doubt. Financial director Ken Gardner sought support to launch a takeover bid and after a visit to Bournemouth, MacDougall volunteered his assistance, 'I made a brief visit to Dean Court in the April of 1994. I walked in, went through the changing rooms, in the boardroom and down the corridors. I didn't see anyone! It was like a ghost town, almost as if the club had been abandoned. Having been away for a long time, I was shocked to see how depressed the mood had become. There was a messy takeover going on but Bournemouth was still my first love, so I hated the thought of seeing them go down, although the club was obviously in disarray.

'When I got back home, I was asked if I would like to have some input and I said I was prepared to invest in the club if the circumstances were right, and that I knew other people who could also put money in. I was prepared to come back and give total commitment myself, and would have been happy to step in as either general manager or director of football. I had a call from someone on the board at 10am one morning, who said they were having a meeting at 1pm that afternoon and asked if I was still prepared to get involved. I said I was and was told they would get back to me. I waited patiently by the telephone but sadly I never got a call back and that did leave a sour taste at the time.

'So instead, I went to California as unfortunately there was no money for coaching in Canada at the time, but there was money to be earned in Los Angeles where I starting coaching inner-city kids.'

The Cherries survived on this occasion without MacDougall's assistance but it would not be the last time that he would go to the club's aid at a time of financial crisis.

Gardner completed a takeover three months later but the deal drove a wedge between himself and Hayward which would resurface three years down the road. Having already dismissed Pulis before the new season started, Gardner eventually appointed Ted's former Cherries team-mate Mel Machin as his successor. Machin, formerly a manager at Manchester City and Barnsley, somehow went on to preside over one of the greatest escape acts in league history as Bournemouth somehow managed to hang on to their third tier status. They had gained just nine points by Christmas but with new signings such as Matt Holland making significant contributions as the season continued, they managed to scramble clear in their final game among memorable scenes at Dean Court.

With debts continuing to mount and bills unpaid, Gardner resigned as chairman in December 1996 and the following month the club became subject to a court winding-up order. A proposed rescue package which would have seen Norman Hayward return as chairman did not meet with a favourable response from the bank, which promptly put the club into receivership with debts amounting to almost £5m.

With no party willing to provide money to keep the club afloat, an independent trust fund headed by lifelong supporter and local solicitor Trevor Watkins started negotiations with the administrators in an effort to save the club. Fans pledged their financial support, with £33,000 raised in one evening alone at a public meeting in the town's Winter Gardens. Everyone seemed to want to play a part in helping the club survive, whether it was by doing sponsored walks or cycle rides, selling cakes or organising mufti days at work. It was a remarkable show of support which resulted in the winding-up being successfully resisted and adjourned. The Trust was then faced with the task of working out a deal that would be acceptable to all the club's creditors, including Hayward, as well as the Football League, 'I first heard about Bournemouth's plight through a reporter from Inverness who just dropped it into the conversation. I couldn't believe it and was very sad to hear about all the problems. I was running a soccer academy back in Canada with over a hundred children aged between 11 and 14 but when the *Bournemouth Echo* contacted me, I said I would do anything I could to help. As soon as I was asked to come over, I flew across like a shot in an attempt to boost the fund raising activities. Trevor was working so hard to try and pull everything together. I made myself available to help the Trust in any way I could and they looked after things for me. They kept me pretty busy too, I signed a lot of merchandise they had produced and the spirit in the town, the club and the supporters was like Custer's last stand!

'I went to a game against Shrewsbury Town at the beginning of March, where I was a guest in the directors' box and afterwards met up again with Mel and our old team-mates Keith Miller and Fred Davies, who was then manager of Shrewsbury. The game ended goalless and I couldn't help noticing that the Bournemouth players seemed to lack a bit of confidence. Mind you, it had to be difficult for them playing under conditions where they were not sure if they would be paid at the end of the month or if they would even still have a job. They were very hard times for everyone at the club.

'The following week the Trust arranged a friendly game against Southampton and Mel asked me if I would be willing to make a "cameo" appearance during the game. I was a little apprehensive because at 50 years of age, I broke into a sweat just watching the players train! I hadn't brought my boots with me but fortunately I had kept myself relatively fit by coaching the lads at my soccer school, so I told Mel I would love to play providing nobody kicks me, although five minutes would be enough!'

MacDougall received a hero's reception from both sets of supporters in the crowd of almost 9,000 when he came off the bench six minutes before the end of the game, which the Cherries won 2-1. Although he twice had chances to score, Ted failed to make contact with the ball on either occasion, 'I remember it like yesterday. The reception I got was fantastic and I definitely should have notched a goal, but I still picked up the man of the match award! I was caught out on the blind side for the first chance. I remember the run, they didn't get the ball in quick enough, Steve Robinson took an extra touch and I told him about it afterwards. Boy did I give him some shit! I just couldn't reach the other one at the near post but I would have done 20 years earlier! I remember the Saints players afterwards saying, "Ted, we couldn't let you score, that would have been taking the piss!"'

The match grossed almost £60,000 and as MacDougall made his way back home to Canada, the Trust tabled its first bid to buy the club. Although not successful, its efforts proved enough to persuade the authorities to grant it the opportunity to run the club for the remainder of the season, and in doing so, further time to strengthen its position. Meanwhile on the pitch, the team displayed a great strength of character which enabled them to scrape through and finish safely in mid-table. Then finally, despite Hayward making a late rival bid for the club, the Trust successfully reached an agreement to take over on 18 June 1997. The Cherries had pulled off another great escape and Europe's first community football club was born, although it had to wait until just days before the new season started to receive the Football League's official backing, 'I can't speak highly enough about Trevor and everyone involved with the Trust. They did a fantastic job in saving the club on behalf of all the club's supporters.'

Amazingly, the same supporters who had been throwing coins into buckets to keep the club alive found themselves at Wembley Stadium the following April, where Bournemouth faced Second Division rivals Grimsby Town in the Auto Windscreens Shield Final. Although the Mariners triumphed through a 'golden goal' winner in extra time, the Cherries' first, and to date, only appearance at the national stadium was a magnificent reward for all those who had fought so hard to save the club.

26

Pompey Times

IN 1998, at the age of 51, MacDougall was offered the opportunity to make a return to English football by his old friend Alan Ball, 'My coaching had taken me from Los Angeles down to Long Beach and then to the Newport coast, where I got a call from Bally. He'd just got the manager's job at Pompey and he wanted me to be his assistant. I told him I was hesitant to make such a big move back to England, so Bally gave the job to Kevin Bond. Then he called me again and said he would like me to be the club's chief scout. I asked him, "How can I be chief scout when I've been out the country for 14 years?" I didn't know why he needed a chief scout anyway, as the club had no money! But, because it was Bally, I decided to give it a go and came over.'

Ball was now in his second spell as manager of Portsmouth and since he and MacDougall had been in charge at Blackpool, he had enjoyed an extension to his playing career at Southampton before bringing things to a close at Bristol Rovers in 1983/84. Pompey had given him a return to management in 1984 and after two near-misses, he finally guided the club back to the First Division in 1987. However, their stay lasted for just one season and Ball was sacked in January 1989 after a falling-out with chairman Jim Gregory. He then had spells in charge at Stoke and Exeter before taking over at Southampton in January 1994. He led Saints to a tenth-place finish in the Premier League the following year before leaving for Manchester City in July 1995. His departure from The Dell was again somewhat acrimonious, Ball having been tempted away by his former England team-mate Francis Lee, who then held the purse strings at Maine Road. Unfortunately his first season at City ended in the club's relegation to the First Division and Ball resigned early in the following campaign.

Since 1976, Portsmouth Football Club had been beset by a series of off-the-field financial difficulties of one kind or another and by the summer of 1996, responsibility for running the club had passed to Gregory's son Martin. Following the excitement of the European Championships held in England that year, Gregory was delighted when he persuaded outgoing England manager Terry Venables to come to Fratton Park, initially as a consultant, by offering him a three-year option to buy a controlling interest in the club for a nominal sum. It was an option Venables took up the following February, when he purchased a 51 per cent stake in the club for a seemingly knock-down price of just £1. Under manager Terry Fenwick, the team enjoyed a run to the quarter-finals of the FA Cup the following season but narrowly missed out on a play-off spot for promotion to the Premier League. As well as taking on the role of Pompey chairman, during the season Venables had surprisingly also accepted the position of national coach to Australia.

The close season saw bulldozers move into Fratton Park to demolish the remains of the old Fratton End of the ground and begin laying the foundations for a long-awaited new stand, which was to cost £2.5m. Meanwhile, Fenwick spent much of the time in Australia casting his eye over his chairman and mentors' World Cup qualification campaign. When he returned for the new season he had spent over £400,000 in bringing several relatively unknown Australian players to the club, together with striker John Alosi, a regular in Venables's side, who joined Pompey in a £300,000 deal from the Italian club Cremonese. Aloisi would replace the previous season's leading goalscorer, the popular 22-year-old Isle of Wight-born striker Lee Bradbury, who was sold to Manchester City for £3m.

Unfortunately, with the notable exception of Aloisi, the new imports failed to make any impact and the £1m sale of 20-year-old striker Deon Burton angered supporters, who had become disenchanted with both Fenwick and Venables's commitment towards the club. Venables's role with Australia meant he was absent from Portsmouth on a regular basis and there were question marks over a number of his business dealings.

After a bright start, Fenwick came under increasing pressure following an 11-match winless run which left the side near the bottom of the league table. Gates dropped alarmingly, with less than 9,000 people turning up upon the opening of the new Fratton End for the match against Swindon at the end of October, which Pompey lost 1-0. Worse still, just 7,072 watched the 2-0 win over Stoke at the beginning of December, by which time the club's debts were seriously mounting. Staff wages went unpaid until Gregory stepped in to arrange funds to cover them and things came to a head in early January 1998, following a 3-0 home defeat to Manchester City in a crucial relegation battle. Cries went out from supporters for both Fenwick and Venables to leave the club and the following Monday, with Pompey bottom of the second tier and apparently losing £150,000 a month, Fenwick was dismissed while Venables agreed a six-figure sum to sell his shareholding back to Gregory.

Ball was contacted by Terry Brady, a Portsmouth director, and with Gregory's authority, he offered him the opportunity of a return to Fratton Park. Ball, however, was reluctant to work again for Martin Gregory because of the way he had been treated previously by his father Jim, but it was the intervention of Brian Howe which persuaded him to take up the challenge. Howe, the former lead singer with the group Bad Company and a staunch Pompey supporter, informed Ball that he was to make a takeover bid for the club and wanted the former manager to take charge once again. Unfortunately though, Howe was unable to complete a deal with Gregory and the takeover failed to come about, although Ball eventually decided to take the manager's job anyway.

He took charge again the following month, and shortly afterwards appointed Kevin Bond as his assistant, but with the club edging closer and closer towards a near-fatal financial crisis, Ball quickly recognised how big a part the Fratton Park crowd could play if his team were to succeed. He set about convincing them that the seemingly inevitable relegation could be avoided and the amazing backing given to his side became part of the club's folklore. They started the home match against Stockport County seven points adrift of safety and in a game they simply had to win, took the lead in the 15th minute with a goal from Steve Claridge, a former Pompey apprentice, who had returned to the club on loan from Leicester. As the game wore on County put the team under relentless pressure, but as the chant of 'Alan Ball's blue and white army' resounded around all four sides of the ground, the home side managed to keep the opposition out, 'Like it did at Bournemouth, the financial problems brought everyone together and the supporters did an enormous amount of fundraising to try and keep the club afloat. Bally had a great affinity with the fans, they loved him and instantly got right behind the team.

'He sent me all over the place watching the following week's opponents because there was no point me looking at anyone to buy. We wanted to sign Claridge permanently but Bally had to let him go back to Leicester before the end of the season because Pompey couldn't afford to pay his wages. We did manage to sign him the following season though.'

Four wins followed from the next five games but were followed by a dreadful run of eight without a victory, which included a 2-1 defeat at relegation rivals Stoke with the Potters scoring the winning goal in the last minute. It eventually came down to the last two games of the season and to have any hope of avoiding relegation, Pompey needed to win both and hope their rivals would drop points. In the lead-up to the first fixture, Gregory announced that Ball had signed a four-year contract and a few days later Portsmouth's fate was back in their own hands following a 3-0 win over Huddersfield and favourable results elsewhere. The Blue Army of 3,600 supporters headed north to Bradford City for the last game, where two goals from former Liverpool utility man John Durnin and another from youth team graduate Sammy Igoe sealed a memorable 3-1 victory, to complete a miraculous escape that saw two of Ball's former sides, Stoke and Manchester City, relegated.

Portsmouth's centenary season of 1998/99 saw the financial crisis deepen and it seemed the 100th year of the club's existence might also be its last. With money so tight, Ball was forced to try and move on the most expensive earners and to trim his playing squad down to around 17 players. Two of the five Australians brought in by Venables, Aloisi and the national team captain Craig Foster, were on long contracts that the club could not afford and eventually both left the club. Aloisi, having scored 17 goals in all competitions for Pompey during the season, was valued in excess of £3m by many experts, but joined Premier League Coventry for just £690,000 in December, while Foster was allowed to leave on a free transfer.

The sale of Aloisi worsened relations between Ball and Gregory, the manager claiming that the seemingly cut-price deal was done behind his back. Soon afterwards, Gregory decided to quit, thus releasing his 97 per cent ownership of the club, which was officially placed in administration. After making a bright start to the season, the team slipped down the table and hovered perilously close to the relegation places, but despite the poor run of results, Ball never lost the supporters' backing at any stage. Under his tutelage, the players managed to maintain a strong team spirit throughout and gave their all to ensure that Pompey finished 19th, thus guaranteeing their safety for another season.

The man who supporters held responsible though was Venables, who had left the club in such a perilous state the previous year, 'It was a question of trying to keep the club going in the hope that a new owner could be found. All the backroom staff took pay cuts – it was either that or lose our jobs. We went on sponsored walks and all sorts and at one point a group of supporters went round the town carrying a coffin. It had "Portsmouth F.C. R.I.P." written on it and people would throw money in.

'After Martin Allen was sacked in February 1999, I became reserve team coach, which I loved. It wasn't so much about coaching but more about psychology and it taught me a lot. You had this mixture of first-team pros pissed off because they were out of the side and young kids wanting to break through. It was great! To deal with the different mindsets was fantastic experience. I needed to get them to play for me and to do that I had to jolly them along sometimes. It wasn't always a question of coaching, I just tried to help them.

'Steve Claridge was into his early thirties and he asked me one day how I knew when I was coming to the end of my career. He asked me if my legs went or whether I had suffered a lot of injuries, and I told him it was none of those things. It was when I didn't want to get on the team bus. I didn't want to drive up to Liverpool or Carlisle or anywhere else. I had had enough, and I think that surprised him.'

In May 1999, Serbian-American businessman Milan Mandaric became Portsmouth's new owner and took the club out of administration. Mandaric had been introduced to the club by David Deacon, a former Pompey director and son of former chairman John Deacon, together with the former Arsenal and England full-back Bob McNab, who had been coaching in America where Mandaric owned a club in San Jose. The deal was duly completed and after a favourable first meeting with the new owner, Ball set about what he believed to be a three-year plan to return the club to order, during which time he would build a new side and restart the club's youth policy.

Rather than spend millions of pounds of Mandaric's money unnecessarily, Ball looked to bring in young, talented players, just as he had tried to do while in charge at Blackpool almost 20 years earlier. But the problem was that Mandaric was used to spending big money and as the season unfolded, Ball's softly, softly approach gradually appealed less and less to the new owner. After an encouraging start Pompey suffered a 6-0 defeat at Barnsley at the end of August which heralded a run of only one victory in nine matches before they beat Walsall at home in late October. The win coincided with the £300,000 return to Fratton Park of Bradbury, who had endured a lean time at Maine Road. Ball brought him back to the south coast to strengthen Pompey's attack and he marked his return with a goal in a comprehensive 5-1 win.

Despite the success against Walsall and another home win against Crystal Palace, a run of nine consecutive defeats made Mandaric increasingly restless until he finally lost patience. Ball's contract was terminated in December, with the club just four places off the bottom of the table. His departure came six months after the club had been rescued from financial oblivion and such was Ball's disillusionment, he never returned to football management.

Pompey were not progressing quickly enough for Mandaric's liking and the writing had perhaps been on the wall as early as August, when young defender Jason Crowe arrived from Arsenal. The £180,000 deal had nothing to do with the manager and when the player reported for training, it became clear that he had been signed on the recommendation of Bob McNab after he had spent a week coaching the Gunners youngsters at Highbury, 'Bob McNab spent most of his time talking about Arsenal's double team of 1970/71! He was certainly Mandaric's man, but he was poor.'

Ball's efforts to rebuild his side had also been disrupted by a number of injuries, central defenders Jason Cundy and club captain Adrian Whitbread each missing a number of games, while 23-year-old goalkeeper Aaron Flahavan suffered blackouts on the pitch and young striker Rory Allen sustained a badly broken ankle. In addition, Claridge had missed the first two months of the season recovering from an operation.

Bond, MacDougall and Ball's son Jimmy, who had been assisting with the youth team, soon followed the manager out of the door.

McNab took caretaker charge of the team for one game, before the club went through a succession of managers in just a matter of months, with Tony Pulis, Steve Claridge and Graham Rix all taking charge before the chairman settled on Harry Redknapp, 'Mandaric came in and all seemed well to start with but he turned out to be a piece of work. He did bring money to the club but Bally, by doing what he thought was right, actually got it all wrong in the end.

'For example he signed Jason Cundy on a free transfer from Ipswich. Cundy was a good professional but he wasn't what Mandaric wanted. Mandaric was prepared to spend money to get instant success and Alan was out of touch in this respect. After all the financial restraints he had been under, Bally thought he was doing a good thing by not spending. If he'd have spent £5m and got promoted that wouldn't have bothered Mandaric.

'Bally and I had some rows towards the end though, he just wouldn't listen to what myself and the rest of his staff were trying to tell him and he lost the dressing room. We all went out one night to try and talk it through, I broke the ice and told him he's got to get something out of the players so he can't treat them like crap. That may have been the way in the past but not now with players earning several thousand pounds a week.

'The next game Bally spoke to the team in the dressing room just before they went out and said, "I've been speaking with people who care about me and they've told me things, and I want to apologise and say thank you to you for being my side." And the lads went out and played their socks off for him but sadly after that it slipped back again. Because Alan was such a great player, a World Cup winner at 21, and so many things were simple for him, he had little time for players who couldn't put in the effort or pass the ball or do what he wanted them to. And then he related this to the money they were on at the time and that became an issue.

'It all ended though when Bally got fired on the Friday, Kevin Bond got fired on the Saturday, and afterwards he phoned me and said, "I think it's coming." And sure enough I had a meeting with the managing director David Deacon on the Monday.

'I think the reserves were lying second in their league at the time and David said how pleased he was with the job I had been doing, but they were going to fire me anyway. Good job I hadn't done crap then! He explained it was a case of a new broom sweeping clean and I thought fair enough, that's football. I had two years' great experience at Pompey, it was fantastic.

'My career had taken me to three south coast clubs but Portsmouth was different to Bournemouth and Southampton. I found the people very hard-working, down-to-earth types – a little insular perhaps. There was an element of "everybody is against us" about them, a bit like people from Newcastle or Scotland and they put the barricades up. They were fantastic supporters though, and deserved much more than they have got over the years.

'So I bought an apartment in Bournemouth, overlooking the sea, and did it all up like I was back into the building business again. I stayed for a year after I left Portsmouth but I couldn't live in England anymore so I sold up and went back to California.

'Bally and his wife Lesley were dear friends. We had fallen out a bit towards the end at Portsmouth, but one evening a few years later I went to a pub just round the corner from where he lived in Warsash just to see if he was there. Sure enough he came in, gave me a hug, put his arm round me and asked if I would come back with him to see Lesley. Unfortunately this was just before Lesley died of ovarian cancer in 2004, so I went back with him and we sat on his patio having steak and wine. It was wonderful to have had the opportunity to see Lesley, who was a dear friend but sadly she was like a little old lady. She had always been vibrant and full of life. We sat chatting, it was like something from the film *Beaches*. Alan was cooking, and it was a lovely sunny evening. Lesley passed away three months or so later but I was so pleased we shared that evening together.

'Bally was a wonderful character, also larger than life. When he was manager at Exeter he was on £50,000 a year and he was spending £65,000 a year maintaining his lifestyle! Then he went to Manchester City on about £250,000 a year but he was the same guy, always charismatic with people. He would spot the old guy in the corner of the room with the flat cap. "All right, Alan?" the guy would enquire, "Ee how are you, you all right lad, get that lad a drink" – that was Alan. He was a quality person, a great guy.

'Then in 2007 I got a call one morning from Jimmy to tell me Alan had passed away suddenly. Jimmy said Alan had looked great just before he died but I said, "Jimmy, did he have checks?" This is one thing that annoys me among English people – the reluctance to undertake health checks. Alan had been watching an England game, then something happened at the bottom of his yard, the fence caught fire and he didn't have a hose so he went running to and fro with buckets of water. The firemen found him in his garden. He was only 61. I wanted to fly back to attend his funeral but Jimmy said Alan would not have expected me to do that and I think in the end there was a lot going on and the family were upset about different stuff. It was so sad – I loved him dearly.

'Unfortunately, there is another very sad postscript to my time at Portsmouth, and that was the tragic death of Aaron Flahavan. He died in a car accident on his way to see a group of young Californian footballers who had arranged to meet him in a club in Bournemouth. It was a group that I had brought over to play a series of games and when I took them to watch Pompey train the previous day, they had all fallen for Flav's good looks and undoubted charm. I received a call from the club early on the morning after the accident and then had to tell the girls what had happened. The funeral was packed with all sorts of players, family and friends and at the end of the service they played The Police's track "Every Breath You Take" and everyone completely lost it.'

27

The American Dream

TED returned briefly to England early in 2001 to help launch an appeal for community facilities in Bournemouth's proposed new stadium. During a meeting at the Bournemouth International Centre, the Ken Dando Stadium Appeal, named in memory of one of the club's late directors, launched a t-shirt and framed photo of MacDougall's goal at Villa Park in 1972. For the next week Ted once again found himself the focus of attention at Dean Court, 'It was only a short visit but I spent hours signing these prints and t-shirts, I couldn't believe how popular they were considering the event they marked had taken place some 30 years previously!'

Later that year Ted returned to watch the Cherries' last game at the old ground, then the following day he acted as auctioneer while the stadium was dismantled and the club sold any object they could to raise some further much-needed funds, 'People were buying their individual seats and cushions from the stand, the dugouts went too and all sorts of signs. I was flogging everything from turnstiles to toilet seats out of the dressing rooms. I cranked up the price by reminding the punters how many famous backsides had sat on them! Some guys were also paying to dig up pieces of turf. It was all a bit surreal really. I couldn't help thinking about all the good times I had been part of on that pitch.

'I enjoyed being back in Bournemouth for a while but I still had no wish to remain there permanently. I just loved the lifestyle in the States. After I left Portsmouth I went to Los Angeles, then on to

Tampa to take my [UEFA] B Licence coaching course. While I was down there a chap told me he could get me a job in Atlanta. I didn't even know where Atlanta was but when I found out, I went there and stayed for ten years.'

MacDougall's first appointment in Atlanta was as assistant director of coaching for boys at the Tucker Youth Soccer Association. Here he worked alongside the former Tottenham and Manchester City player Neil McNab, 'Neil mainly looked after the girls' section of the club while I coached the boys and while there I went on to get my A Licence. I was still a regular visitor to the UK though, because I came over to arrange trials with English clubs for some of our best young players. I regularly called in at Bournemouth and we had an extended stay in August 2006, when Neil and I brought under-13 and under-14 boys' teams over to play matches in England, including a game against the Cherries' youngsters.'

In 2007, Ted became director of youth coaching at the Atlanta Silverbacks, where he coached under-12, under-14 and under-16 boys' teams, but during his time at the North American Soccer League club, the one lingering injury from his playing career worsened considerably and he was eventually forced to undergo surgery, 'I'd had a dodgy back which had deteriorated over the years. I didn't miss many games as a player but my back was always an issue. However, by now I was in a bad way and had to have an operation. It cost me $86,000 for eight days in hospital. Afterwards I was in a wheelchair and then I had to learn to walk again. The surgeon was a genius, he did a great job and I've no problems now. I do a lot of stretching in the morning and every day I wake up enthusiastic, you know, like I've got things to do!'

In 2009, 40 years after he first signed for the Cherries, MacDougall was voted as Bournemouth's all-time fans' favourite player in an online poll conducted on behalf of *The Times*. He headed a 50-man list which also included the club's long-serving striker Steve Fletcher, who was runner-up, and former strike partner Phil Boyer who came third, 'I thought it was a great honour and I was very, very flattered at the time. I certainly wasn't the club's best-ever player but I did a specific job and the one things that fans always relate to is goals and goalscorers.'

The same year, back in Atlanta, MacDougall launched his own football club. Together with the former Nottingham Forest player Paul Smith, he helped to create Atlanta Spurs, and was installed as the club's president, 'I had never been a president before so it was wonderful.

We ran the club as a business, but there was no board of directors or volunteers telling me what to do, just as well with my personality!'

One of the club's youth teams, the under-14 boys, won the State Cup during Ted's time in charge, in addition to making the last eight of the regional finals, 'They were probably the best side I ever had as a coach. At its peak, the club had around 200 select players and 300 recreational players. We had an academy for ages eight to 12, before they reached full youth status at 13. Our aim was to give them individual attention and bring them along to whatever level they could achieve.

'My philosophy when working with young kids, has always been to try to find out what it is they have got and how it can be used to the advantage of the team. I believe that's the same with all the top sportsmen. Everybody at their level has talent and ability but it is those who have the mental ability to take in and disseminate the information they are given, that win the prize money. The majority of kids and professionals are no different, you tell them something and they say they understand it but unfortunately the majority actually don't.'

MacDougall brought groups of the club's youngsters over to the UK in both 2010 and 2011 before his next move to Florida in 2012, where he spent a year at the Jacksonville Soccer Club. Shortly after he had made a further visit to Bournemouth later that summer, came the sad news that former manager John Bond had passed away at the age of 79. Bond had left Norwich in 1980 to succeed Malcom Allison as manager of Manchester City, taking with him his assistants John Benson and John Sainty, while his long-time right-hand man Ken Brown was appointed as his successor at Norwich. By the end of his first season at Maine Road, John had taken Manchester City to Wembley for an FA Cup Final against Tottenham, and ironically, City's cup run had included a 6-0 victory over Norwich at Maine Road in the fourth round, after which the City manager was the first to commiserate with his son Kevin, who had been playing for the Canaries.

The following season Bond oversaw a tenth-place finish in the First Division but he fell out with City chairman Peter Swales over the purchase of England international forward Trevor Francis. He threatened to walk out if the deal failed to go through but though Francis arrived, his appearances were restricted due to a succession of injuries and the friction between Bond and Swales returned, eventually leading to his resignation in 1983. John later had short spells in charge at Burnley, Swansea, Birmingham and Shrewsbury, then in September 1999, nearing his 67th birthday, he was brought out of retirement by his good friend John Benson, who was then manager of Wigan and wanted Bond to assist with coaching and scouting at the club.

However, John left after less than a year following Benson's move to the role of director of football, 'John was fantastic with me, I was very sad when I heard he had passed away. I last saw him in 2008 at Norwich, when I attended their "Greatest Ever" event, where I was honoured to be inducted to their Hall of Fame. It was a joy to see him along with Ken Brown, Martin Peters and Kevin Keelan. I have been blessed to have known John and his family because they changed my life, although John didn't know what he was dealing with when he first met me. I didn't know either, as I was always on the edge.

'Bondy could never disguise his feelings, he wore his heart on his sleeve, so you always knew whether or not he was happy. He liked to be flamboyant at times, a bit like Malcolm Allison, and could be very outspoken. The press loved him for it of course and he put clubs like Bournemouth and Norwich on the map. He was desperate for success and that's what was behind his move to Manchester City.

'So much of my success was down to John. Each day he taught me something new in training, he captured all the players' imagination and made us think about the game. But not only did I learn from him as a player, I also learnt from him as a person. God bless him.'

MacDougall was invited to return to his old club once again the following July, this time to open their stadium's new South Stand. Known as the Ted MacDougall Stand in recognition of Ted's service at the club, it was duly opened prior to the Cherries' prestige friendly against Real Madrid, 'While I was cutting the ribbon, I couldn't help thinking about the penniless days the club had been through in the past. Now here I was opening a stand bearing my own name, it was a great honour but I'm sure one day it will be renamed the Eddie Howe Stand!'

In 2013 Ted's career took a slightly different direction when, at the age of 66, he was recruited by the biggest computer software company involved in youth soccer administration in the United States. As the company's chief executive, his latest and current challenge is to help it break in to the British market, 'I met the owner, Gavin Owen-Thomas a few years earlier on a USA Soccer License course, we became friends and stayed in touch. Then, when I made the move to Florida, I was given the opportunity to get involved with the company. GotSoccer is used in 27 states in America and administers for around half of the four million kids registered to play youth soccer and is used for something like 1,700 of the 2,000 tournaments held each season. It's used for the Disney tournaments and most of the biggest showcase tournaments played throughout the states.

'The system calculates all the official rankings throughout America, and in doing so determines the level of playing ability needed to enter tournaments from the under-11 to under-18 age groups. The rankings mean you are competing at the right level and then when the players reach college age, the rankings can be seen by all the colleges in America. This is what all the parents are enthusiastic about, as a good ranking carries some weight when the lads are looking to get a scholarship.

'There are a lot of English people coaching kids in the States, the money is good, and it's run very professionally which is the reason it's taking off. GotSoccer looks after all the player registrations, team fixture scheduling, referee appointments, in fact anything you can think of involved in running a league, club or a team within a club.

'What I have been doing for the last couple of years is to try and help to establish GotSoccer in England, where it's known as GotFootball. I make frequent visits to the UK to try and arrange introductory discussions with leagues, then follow up with a return visit with a technician to demonstrate the system's capabilities. When a new league comes on board we do the training for the clubs and the league before they start to use our system.

'I believe the potential of the product is enormous. It has revolutionised the way grassroots clubs and competitions can be run but it is sometimes difficult to convince administrators to break away from systems that have been in use for many years. Nonetheless, GotFootball continues to expand all over the country and we now have some 50,000 players registered. In addition, we have met with Martin Glenn, the new head of the Football Association, and with their IT staff to hopefully take the system to the next level.'

28

Reflections Past and Present

'HOW'S this for starters – if blood had run its course, I would have been a goalkeeper!

'Seriously, I've learned one thing above all else in my travels – there's more to life, much more, than just money, big clubs and glamour. Happiness is far more important than those qualities. You've got to be happy in what you're doing and where you're doing it – and if you're not, it's the worst thing in the world.

'Throughout my career there was only one major issue – that was me, I was a big issue. I was not a great person to be around. Certain people react in certain ways and I would have called myself a reactionary. Nowadays when I go back and see people the first thing I have to do is apologise to everyone for being such an arsehole! When I went back to Norwich a few years ago, Duncan Forbes said to me in his inimitable way, "You were always a bit of a complex character!" That about summed me up! Thankfully you change as you get older and I think I have become a lot better person over the years.

'I could be a difficult guy to play with because I only had one thing in my mind – to score goals. I only really came to life when I got in front of goal. I was happy to be left out of the build-up play as much as possible, provided the ball eventually came in my direction inside the penalty area.

'I was selfish, very much into myself because I wanted to be so great. A team is made up of different types of people but why are you there? Some people are happy to be there, just happy to be in the team, some are playing out a contract – I wanted to be the best goalscorer in the country. I didn't want to know about midfield and that sort of thing. We're all in the same team but are our goals the same? Is what we are trying to achieve the same? I don't think so.

'I was so strong in my opinions, I was just there to score goals and I didn't care how I did it because each goal counted the same as long as I scored. I always said to managers, "Look I'll miss chances because I'm there to miss them. If I am missing chances they are being created and eventually I'll get one. In one game I might get four or five goals – in another I might not get anything."

'Shortly before I left Bournemouth in 1972, the commentator Brian Moore interviewed me after a game at Brentford and I told him that I wasn't bothered about playing well, and that it didn't interest me how well I might have played if I didn't score. That was pretty much my mantra and I don't hear any player say that now. Maybe they're not allowed to as they have to be involved in other aspects of play nowadays.

'My job was not about building things, it was about getting on the end of them. I was always contentious, really prickly, very hard to handle and very single-minded. I didn't really care about anyone else, it was all about me scoring.

'On Facebook a couple of years ago, a writer and Norwich City supporter, Edward Couzens-Lake, posted an article which really summed up my career. He mentioned all the doubters who never believed I could make it in the top division, then added that I was "a loose cannon, a maverick, an opinionated and argumentative individual who had to get his own way and be number one at his club". Pretty strong stuff, not the usual sort of comment I'd expect to hear from a Norwich type of person.

'He went on to say that John Bond's faith and tolerance paid off in the end and that I "made the game look easy and played like we all did, just wanting to score goals and became a classic goal hanger". I further endeared myself to the writer, a young schoolboy at the time, during a lull in a game at Carrow Road. I was stood "hands on hips, near the opposing team's penalty area" which infuriated his father who yelled out, "Come on MacDougall, put some bloody effort in!" Apparently, my reaction was to glance over and "simply and with feeling" tell him to "fuck off"!'

* * * * *

'When I was at Norwich, I thought the world of the chairman, Sir Arthur South, who was a big teddy bear of a man. After he was knighted, I started calling him Sir Arthur and he loved that! Once, when I had been offered a new contract and the club were desperate to keep me, Sir Arthur and his wife took my wife and I out to dinner. They arrived in his chauffeur-driven Rolls-Royce and duly wined and dined us and I always remember one piece of advice he gave me during the evening, "Always put your money in to land." Funnily enough, that resonated and stayed with me and as the years went by it remained one thing I believed in.'

* * * * *

'Every day we trained under John Bond it was about finishing and movement. His philosophy to the other players was, "We've got the best striker in the country so you better get him in!" My job was to create space, the defender's job was to deny space, but our end product was me. I had such a desire for knowledge because I knew I scored goals but I wanted to know why. John began to teach me about movement, angles and stuff, and creating space for yourself in a small area. Movement creates space – today top players will make one run, but if the ball doesn't come to them they won't do it again.

'I learned how to make a run towards the ball. I was good in the air, I could hang there but I couldn't do it from a standing jump, I had to move in and attack the ball. That way I would drag my marker away, then go back and use the space I had created and the power I could generate on the ball.

'To be a good striker I think you have to be born with a talent and desire for scoring goals. It's purely instinctive. You must be single-minded and have the kind of nasty streak that makes you want to be the best, to go into areas others fear to tread. Naturally you must have the basics required to play football but, for me, the right attitude and approach is half the battle. Average strikers could improve if they were given advice by qualified people.

285

'While at Bournemouth it was once said to me that the goals are the same size, no matter which division you are playing in. In fact I found the higher you went, the easier it was. The chances come at any level, whether you're a Premier League player today or a Fourth Division player when I was around. Yes, you got fewer chances at the top level, but there's a bit more time because people respect your ability. There wasn't as much cut and thrust and I didn't get hacked down so much in the First Division. But when the ball is loose in the goalmouth I stood an equal chance of scoring – and that's how I got a lot of my goals.

'I used to look in the mirror, look at my hair and think, "What am I good at? What am I not good at? So what am I going to do? Am I going to work at what I'm not good at or am I going to eliminate it?" I decided to eliminate it and let Phil Boyer do it – running, showing, linking, pushing down the wings. My game was primarily running away from the ball until the cross came in. Now I thought if that's all I do, I'd better do it well!

'I've been told on a number of occasions that my celebrations after scoring a goal were a bit lame by today's standards. My answer to that is quite simple, I was a goalscorer and I was simply doing my job, there was nothing special about it. Why should I have to celebrate something I should be doing anyway? We would train all week to achieve this and it was simply the culmination of everything we had worked for and planned.'

* * * * *

'Me and "Charlie" Boyer? It was just like being married – I bossed him around and he just accepted it! I went on to love him to death though and we roomed together all over the world. He wasn't just a willing workhorse, he was a marvellous player who created so many chances in the box. Although he was a couple of inches shorter than me he had great upper body strength and that gave him the ability to hold the ball up. I needed him more than he needed me, I was brave in the box, but not outside it whereas Phil was brave everywhere.

'He wasn't just my goal provider, he had a lot of skill and a good footballing brain, plus he knew where the goal was and could have played successfully alongside plenty of other forwards. He didn't have exceptional pace but he was sharp enough and he could move the ball about quickly and accurately. He was tireless – he had to be to do all my running as well!

'People used to say we had telepathic awareness, I'm not sure what it was but I always found it easy to work with "Charlie" and we just hit it off together. There was never any friction between us. I may have gained more plaudits but that was just the press, people in the game knew what each of us could do.'

The importance of the Boyer and MacDougall strike pairing was very evident in promotion seasons for Bournemouth and Norwich respectively, where the pair were responsible for over 65 per cent of the total number of league goals scored at each club, while in Southampton's successful Second Division campaign in 1977/78 their share was almost 45 per cent. Saints' success was remarkable also in that it was the only instance where Boyer outscored MacDougall, by scoring 17 goals to Ted's 14. When playing together for their various clubs, Ted and Phil scored an aggregate total of 195 goals.

Boyer's careered spanned 510 league matches in which he scored 157 goals, quite apart from his numerous appearances and goals in various cup competitions. He won two England under-23 international caps and became the first Norwich City player to win a full England cap in 1976 when he made his only senior appearance. Despite becoming unsettled at Norwich after MacDougall's departure, Boyer decided to stay with the Canaries but he picked up an injury which kept him out for almost half the 1976/77 season. His best campaign at Carrow Road was 1974/75 when he finished with 21 goals in 54 league and cup games and he went on to make 137 appearances for Norwich, scoring 40 times before Lawrie McMenemy reunited him with Ted at Southampton.

Apart from his England cap, the highlight of Boyer's career came when he was the First Division's leading goalscorer in 1979/80. Ever-present in the Saints side throughout the league season, his final tally of 23 goals included three hat-tricks. He remained at Southampton until the autumn of 1980, scoring 61 goals in all from a total of 162 league and cup appearances, and latterly forged a new striking partnership with Mick Channon.

The arrival of Kevin Keegan at The Dell the following season persuaded McMenemy to allow Boyer to link up again with John Bond upon the latter's appointment as manager of Manchester City. Bond paid Southampton £220,000 for Boyer's services but unfortunately injury restricted his career at Maine Road to just 20 league appearances and three goals. He spent a period in Hong Kong on loan to Bulova in 1982 and then joined Northern Premier League Grantham Town in September 1983, before brief stays at Stamford and Shepshed Charterhouse. He returned to Grantham as assistant manager during the 1985/86 season but by this time the club had been relegated to the Midland Division of the Southern League. His last goal for the Gingerbreads came in April 1987 in a defeat at Bridgnorth Town and his final appearance for the club came against Banbury United in the final fixture of that season.

Boyer appeared to enjoy the coaching side of his responsibilities at Grantham, and later briefly undertook a management role at Midlands Regional Alliance club Harrowby United before becoming a bank courier. He remained in touch with the game by acting as a scout for a number of clubs, but never one to seek the limelight during his career, Boyer remained the same once his playing days were over, preferring to remain very much out of the spotlight while living at home in Nottingham with his wife Sonia. Despite being inducted in the Norwich City Hall of Fame he has through his own choice maintained only minimal contact with his former playing colleagues.

Ted recalls, 'I love him dearly to this day and there is a true story about Charlie. After we had known each other quite a few years, he said to me one day, "You know Ted, I really can't but admire you with all the travelling you've done around the world and all the things you've seen." So I said, "Well why don't you do that?" He replied, "Well, I can't." So I asked him, "What do you mean you can't?" He said, "Well I've got a budgie." I thought he was taking the piss, so I said, "You've got a budgie?" and he says, "Yes, and I can't leave him." Anyway a few months later he comes to me and says, "The budgie's died." So I said, "You're all right now then, you can go and travel wherever you want to." He says, "No, I can't," so I asked, "Why's that?" And he said, "I've bought another budgie." You can't make this stuff up!'

* * * * *

'A couple of years ago, I met up with Ian Storey-Moore. I hadn't seen him for years and he told me he had been chief scout at Nottingham Forest. His wife remembered making me dinner when I first signed for Manchester United! Ian's a lovely, lovely guy. Brian Clough was bluffing when he said Ian had agreed to sign for Derby just before he joined United. It put Ian in a difficult situation that was not of his own doing. He scored an awful lot of goals as a winger and was always dangerous when he cut in to his right side. Unfortunately his career was finished by injury because he didn't receive the treatment he needed.

'Was I a Manchester United player? Probably not, because I relied too much on other people. But they were not worried about me, they were all vying to be "The Man" and I think Manchester United is still a bit like that. I believe this is where [Javier] Hernandez had a problem a couple of seasons ago, I didn't play like him and he doesn't play like me although we were both similar in the box. He made a lot of runs but didn't receive the ball at the right times.'

* * * * *

'I think I only missed about ten games in my entire career through injuries. The only time I got hurt was when a tackle came from behind and I didn't see it. I went over the top on occasions, when it was about me and the other player I protected myself, I had to. In those days most defenders went around with cauliflower ears and broken noses and they would threaten to break your legs, it was all about intimidation. But I think you got more respect from them if they knew you could handle yourself. I was good in the air, I was brave. I've had split eyes, tons and tons of stitches over my eyes but I was brave because I wanted to score goals. It was the only thing I could do, if I was scoring goals I knew I would remain in the side, if I wasn't then I should have been out.

'I had a dodgy back which deteriorated over the years, but I was lucky as I didn't miss many games. When I retired there was only one league ground I had never played on and that was Swindon Town's County Ground. I think players pick up more injuries today because they are more finely tuned, they're like racehorses. We weren't like that in my day, we were more like dray horses!

'My pre-match stretching exercise with Alan Ball at Southampton consisted of having a "slipper" bath – that's two of us in a single bath of hot water. The lads would go and get us a bar of chocolate each and we would eat that while in the bath, then we would get out, do a couple of stretches just before five to three and run out! All the way through my career, right up to Southampton, we'd always have a case of beer in the dressing room after the game and when you came off you went and had your beer!

'I think most clubs were the same, mind you at some of them you could have filled the bath with champagne and the players would have drunk it all! We had big Kevin Keelan in goal at Norwich and he used to have a big tot of whisky before he went out for a game. I once asked him if it did him any good, he told me he didn't know, but he liked it. At Manchester United there would be Denis Law and Bobby Charlton smoking while they put their kit on.'

* * * * *

'Alan Ball was just 21 when England won the World Cup in 1966 and I believe he was the best player on the park by a mile. He was probably the best captain I played under as well, because he was pretty special. Mind you, Bobby Moore was fabulous too, a great character. Bally used to say that Mooro was so neat he used to iron his money beside the bed!

'I was lucky to have the opportunity to play with some great players like Eusebio, Mackay, Moore, Ball, Osgood, Best, Law. Dennis Law was my hero. He was great to me at United, always happy to go and have a cup of tea – he drank a lot of tea! I played and met so many great characters and most responded well to me. On the other hand, players who were a bit "iffy" didn't respond so well. Someone like say Trevor Brooking, he must have got splinters in his backside because he spent so long sitting on the fence. We used to call him "The Arbitrator"! I didn't like that kind of character because they didn't have the conviction of their own beliefs and would wait to hear what someone else had to say to see if they were on common ground before speaking. I was the opposite and needless to say I wasn't one of Trevor's favourites. Then there was Bobby Charlton – he could send a glass eye to sleep!

'Mick Channon was a very good player and another great character. I went up to see him at his stables when he was working with the former Newcastle, Portsmouth and Coventry player, Micky Quinn. Then, in the early 1990s Lyne and I came over to England and one day Lyne saw that Mick had a horse running at Wincanton. I don't normally go horse racing, but we were in Bournemouth so she suggested we went along. When we got there, I saw this guy bending over this horse – I wasn't sure who had the biggest arse, him or the horse! I knew it wasn't Mick because he was still as thin as a rake, but in the typical Channon way,

Mick didn't say hello, he just told me to get hold of the horse's head and help put this fucking bridle on him!

'So I was looking around this horse's head and I said, "Hello Mick, nice to see you," and he told me to say this was my horse. "It's an apprentice race," he said. "And we'll all be owners." I hadn't seen him for almost 20 years!

'In the parade ring, this little jockey came in, about three feet tall, and he says, "Hello Mr and Mrs MacDougall," touching his forelock in the usual style before Channon gives him his team talk. "It's a good little horse and if you whip the little fucker, I'll whip you afterwards and if you don't finish in the top three don't bother fucking coming back!" Well the guy's gone ashen and I just pissed myself laughing. He finished third at 20/1 and my wife, not knowing anything about place money, thought I had asked her to put money on him to win, but I had asked her to put money on him to finish in the first three, so we never won anything!'

* * * * *

'I still follow the fortunes of my former clubs and have been puzzled by a number of the players that have arrived at Anfield over the last few years in big-money transfers. The sad thing is I'm not sure some of them ever wanted to play for the great Liverpool Football Club. Money and agents are what turns many a player's head these days. There are too many outside influences involved in a player's decision-making progress. I was lucky enough to play with or against most of the England World Cup-winning squad of 1966 and I believe they were successful because their attitude was, "Fuck you, I'm going for it." I don't believe that attitude exists in a lot of players at the top level today. The "Boys of '66" all had it and it's what made them stand out.

'I think Brendan Rodgers did well at Swansea but lost it a bit at Liverpool and began to pontificate about the club's ability to develop players, as if no other club could match them. He even believed he could handle Mario Balotelli, but that didn't work! Jurgen Klopp looks to be a loose cannon at times, but I really prefer his style. He's more pragmatic and when things haven't gone so well, rather than blame injuries or something else, he just accepts things and gets on with it.

'Looking in from afar, I never quite saw the long-term picture that Louis van Gaal was working towards at Manchester United. His style of play seemed to be either a slow, predictable build-up or if that failed, put Fellaini on and go over the top. Ashley Young had a brilliant season for United in 2014/15 yet the following season he barely gets a game? Darmian and Rashford are both very promising but I think it was the progress made by Martial that kept van Gaal at Old Trafford until the end of his second season. He said originally, that it would take the players three months to understand his system but just before he left he was telling everyone it would take three years! How long was his contract? Oh, three years, that's handy!

'I went back to York a year or so ago and the chief executive handed me this huge book detailing the history of the club. It was about four inches thick so I thanked him but told him I would never get it on the aeroplane! Since then, they have lost their place in the Football League but they have always had that sort of existence, only re-election saved them in my time. My former team-mates Chris Topping and Barry Jackson are still around apparently and inside the dressing room nothing had changed. It might have been painted but that's about all!

'Apparently a little old guy turned up at the ground the previous week, he was a former player who suffered from dementia and he was allowed to sit in the dressing room. While he was there he spotted what used to be his peg and pointed out that the picture on the wall had been there when he played. Then he asked a member of staff to look at the peg, because he remembered there used to be a loose screw just below it. So they looked and the screw was there and it was still loose! That screw had been loose for 70 years – that's one of the characteristics of football!

'I think Norwich have become a "boomerang" club, going back and forth between the Championship and the Premier League. I think their relegation this time showed you have to have a certain amount of depth in your squad to survive at the highest level. Fighting relegation is physically demanding and it drains you. When you concede a goal, it's difficult to pick yourselves up. While someone with the experience of Sam Allardyce can perhaps deal with that, Norwich manager Alex Neil was at the opposite end of the scale and it was asking an awful lot of him.

'I was at Portsmouth in 2014 when Andy Awford was in charge and I found the place depressing, the ground in particular. I thought Mandaric was going to build a new stadium when he was there? There's still a lot of work to be done before the club can be successful again, the supporters deserve better but most just seem grateful that the club is still in existence. On the other hand, Bournemouth's rise to the Premier League has been absolutely fantastic. Although I live 4,000 miles away, I love the club even more now than when I played for them. Only seven years before, they were very close to dropping out of the Football League, but their achievements since then have been absolutely stunning. The arrival of owner Maxim Demin provided Eddie Howe with the financial backing he needed to move the club up to a different level.

'Eddie and his assistant Jason Tindall have done an unbelievable job, they interact so well together and I believe the experience they had briefly at Burnley was important for them. I've watched them in training over recent seasons and I took some of what I saw back to Atlanta and did the same with my kids. Their passing and movement drills are great and they all lead up to a finish. In America you're always looking for something new and I learnt a lot of stuff from them.

'It will be fascinating to see what a second season in the Premier League will hold for them. Eddie needs to strengthen their squad, that's for sure, but he knows that. Football moves on and as much as a manager might want to remain loyal to those players who have brought him success in the past, there comes a time when everyone has to move on, and I think Eddie has a bit of that to sort out now. There are players there that are not able to give him anything more and if he can bring in three or four new signings – without going through the roof with transfer fees – players who are a little bit better, stronger and younger, then I think that is the way forward. He doesn't need any superstars or anyone who is going to rock the boat, and I'm sure he won't allow that to happen. Eddie needs players who are ready to learn and enjoy the environment that they are coming in to.

'Steve Fletcher is a wonderful character to still have around the club, I love him to death, I think he's fantastic. His persona, his character is larger than life. He's like a big kid and to have that from an ex-player who is 100 per cent on your side, it's priceless.

'Another important element in Bournemouth's success has been the quality of their pitch. It has to be good to enable them to play their passing game. The improvement in pitches is one of the biggest changes in the game today, they enable players to play better, control the ball better. The players' nutrition has improved alongside the training methods with cooling and warming down, fitness and stretching –

these factors have all advanced 100 per cent from when I played. Apart from that, the Football League hasn't changed that much but at the top level it's certainly entered a different hemisphere.

'The money has changed the game, I've got no problem with that and no problem with the players earning what they can, although I believe it's changed their strength and impetus. Nowadays players are under such great pressure to succeed and if they are involved in the Premier League and the Champions League they are travelling about so much and playing two high-profile games a week. We used to come off the park and go and sign autographs for the kids – players rarely do that now, instead they go straight to the dressing room or straight to their cars or coach. They can't converse with people. Money changed it and not all for the better.

'My time at Norwich was mostly successful and it occurred to me that when you are doing well, you never have to chase money. Magazine articles, billboard advertising and television appearances all come calling, and I watch a lot of football today and assess how different young talents handle the limelight. The difference between Harry Kane and Memphis Depay for example could not be starker. One appears to be able to get on with the "circus" while the other becomes the "circus". The basic situation hasn't changed much from my day, although the monetary rewards certainly have.

'I tell you what though, we often played two games a week as well but we didn't get much money so where the hell did it all go? You had 50–60,000 people at Old Trafford for a game – where did all that money go? It makes you wonder! [Earning] £160–£200 a week was good money to us, now you've got players on £250,000 a week. It makes me wonder just how much I would be worth as a player now. When I joined Manchester United, they paid the equivalent of £1.8m today. But that would not buy a similar player to me today, you would be looking at more like ten times as much!

* * * * *

'I don't think the Premier League is as good today as it has been in the past, because I think the players are not as good as they were. There is nobody anywhere near the class of Henry, Bergkamp, Vieira or Vialli. Instead you are seeing mush lesser players coming in from all over the world, some of whom most people haven't even heard of! Mind you, if clubs can get a good lad who is not a mercenary then they have a chance. I'm sure some clubs sign players these days just because they have the money and to stop their rivals from getting them.

'What amuses me is that there always seems to be a certain type of player that most teams promoted to the Premier League will be in for. The manager will say he signed him because he is experienced at that level – yes he's experienced, he's played for a team that has been relegated from the Premier League in each of the last four seasons!

'Quality British players have been increasingly sought-after as, until recently, there have not been many of them despite clubs spending millions on academies. Where do all these players go then? A couple of seasons ago, Chelsea had over 40 players out on loan and they make money on many of them with clubs covering their wages and paying a loan fee. Most of the bigger clubs make money this way, it's not just a matter of bringing on the players.

'When Roy Hodgson went to watch a Premier League game, at times he'd be lucky to find three English players on the pitch. But I believe it will soon go full circle because I think England has the best group of young lads coming through anywhere in the world at the moment, and the nucleus of a squad that could do something really special. The only position I see a weakness is in the centre of defence. It can all be screwed up if they don't receive the opportunity to play at the top level of course, if the manager doesn't pick them or if the press elevate them too quickly.

'But I honestly believe England will win a major tournament very soon and I think there will be a significant increase in the number of young British players involved at the top level of the game all over Europe.'

* * * * *

'I don't believe there is very much coaching at all done at the top level today. The players get coached on how they are required to play "the system" but individually they get very little. At that level, the individual coaching will have occurred when they were much younger. How many players have you seen playing well week after week in the local park, and you wonder why they never made it? Unfortunately you will never become a professional footballer on ability alone, you must have the right attitude to go with it.

'For example, all the golfers on the PGA Tour are undoubtedly good golfers but why do the same three or four keep winning? Because they have the "je ne sais quoi" factor, or, "Fuck you, I'm going for it." The more intellectually sound you are, the better the player you will become. Let's face it, you're going to be playing with a load of dozy bastards who can be coached till the cows come home, but they cannot absorb anything! The brighter player wants to think about his game, understand it and know what he's good at.

'I've got a better love and understanding for football now than I believe I've ever had. I love watching games and I love the things I see in them as a coach. I don't coach from a book, I coach what I see with my own eyes. The new formations, the movement of players, little things I see changing – when you see this you can coach it but you have to know what you are looking for. The difference for me between a good player and a bad player are the decisions he makes on the pitch.

'If he makes the right decisions enough, then I would deem he was a good player. It's not the first thing he does with the ball, it's the last – the end product. How many wingers do you see make a great run then put in a poor cross? The crowd may think it's good and cheer and wow, but let's see the end product then – ooh, it's not there!

'When I played there was always plenty of aggression in the game which often led to an intimidation factor, but this seems to have gone out of the game today. I would struggle to name five or six top central defenders of Gordon McQueen's type because the art of defending has changed and you can no longer intimidate players in the same way, you can't just go through people when you tackle. When I played, most defenders had broken noses and cauliflower ears and would growl at you, "Go past me and I'll break your legs." But now they have got to be able to play as well so the game has changed for the better.

'I was going to say I feel sorry for defenders but I don't really! It's just a different game today. Players have got to be so careful because their opponents are jumping and diving everywhere and the referees are seeing things that maybe aren't there. Some of the tackles made by Vinny Jones in the late 1980s were criminal, but things often go in cycles and maybe eventually things will turn this way again, although I think it's probably gone too far the other way to change back now. I have to say that nowadays, I think it's very difficult to be a defender.

'In my day, we used to get told by the club secretary about new rules and then we would go out on the training ground and work out how we could get around them! It wasn't cheating, it was being professional and you had to do things to the best of your advantage. I'm sure the players do just the same today. Mind you, if they were allowed to, referees could stop all this tugging and pulling in the penalty area at corner kicks with a memo on the Monday to all clubs and again in the dressing room before the game. They just need to make it clear that any of that stuff will result in a penalty, free kick, red card, yellow card whatever, and it would stop there and then. If it happened on the halfway line it would be a free kick so what's the difference? All this tugging and pulling is like wrestling, but the change can't come from the players, the clubs or the referees, it's got to come from FIFA.

'I see things in the game today that are different from my time but I don't always understand why they are happening. I was with Harry Redknapp, Kevin Bond and Joe Jordan in the Spurs dressing room a couple of years ago and I asked a question. I wasn't trying to be "Billy Big Balls" or anything, but I couldn't work out why, when teams concede a free kick 30 yards or so from goal, defenders hold the line on the edge of the penalty area? Years ago you would do this on the six-yard box and run out. I think the goalkeeper's life is made far more difficult when he has a dozen or so players running towards him chasing after a ball played in at the correct angle and speed. If you get the ball over the first man, the defenders are all running back so all they can do is head the ball out for a corner. If you ask me as a forward whether I would prefer to be running towards the goal or away from it – well I don't need to answer that!

'The answer I got to my question was, "We don't know, everybody does it." It's crazy, they're now moving further forward and are often on the edge of the D. The chances of the goalkeeper being able to come out to the edge of the 18-yard line and collect the ball in are nil. Then if the keeper parries it, the forward is running in for the rebound. I watched a game between Liverpool and Manchester United where Liverpool employed zonal marking and from a corner the three big defenders are stationed in the middle of the penalty area, leaving Raheem Sterling to mark Marouane Fellaini! That can't be right?'

* * * * *

'Football has always been about players, but nowadays everybody gets wrapped up about "stats". To me the most important statistics are who scores goals and how many goals a goalkeeper may concede. As for an "assist", well when I played if somebody got one of those, he went to the doctor and got it squeezed!

'Managers are called "coaches" more and more often now, well, with respect, in these days of two games a week with lots of travelling, when are they doing this coaching? I'm telling you a lot of it is bullshit. You watch a coach on the touchline when he is about to bring a player on, he's telling the lad this and that and showing him diagrams, and the player is nodding his head. Do they think the player is really listening? I believe it's the power of showing people you are specialised and good at what you are doing.

'When John Bond used to shout at me from the touchline, I used to stand on the other side of the pitch and gesture that I couldn't hear him. This is and always has been a players' game not a coaches' game. When you play, you play and you express yourself. As a coach your job is to perform in training and to make me as a player, as aware as you can of situations I might face in the game. How good I am as a player will be determined by what decisions I make on the pitch. Do I dribble or do I shoot, do I stop or do I pass? If I make the right decisions then I have had a good game. As a player, you are only as good as your decisions on the pitch and you are only as good as the last thing you do with the ball. As a coach you coach me to make the right decisions.

'For example, Sterling does a trick, then he does a dribble but what happens with his final touch of the ball – too often it's nothing. I've watched him running down the left wing and the defenders are pushing him on to his left foot. Why, because the kid is 21 years old, he clearly thinks he's arrived but I guarantee he is not working on his left foot. That is where the coach should be helping him. He is awful with his left foot. So Manchester City paid £49m for a player with one foot – how much for one with two feet then?

'I believe the concept of the coach has come from the American culture seen in the NFL. The better ones are those that can communicate with players at the correct level, get them organised to play in the way they want, making sure they understand the part they have to play within the group. Jose Mourinho operates in this way, you can always tell one of his teams because of the way they play and the way he sets them up to play. However, if somebody doesn't perform their role then everything falls down. It's about repetition, is that a part of coaching? Yes I believe so and it centres around a good team discipline.

'You only see the true value of managers and coaches when they are losing matches, you don't see it when they win because it's easy to be nice. When you are under pressure, you look back and probably wish you had done things differently. Your true character comes out when you are in a tight spot, and it can be a lonely profession. Everybody wants to be your friend when you are doing well – I'm sure Claudio Ranieri didn't have an enemy in the world at the end of last season!'

* * * * *

'That brings me nicely on to Leicester. Their success in winning the Premier League in 2015/16 was phenomenal but I can't honestly see something like that happening again. Looking through their team, a number of them are journeymen – both Danny Drinkwater and Danny Simpson didn't make it at Manchester United and had both been on loan to a number of different clubs, Robert Huth seemed past his best five or six years ago, and Wes Morgan had spent ten years at Nottingham Forest. Okasaki and Mahrez have been fantastic, and Vardy has worked really hard to get where he is and is now getting the rewards.

'The great thing is, Ranieri was able to work with them throughout each week because they have not had the commitment of playing in Europe. They were also fortunate with injuries and therefore able to use the same 13 or 14 players each week.

'Some people said they would crack under pressure, but when you're winning each week and the supporters are behind you, you can't wait to get back into training and for the next game. That's not pressure – Leicester experienced pressure when they were fighting relegation the previous season. It will be interesting to see if the team stays together and how they fare in Europe in 2016/17.'

* * * * *

'I still love working with kids whenever I get the opportunity, although my current involvement with GotSoccer means I don't have as much time to get involved in coaching at the moment. Kids are so honest and you're developing a personality not just a player. You're working on their self-esteem and their confidence, to enable them to walk into a crowded room and say "hi" rather than, "No, I can't go in there."

'But I'm very happy with the life I've been blessed with – my career, my health and the opportunities I've had to make money and be successful. I work out most days. I don't do a lot of jogging because of my back but I feel I've been given a second chance. I've changed my philosophy and outlook on life too. I no longer have to get fit, just maintain the fitness I have already got. I've never been on a diet in my life and I'm only five or six pounds heavier than when I was a player. I've never had a weight problem in all my life. Now my back is sorted I feel blessed that I have something to wake up for each morning.

'Sadly, my Mum and Dad have long since passed on but my wife and my ex-wife are fortunately on friendly terms. Mind you, I don't know who or what they talk about! Lyne has given up the ladies' fashions and is now an accomplished artist, although she's not painted me yet! She prefers me to be out of the house to give her peace to paint. My daughter Alison lives in Poole, Dorset, and I have two fantastic, lovely grandsons, Harry and Jackson, while Lyne's boy David became an accomplished ski racer and now lives in Asheville, North Carolina.

'I'm fit and healthy and I love what I do. I love every day and am thankful for each day. I don't feel like an OAP yet, though people sometimes ask me when I'm going to retire, but I tell them you only retire from work. I'm doing something I love doing so why should I stop doing it? These are exciting times.

'Could I make an impact as a player in the game today? Yes, I think I could, well in my head anyway!'

Appendix

Career Statistics

A record of matches played and goals scored by Ted MacDougall in international, European, Football League, FA Cup and Football League Cup competitions.

*indicates an appearance as a used substitute

YORK CITY
1967/68
21st in the Fourth Division – re-elected

Aug 19	Workington (A) D 1-1 (1 Goal)
Aug 26	Rochdale (A) L 2-3
Sep 2	Brentford (H) L 0-1
Sep 5	Newport (A) L 1-2
Sep 9	Bradford PA (A) D1-1
Sep 16	Doncaster (H) L 1-2
Sep 23	Luton (A) L 1-3 (1 Goal)
Sep 25	Newport (H) L 0-1
Sep 30	Southend (H) D 2-2
Oct 3	Swansea (A) D 1-1 (1 Goal)
Oct 7	Halifax (A) L 1-2
Oct 14	Bradford City (H) L 0-1
Oct 21	Crewe (A) D 0-0
Oct 23	Swansea (H) W 2-1
Oct 28	Notts Co. (H) W 4-2
Nov 4	Port Vale (A) L 0-1
Nov 11	Chester (H) W 4-1 (1 Goal)
Nov 14	Brentford (A) L 1-3 (1 Goal)
Nov 18	Chesterfield (A) L 1-3
Nov 25	Exeter (H) W 4-0 (1 Goal)
Dec 2	Darlington (A) L 1-3
Dec 23	Rochdale (H) W 4-1 (2 Goals)

Dec 26   Barnsley (H) D 1-1 (1 Goal)
Dec 30   Barnsley (A) L 0-1
Jan 19   Doncaster (A) L 0-2
Feb 24   Chesterfield (H) L 0-2
Mar 2   Bradford City (A) D 0-0
Mar 9   Lincoln (H) W 1-0
Mar 16   Crewe (H) D 1-1
Mar 23   Notts Co. (A) D 1-1
Mar 25   Bradford PA (H) W 6-2 (2 Goals)
Mar 30   Port Vale (H) W 5-1 (3 Goals)
Apr 6   Chester (A) D 1-1
Apr 13   Halifax (H) L 1-2
Apr 15   Hartlepool (H) L 0-2
Apr 27   Darlington (H) D 1-1
May 4   Aldershot (A) D 2-2 (1 Goal)
May 11   Wrexham (A) L 1-3

FA Cup
Dec 9   (first round) Doncaster (H) L 0-1

Football League Cup
Aug 23   (first round) Darlington (A) L 0-1

Total appearances in all competitions 40; goals scored 15

YORK CITY
1968/69
21st in the Fourth Division – re-elected

Aug 10   Chester (A) L 0-2
Aug 17   Doncaster (H) D 1-1
Aug 24   Chesterfield (A) D 1-1
Aug 26   Bradford City (H) D 1-1
Aug 31   Peterborough (H) W 2-1
Sep 7   Colchester (A) L 0-1
Sep 14   Scunthorpe (H) W 2-1 (1 Goal)
Sep 16   Port Vale (A) L 0-3
Sep 21   Brentford (A) L 1-5
Sep 28   Rochdale (H) D 0-0
Oct 5   Bradford PA (H) W 4-2 (2 Goals)
Oct 9   Bradford City (A) L 0-5
Oct 12   Lincoln (A) L 0-3
Oct 19   Southend (H) D 1-1
Oct 26   Newport (A) L 0-1
Oct 28   Exeter (H) L 0-2
Nov 4   Aldershot (H) W 2-1
Nov 9   Grimsby (A) L 0-3
Nov 23   Notts Co. (A) D 0-0
Nov 30   Darlington (H) D 1-1
Dec 14   Lincoln (H) D 1-1
Dec 20   Southend (A) W 2-1 (1 Goal)
Dec 28   Newport (H) D 0-0
Jan 11   Halifax (A) W 4-0 (1 Goal)
Jan 18   Grimsby (H) L 2-5 (1 Goal)
Jan 25   Aldershot (A) L 0-2

Feb 24   Wrexham (H) W 1-0
Mar 7   Doncaster (A) L 1-2 (1 Goal)
Mar 10   Workington (H) W 2-1 (1 Goal)
Mar 15   Chesterfield (H) W 3-1 (2 Goals)
Mar 18   Swansea (A) L 1-2
Mar 22   Peterborough (A) L1-2 (1 Goal)
Mar 26   Bradford PA (A) L 0-1
Mar 29   Colchester (H) W 2-0
Apr 4   Port Vale (H) W 3-1
Apr 5   Rochdale (A) L 1-2 (1 Goal)
Apr 9   Exeter (A) L 0-5
Apr 12   Brentford (H) W 2-1 (1 Goal)
Apr 16   Wrexham (A) L 1-2 (1 Goal)
Apr 18   Scunthorpe (A) L 1-2 (1 Goal)
Apr 21   Darlington (A) L 2-3 (1 Goal)
Apr 23   Notts Co. (H) W 2-0 (1 Goal)
Apr 28   Chester (H) W 4-2 (2 Goals)
Apr 30   Workington (A) L 0-2
May 2   Swansea (H) L 0-2
May 5   Halifax (H) D 0-0

FA Cup
Nov 16   (first round) South Shields (A) W 6-0 (2 Goals)
Dec 7   (second round) Morecambe (H) W 2-0 (2 Goals)
Jan 4   (third round) Stoke (A) L 0-2

Football League Cup
Aug 14   (first round) Barnsley (H) L 3-4 (2 Goals)

Total appearances in all competitions 50; goals scored 25

BOURNEMOUTH AND BOSCOMBE ATHLETIC
1969/70
21st in the Third Division – relegated

Aug 9   Barnsley (A) L 0-1
Aug 16   Luton (H) L 0-1
Aug 23   Brighton (A) D 1-1 (1 Goal)
Aug 26   Bury (A) L 0-1
Aug 30   Rotherham (H) W1-0
Sep 6   Tranmere (A) W 5-1 (1 goal)
Sep 13   Torquay (H) L 1-2
Sep 20   Shrewsbury (H) D 3-3 (1 Goal)
Sep 27   Halifax (H) D 0-0
Oct 4   Southport (A) L 0-3
Oct 7   Luton (A) D 0-0
Oct 11   Fulham (H) D 2-2 (1 Goal)
Oct 18   Walsall (A) L 1-2
Oct 25   Bristol Rov. (H) D 2-2 (2 Goals)
Nov 1   L. Orient (A) L 0-3
Nov 8   Stockport (H) W 1-0
Nov 22   Gillingham (H) W 2-1 (1 Goal)
Nov 26   Doncaster (H) W 3-1 (1 Goal)
Nov 29   Plymouth (A) W 1-0

Dec 13   Torquay (A) D 2-2 (1 Goal)
Dec 20   Tranmere (H) D 2-2 (1 Goal)
Dec 26   Brighton (H) D 0-0
Dec 27   Rotherham (A) L 0-3
Jan 10   Reading (H) L 1-2 (1 Goal)
Jan 17   Halifax (A) L 1-4 (1 Goal)
Jan 24   Bradford City (A) L 1-8
Jan 26   Rochdale (A) W 1-0 (1Goal)
Jan 31   Southport (H) W 1-0 (1 Goal)
Feb 6   Fulham (A) D 1-1 (1 Goal)
Feb 14   Barnsley (H) W 3-1 (3 Goals)
Feb 21   Bristol Rov. (A) L 2-5 (1 Goal)
Feb 28   L. Orient (H) L 0-2
Mar 4   Barrow (H) D 0-0
Mar 14   Plymouth (A) L 1-3 (1 Goal)
Mar 16   Mansfield (A) L 0-2
Mar 21   Barrow (A) D 1-1
Mar 27   Walsall (H) D 2-2 (1 Goal)
Mar 28   Bradford City (H) D 0-0
Mar 30   Stockport (A) W 2-0
Apr 4   Bury (H) W 2-0
Apr 7   Doncaster (A) L 1-2
Apr 15   Shrewsbury (A) L 0-2
Apr 18   Mansfield (H) W 1-0
Apr 25   Gillingham (A) D 0-0

FA Cup
Nov 15   (first round) Luton (H) D 1-1
Dec 18   (replay) Luton (A) L 1-3

Football League Cup
Aug 13   (first round) Bristol Rov. (H) W 3-0 (2 Goals)
Sep 3   (second round) Sheffield Wed. (A) D 1-1
Sep 9   (replay) Sheffield Wed. (H) W 1-0
Sep 24   (third round) Leicester (H) L 0-2*

Total appearances in all competitions 50 + 1*; goals scored 23

BOURNEMOUTH AND BOSCOMBE ATHLETIC
1970/71
Second in the Fourth Division – promoted

Aug 15   Aldershot (A) L 0-2
Aug 22   Grimsby (H) W 2-1
Aug 29   Newport (A) W 2-0 (1 Goal)
Aug 31   Peterborough (H) W 1-0 (1 Goal)
Sep 5   Stockport (H) W 2-0 (2 Goals)
Sep 11   Southend (A) W 2-1
Sep 18   Colchester (H) W 4-1 (4 Goals)
Sep 23   Workington (H) W 1-0 (1 Goal)
Sep 26   York (A) D 1-1
Sep 30   Scunthorpe (H) L 0-2
Oct 3   Cambridge (H) W 3-0 (2 Goals)
Oct 10   Brentford (A) W 2-1 (1 Goal)

Oct 17   Aldershot (H) D 1-1 (1 Goal)
Oct 20   Oldham (A) D 2-2 (1 Goal)
Oct 24   Chester (A) L 2-4 (1 Goal)
Oct 31   Lincoln (H) W 3-0 (1 Goal)
Nov 7   Darlington (A) L 0-1
Nov 10   Southport (A) W1-0 (1 Goal)
Nov 14   Hartlepool (H) W 3-0 (1 Goal)
Nov 28   Crewe (H) D 2-2
Dec 5   Notts Co. (A) L 1-2 (1 Goal)
Dec 19   Grimsby (A) L 0-1
Jan 2   Barrow (A) W 2-1 (2 Goals)
Jan 9   Scunthorpe (A) D 1-1
Jan 16   Oldham (H) W 5-0 (1 Goal)
Jan 23   Northampton (H) W 4-2 (2 Goals)
Jan 27   Exeter (H) W 4-1 (2 Goals)
Jan 30   Crewe (A) D 3-3 (2 Goals)
Feb 6   Notts Co. (H) D 1-1
Feb 13   Northampton (A) W 4-2 (2 Goals)
Feb 20   Southport (H) L 0-1
Feb 27   Lincoln (A) W 2-1 (1 Goal)
Mar 6   Chester (H) W 3-1 (1 Goal)
Mar 10   Workington (A) L 0-1
Mar 13   Hartlepool (A) L 1-2
Mar 17   Barrow (H) D 0-0
Mar 20   Darlington (H) W 1-0 (1 Goal)
Mar 26   Stockport (A) D 1-1 (1 Goal)
Apr 3   Newport (H) D 2-2 (2 Goals)
Apr 9   Southend (H) W 4-0 (1 Goal)
Apr 10   Exeter (A) D 0-0
Apr 13   Cambridge (A) W 2-0 (1 Goal)
Apr 17   Brentford (H) W 1-0
Apr 23   Colchester (A) D 1-1 (1 Goal)
Apr 28   Peterborough (A) L 1-3 (1 Goal)
May 1   York (H) W 4-0 (2 Goals)

FA Cup
Nov 21   (first round) Oxford City (A) D 1-1 (1 Goal)
Nov 25   (replay) Oxford City (H) W 8-1 (6 Goals)
Dec 12   (second round) Yeovil (H) L 0-1

Football League Cup
Aug 19   (first round) Torquay (A) D 1-1
Aug 26   (replay) Torquay (H) L 1-2

Total appearances in all competitions 51; goals scored 49

BOURNEMOUTH AND BOSCOMBE ATHLETIC
1971/72
Third in the Third Division

Aug 14   Shrewsbury (H) W 3-1 (1 Goal)
Aug 21   Bolton (A) D 0-0
Aug 28   Rotherham (H) W 3-1 (1 Goal)
Aug 31   Blackburn (H) W 1-0
Sep 4   Halifax (A) L 0-1

Sep 11   Rochdale (H) W 4-1 (3 Goals)
Sep 18   Wrexham (A) W 3-1
Sep 25   Chesterfield (H) W 1-0 (1 Goal)
Sep 29   Notts Co. (A) D 1-1 (1 Goal)
Oct 2   Plymouth (A) D 1-1
Oct 9   Swansea (H) W 2-1
Oct 15   Shrewsbury (A) L 2-3 (2 Goals)
Oct 19   Port Vale (H) W 3-2 (1 Goal)
Oct 23   Aston Villa (H) W 3-0 (1 Goal)
Oct 29   Mansfield (A) W 5-0 (3 Goals)
Nov 6   Torquay (H) W 1-0 (1 Goal)
Nov 13   Bradford City (A) D 2-2 (2 Goals)
Nov 27   Barnsley (A) D 0-0
Dec 4   York (H) D 2-2 (2 Goals)
Dec 18   Halifax (H) W 3-1
Dec 27   Brighton (A) L 0-2
Jan 1   Wrexham (H) W 4-0
Jan 8   Rotherham (A) D 0-0
Jan 22   Notts Co. (H) W 2-0 (1 Goal)
Jan 29   Port Vale (A) D 1-1
Feb 5   Plymouth (H) W 1-0 (1 Goal)
Feb 12   Aston Villa (A) L 1-2 (1 Goal)
Feb 19   Mansfield (H) D 1-1
Feb 23   Walsall (H) D 0-0
Feb 26   Torquay (A) W 2-0 (2 Goals)
Mar 4   Bradford City (H) W 3-0 (1 Goal)
Mar 8   Bristol Rov. (H) W 2-0 (1 Goal)
Mar 11   Swansea (A) W 2-1
Mar 14   Walsall (A) D 1-1 (1 Goal)
Mar 18   Bolton (H) L 1-2 (1 Goal)
Mar 21   Oldham (A) L 1-3
Mar 25   Rochdale (A) D 1-1 (1 Goal)
Apr 1   Brighton (H) D 1-1 (1 Goal)
Apr 5   Chesterfield (A) D 0-0
Apr 7   Tranmere (A) W 2-1 (2 Goals)
Apr 15   Barnsley (H) D 0-0
Apr 18   Bristol Rov. (A) W 2-1
Apr 22   York (A) W 2-0 (1 Goal)
Apr 26   Blackburn (A) L 1-2 (1 Goal)
Apr 29   Oldham (H) W 2-0 (1 Goal)
May 3   Tranmere (H) D 0-0

FA Cup
Nov 20   (first round) Margate (H) W 11-0 (9 Goals)
Dec 11   (second round) Southend (H) W 2-0 (1 Goal)
Jan 15   (third round) Walsall (A) L 0-1

Football League Cup
Aug 17   (first round) Portsmouth (H) W 2-1 (2 Goals)
Sep 8   (second round) Blackpool (H) L 0-2

Total appearances in all competitions 51; goals scored 47

AFC BOURNEMOUTH
1972/73
Seventh in the Third Division

Aug 12   Bolton (A) L 0-3
Aug 19   Chesterfield (H) D 2-2
Aug 26   Watford (A) L 2-3 (2 Goals)
Aug 29   Halifax (H) W 1-0
Sep 2   Scunthorpe (H) D 1-1 (1 Goal)
Sep 9   York (H) D 0-0
Sep 16   Southend (H) W 2-0
Sep 23   Brentford (A) D 1-1 (1 Goal)
Sep 26   Port Vale (H) W 4-0 (1 Goal)

Football League Cup
Aug 15   (first round) Plymouth (A) W 2-0 (2 Goals)
Sep 6   (second round) Blackpool (H) D 0-0
Sep 11   (replay) Blackpool (A) D 1-1 aet
Sep 18   (second replay) Blackpool L 1-2 aet

Total appearances in all competitions 13; goals scored 7

MANCHESTER UNITED
1972/73
18th in the First Division

Oct 7   WBA (A) D 2-2
Oct 14   Birmingham (H) W 1-0 (1 Goal)
Oct 21   Newcastle (A) L 1-2
Oct 28   Tottenham (H) L 1-4
Nov 4   Leicester (A) D 1-1
Nov 11   Liverpool (H) W 2-0 (1 Goal)
Nov 18   Manchester City (A) L 0-3
Nov 25   Southampton (H) W 2-1 (1 Goal)
Dec 2   Norwich (A) W 2-0 (1 Goal)
Dec 9   Stoke (A) L 0-2
Dec 16   Crystal Palace (A) L 0-5
Dec 23   Leeds (H) D 1-1 (1 Goal)
Dec 26   Derby (A) L 1-2
Jan 20   West Ham (H) D 2-2
Jan 24   Everton (H) D 0-0
Jan 27   Coventry (A) D 1-1
Feb 10   Wolves (H) W 2-1
Feb 17   Ipswich (A) L 1-4

Total appearances in all competitions 18; goals scored 5

WEST HAM UNITED
1972/73
6th in the First Division

Mar 10   Sheffield Utd. (A) D 0-0
Mar 17   Manchester City (H) W 2-1 (1 Goal)

Mar 24   Crystal Palace (A) W 3-1 (1 Goal)
Mar 31   Everton (H) W 2-0
Apr 7   Newcastle (A) W 2-1 (2 Goals)
Apr 14   Leeds (H) D 1-1
Apr 20   Southampton (H) W 4-3
Apr 21   Derby (A) D 1-1
Apr 23   Birmingham (A) D 0-0
Apr 28   Arsenal (H) L 1-2

Total appearances in all competitions 10; goals scored 4

WEST HAM UNITED
1973/74
18th in the First Division

Aug 25   Newcastle (H) L 1-2
Aug 27   Ipswich (H) D 3-3
Sep 1   Norwich (A) D 2-2
Sep 8   Tottenham (H) L 0-1
Sep 15   Manchester Utd. (A) L 1-3
Sep 22   Leicester (H) D 1-1
Sep 29   Stoke (A) L 0-2
Oct 6   Burnley (H) L 0-1
Oct 13   Everton (A) L 0-1
Nov 3   Leeds (A) L 1-4 (1 Goal)
Nov 10   Sheffield Utd. (H) D 2-2
Nov 17   Wolves (A) D 0-0
Nov 24   Arsenal (H) L 1-3
Dec 1   Liverpool (A) L 0-1

Football League Cup
Oct 8 (second round) Liverpool (H) D 2-2 (1 Goal)

Total appearances in all competitions 15; goals scored 2

NORWICH CITY
1973/74
23rd in the First Division – relegated

Dec 8   Burnley (A) L 0-1
Dec 15   Liverpool (H) D 1-1
Dec 22   Leeds (A) L 0-1
Dec 26   Ipswich (H) L 1-2 (1 Goal)
Dec 29   Manchester City (H) D 1-1 (1 Goal)
Jan 1   West Ham (A) L 2-4 (2 Goals)
Jan 12   Arsenal (A) L 0-2
Jan 19   Wolves (H) D 1-1 (1 Goal)
Feb 2   Liverpool (A) L 0-1
Feb 5   QPR (A) W 2-1
Feb 9   Sheffield Utd. (H) W 2-1 (1 Goal)
Feb 23   Derby (H) L 2-4
Feb 26   Coventry (A) L 0-1
Mar 2   Ipswich (A) D 1-1
Mar 9   Chelsea (H) D 2-2 (1 Goal)

Mar 16   Tottenham (A) D 0-0
Mar 20   Birmingham (H) W 2-1
Mar 25   Stoke (H) W 4-0 (1 Goal)
Apr 4   Manchester Utd. (H) L 0-2
Apr 13   Everton (A) L 1-4 (1 Goal)
Apr 15   Newcastle (A) D 0-0
Apr 17   Newcastle (H) D 1-1 (1 Goal)
Apr 20   Burnley (H) W 1-0 (1 Goal)
Apr 27   Birmingham (A) L 1-2
Apr 29   Leicester (A) L 0-3

FA Cup
Jan 5 (third round) Arsenal (H) L 0-1

Total appearances in all competitions 26; goals scored 11

NORWICH CITY
1974/75
Third in the Second Division – promoted

Aug 17   Blackpool (H) W 2-1 (1 Goal)
Aug 21   Southampton (H) W 1-0
Aug 24   Aston Villa (A) D 1-1
Aug 27   Southampton (A) D 1-1
Aug 31   Sheffield Wed. (H) D 1-1
Sep 7   Hull (A) D 0-0
Sep 14   Notts Co. (H) W 3-0 (1 Goal)
Sep 21   Fulham (A) L 0-4
Sep 24   Sunderland (A) D 0-0
Sep 28   Manchester Utd. (H) W 2-0 (2 Goals)
Oct 5   Millwall (H) W 2-0 (1 Goal)
Oct 12   Nottm. For. (A) W 3-1
Oct 19   Portsmouth (H) W 2-0
Oct 26   Orient (A) W 3-0 (1 Goal)
Nov 2   WBA (A) D 1-1 (1 Goal)
Nov 9   Bristol Rov. (H) L 0-1
Nov 16   Oldham (A) D 2-2
Nov 23   Bolton (H) W 2-0
Nov 30   York (A) L 0-1
Dec 7   Cardiff (H) D 1-1
Dec 14   Blackpool (A) L 1-2
Dec 21   Bristol City (H) W 3-2
Dec 26   Notts Co. (A) D 1-1 (1 Goal)
Dec 28   Oxford (H) W 1-0
Dec 11   Cardiff (A) L 1-2 (1 Goal)
Jan 18   York (H) L 2-3
Jan 25   Oxford (A) L 1-2 (1 Goal)
Feb 1   Bristol Rov. (A) W 2-0 (1 Goal)
Feb 8   WBA (H) W 3-2 (2 Goals)
Feb 15   Bolton (A) D 0-0
Feb 22   Oldham (H) W 1-0
Mar 8   Sunderland (H) D 0-0
Mar 15   Manchester Utd. (A) D 1-1 (1 Goal)
Mar 22   Hull (H) W 1-0 (1 Goal)

Mar 29   Bristol City (A) W 1-0
Mar 31   Fulham (H) L 1-2
Apr 5   Orient (H) W 2-0 (1 Goal)
Apr 8   Sheffield Wed. (A) W 1-0 (1 Goal)
Apr 12   Millwall (A) D 1-1
Apr 19   Nottm. For. (H) W 3-0
Apr 26   Portsmouth (H) W 3-0
Apr 30   Aston Villa (H) L 1-4

FA Cup
Jan 4   (third round) Coventry (A) L 0-2

Football League Cup
Sep 9   (second round) Bolton (A) D 0-0
Sep 17   (replay) Bolton (H) W 3-1 (1 Goal)
Oct 9   (third round) WBA (A) D 1-1
Oct 16   (replay) WBA (H) W 2-0 aet (1 Goal)
Nov 12   (fourth round) Sheffield Utd. (A) D 2-2 (2 Goals)
Nov 27   (replay) Sheffield Utd. (H) W 2-1
Dec 4   (fifth round) Ipswich (H) D 1-1
Dec 10   (replay) Ipswich (A) W 2-1
Jan 15   (semi-final first leg) Manchester Utd. (A) D 2-2 (1 Goal)
Jan 22   (second leg) Manchester Utd. (H) W 1-0
Mar 1   (final) Aston Villa (Wembley) L 0-1

Total appearances in all competitions 54; goals scored 22

SCOTLAND
1975
Apr 16   Sweden (A) Friendly D 1-1 (1 Goal)
May 13   Portugal (H) Friendly W 1-0
May 17   Wales (A) Home International Champ. D 2-2
May 20   N. Ireland (H) Home International Champ. W 3-0 (1 Goal)
May 24   England (A) Home International Champ. L 1-5
Oct 29   Denmark (H) European Nations Cup W 3-1 (1 Goal)
Dec 17   Romania (H) European Nations Cup D 1-1*

Total appearances 6 + 1*; goals scored 3

NORWICH CITY
1975/76
Tenth in the First Division

Aug 16   Manchester City (A) L 0-3
Aug 20   Leeds (H) D 1-1
Aug 23   Aston Villa (H) W 5-3 (3 Goals)
Aug 26   Arsenal (A) L 1-2
Aug 30   Tottenham (A) D 2-2 (1 Goal)
Sep 6   Everton (H) W 4-2 (3 Goals)
Sep 13   Burnley (A) D 4-4 (2 Goals)
Sep 20   Leicester (H) W 2-0 (2 Goals)
Sep 23   Ipswich (A) L 0-2
Sep 27   Sheffield Utd. (A) W 1-0 (1 Goal)

Oct 4   Stoke (H) L 0-1
Oct 11   Derby (H) D 0-0
Oct 18   Newcastle (A) L 2-5 (1 Goal)
Oct 25   Birmingham (H) W 1-0
Nov 1   Manchester Utd. (A) L 0-1
Nov 8   Middlesbrough (H) L 0-1
Nov 15   Coventry (A) L 0-1
Nov 22   Newcastle (H) L 1-2
Nov 29   Liverpool (A) W 3-1 (1 Goal)
Dec 6   West Ham (H) W 1-0 (1 Goal)
Dec 13   Aston Villa (A) L 2-3 (1 Goal)
Dec 20   Manchester City (H) D 2-2
Dec 26   QPR (A) L 0-2
Dec 27   Wolves (H) D 1-1
Jan 10   Burnley (H) W 3-1
Jan 17   Everton (A) D 1-1
Jan 31   Leeds (A) W 3-0 (2 Goals)
Feb 7   Arsenal (H) W 3-1 (1 Goal)
Feb 21   Coventry (H) L 0-3
Feb 28   Birmingham (A) D 1-1
Mar 6   Tottenham (H) W 3-1 (1 Goal)
Mar 13   Derby (A) L 1-3
Mar 17   Manchester Utd. (H) D 1-1
Mar 20   Liverpool (H) L 0-1
Mar 27   West Ham (A) W 1-0 (1 Goal)
Mar 31   Ipswich (H) W 1-0
Apr 3   Sheffield Utd. (H) L 1-3
Apr 6   Middlesbrough (A) W 1-0
Apr 10   Leicester (A) D 0-0
Apr 17   QPR (H) W 3-2 (1 Goal)
Apr 19   Wolves (A) L 0-1
Apr 24   Stoke (A) W 2-0 (1 Goal)

FA Cup
Jan 3   (third round) Rochdale (H) D 1-1 (1 Goal)
Jan 6   (replay) Rochdale (A) D 0-0 aet
Jan 13   (second replay) Rochdale (H) W 2-1 (1 Goal)
Jan 24   (fourth round) Luton (H) W 2-0
Feb 23   (fifth round) Bradford City (H) L 1-2

Football League Cup
Sep 10   (second round) Manchester City (H) D 1-1 (1 Goal)
Sep 17   (replay) Manchester City (A) D 2-2 (2 Goals)
Sep 29   (second replay) Manchester City (Chelsea) L 1-6

Total appearances in all competitions 50; goals scored 28

NORWICH CITY
1976/77
16th in the First Division

Aug 28   WBA (A) L 0-2
Sep 4   Birmingham (H) W 1-0
Sep 11   Coventry (A) L 0-2

Football League Cup
Aug 31 (second round) Exeter (A) W 3-1 (1 Goal)

Total appearances in all competitions 4; goals scored 1

SOUTHAMPTON
1976/77
9th in the Second Division

Sep 18	Nottm. For. (H) D 1-1
Sep 24	Charlton (A) L 2-6 (1 Goal)
Oct 2	Fulham (H) W 4-1 (2 Goals)
Oct 5	Wolves (A) W 6-2
Oct 16	Hereford (H) W 1-0
Oct 23	Luton (A) W 4-1 (1 Goal)
Oct 30	Chelsea (A) L 1-3 (1 Goal)
Nov 6	Orient (H) D 2-2 (1 Goal)
Nov 10	Cardiff (A) L 0-1
Nov 20	Bolton (H) L 1-3 (1 Goal)
Nov 27	Oldham (A) L 1-2
Dec 4	Notts Co. (H) W 2-1
Dec 7	Chelsea (H) D 1-1 (1 Goal)
Dec 18	Blackpool (A) D 3-3
Dec 27	Plymouth (A) D 1-1 (1 Goal)
Dec 29	Bristol Rov. (H) W 2-1
Jan 15	Millwall (H) L 0-2
Jan 22	Carlisle (A) W 6-0 (1 Goal)
Feb 5	Hull (H) D 2-2 (2 Goals)
Feb 12	Sheffield Utd. (A) D 2-2 (1 Goal)
Feb 19	Burnley (H) W 2-0 (1 Goal)
Mar 5	Charlton (H) W 2-1 (1 Goal)
Mar 22	Nottm. For. (A) L 1-2
Apr 2	Luton (H) W 1-0
Apr 8	Plymouth (H) W 4-1 (2 Goals)
Apr 9	Bristol Rov. (A) W 3-2 (1 Goal)
Apr 11	Cardiff (H) W 3-2 (1 Goal)
Apr 16	Bolton (A) L 0-3
Apr 20	Blackburn (A) L 0-3
Apr 23	Oldham (H) W 4-0 (1 Goal)
Apr 26	Orient (A) W 3-2 (2 Goals)
Apr 30	Notts Co. (A) L 1-3 (1 Goal)
May 3	Wolves (H) 1-0
May 7	Blackburn (H) W 2-0
May 11	Hereford (A) L 0-2
May 14	Blackpool (A) L 0-2

European Cup Winners' Cup
Mar 2 (third round first leg) Anderlecht (A) L 0-2
Mar 16 (third round second leg) Anderlecht (H) W 2-1 (1 Goal)

Anglo-Italian Cup Winners' Cup
Sep 21 Napoli (H) W 1-0
Nov 14 Napoli (A) L 0-4

FA Cup
Jan 8 (third round) Chelsea (H) D 1-1

Jan 12   (replay) Chelsea (A) W 3-0 aet (1 Goal)
Jan 29   (fourth round) Nottm. For. (A) D 3-3
Feb 1   (replay) Nottm. For. (H) W 2-1 (1 Goal)
Feb 26   (fifth round) Manchester Utd. (H) D 2-2
Mar 8   (replay) Manchester Utd. (A) L 1-2

Total appearances in all competitions 46; goals scored 26

SOUTHAMPTON
1977/78
Second in the Second Division – promoted

Aug 20   Brighton (H) D 1-1
Aug 24   Stoke (A) L 0-1
Aug 27   Mansfield (H) W 1-0
Sep 3   Notts Co. (A) W 3-2
Sep 10   Burnley (H) W 3-0
Sep 17   Millwall (A) L 0-3
Sep 24   Hull (H) W 1-0 (1 Goal)
Oct 1   Sheffield Utd. (A) L 2-3 (1 Goal)
Oct 4   Orient (H) W 1-0
Oct 8   Sunderland (H) W 4-2
Oct 15   Crystal Palace (A) W 2-1
Oct 22   Bolton (H) D 2-2
Oct 29   Bristol Rov. (A) D 0-0
Nov 5   Blackburn (A) L 1-2
Nov 26   Fulham (H) W 2-0
Dec 3   Tottenham (A) D 0-0
Dec 10   Luton (H) L 0-1
Dec 17   Blackpool (A) W 1-0 (1 Goal)
Dec 26   Cardiff (H) W 3-1 (1 Goal)
Dec 27   Charlton (A) W 3-1 (1 Goal)
Dec 31   Stoke (H) W 1-0
Jan 2   Brighton (A) D 1-1
Jan 14   Mansfield (A) W 2-1 (1 Goal)
Jan 21   Notts Co. (H) W 3-1
Feb 4   Burnley (A) D 3-3 (1 Goal)
Feb 11   Millwall (H) L 2-3 (1 Goal)
Feb 25   Sheffield Utd. (H) W 2-1 (1 Goal)
Mar 4   Sunderland (A) D 0-0
Mar 11   Crystal Palace (H) W 2-0
Mar 18   Bolton (A) D 0-0
Mar 25   Charlton (H) W 4-1 (1 Goal)
Mar 27   Bristol Rov. (H) W 3-1 (1 Goal)
Mar 29   Cardiff (A) L 0-1
Apr 4   Blackburn (H) W 5-0 (1 Goal)
Apr 7   Fulham (A) D 1-1
Apr 11   Hull (A) W 3-0 (1 Goal)
Apr 15   Oldham (H) D 2-2
Apr 22   Luton (A) W 2-1 (1 Goal)
Apr 25   Orient (A) D 1-1
Apr 29   Tottenham (H) D 0-0

FA Cup
Jan 7   (third round) Grimsby (A) D 0-0

Jan 10   (replay) Grimsby (H) D 0-0 aet
Jan 16   (second replay) Grimsby (Leicester City) W 4-1 (1 Goal)
Jan 28   (fourth round) Bristol Rov. (A) L 0-2

Football League Cup
Aug 30   (second round) Crystal Palace (A) D 0-0
Sep 13   (replay) Crystal Palace (H) W 2-1 aet
Oct 25   (third round) Arsenal (A) L 0-2

Total appearances in all competitions 47; goals scored 15

SOUTHAMPTON
1978/79
14th in the First Division

Aug 19   Norwich (A) L 1-3 (1 Goal)
Aug 22   Bolton (H) D 2-2 (1 Goal)
Aug 26   Middlesbrough (H) W 2-1
Sep 2   Aston Villa (A) D 1-1
Sep 9   Wolves (H) W 3-2 (1 Goal)
Sep 16   Bristol City (A) L 1-3
Sep 30   Ipswich (H) L 1-2 (1 Goal)
Oct 7   Everton (A) D 0-0
Oct 14   QPR (H) D 1-1 (1 Goal)
Oct 21   Arsenal (A) L 0-1

Football League Cup
Aug 19   (second round) Birmingham (A) W 5-2 (2 Goals)
Oct 3   (third round) Derby (H) W 1-0

Total appearances in all competitions 12; goals scored 7

AFC BOURNEMOUTH
1978/79 18th in the Fourth Division

Nov 11   Hartlepool (A) D 0-0
Nov 18   Darlington (H) D 2-2
Dec 9   York (H) L 1-2
Dec 23   Wimbledon (H) L 1-2
Dec 26   Reading (A) L 0-1
Dec 30   Bradford City (A) L 1-2
Jan 13   Crewe (H) L 0-1
Feb 3   Doncaster (H) W 7-1 (2 Goals)
Feb 6   Port Vale (H) W 3-1 (1 Goal)
Feb 10   Portsmouth (A) D 1-1
Feb 21   Northampton (H) D 0-0
Feb 24   Hereford (H) D 1-1
Mar 3   Grimsby (A) L 0-1
Mar 6   Barnsley (A) L 0-1
Mar 10   Halifax (H) W 1-0 (1 Goal)
Mar 13   Huddersfield (A) L 1-2
Mar 17   Torquay (H) W 1-0 (1 Goal)

Mar 20   Aldershot (A) L 0-1
Mar 24   Scunthorpe (H) D 0-0
Mar 31   Wigan (A) L 0-1
Apr 3   Rochdale (A) L 1-2
Apr 10   Wimbledon (A) L 0-4
Apr 14   Reading (H) D 0-0
Apr 16   Northampton (A) L 2-4 (1 Goal)
Apr 21   Bradford City (H) W 1-0 (1 Goal)
Apr 23   Stockport (H) W 3-1 (1 Goal)
Apr 28   York (A) L 1-2
May 1   Newport (A) L 0-2
May 5   Wigan (H) W 2-1

FA Cup
Nov 25   (first round) Hitchin (H) W 2-1
Dec 16   (second round) Wimbledon (A) D 1-1 (1 Goal)
Dec 28   (replay) Wimbledon (H) L 1-2 aet (1 Goal)

Total appearances in all competitions 32; goals scored 10

AFC BOURNEMOUTH
1979/80
11th in the Fourth Division

Aug 25   Newport (H) W 3-2
Sep 1   Scunthorpe (A) L 1-2
Sep 8   Wigan (H) L 1-2
Oct 20   Huddersfield (H) L 1-3*
Oct 23   Hereford (H) D 2-2
Oct 27   Bradford City (A) D 2-2 (1 Goal)
Nov 3   Rochdale (H) W 4-0 (1 Goal)
Nov 7   Hereford (A) L 1-2 (1 Goal)
Nov 10   Lincoln (A) D 1-1
Nov 17   Doncaster (H) D 0-0
Dec 1   Peterborough (H) D 0-0
Dec 7   Crewe (A) D 0-0
Dec 21   Northampton (H) D 2-2 (1 Goal)
Dec 26   Aldershot (A) W 1-0
Dec 29   Darlington (H) W 1-0
Jan 1   Torquay (H) L 1-2 (1 Goal)
Jan 5   Port Vale (A) D 1-1
Jan 26   Newport (A) D 0-0
Feb 2   Stockport (H) W 2-0 (1 Goal)
Feb 6   Wigan (A) L 1-2 (1 Goal)
Feb 9   Halifax (A) L 0-2
Feb 16   Tranmere (H) W 2-1 (1 Goal)
Feb 23   York (H) D 0-0

FA Cup
Nov 24   (first round) Peterborough (A) W 2-1
Dec 15   (second round) Colchester (A) L 0-1

Total appearances in all competitions 24 + 1*; goals scored 8

BLACKPOOL
1979/80
18th in the Third Division

Mar 15   Exeter (H) W 1-0
Mar 18   Carlisle (A) L 0-2
Mar 29   Millwall (H) D 2-2
Apr 4   Barnsley (H) D 1-1
Apr 5   Hull (A) L 1-3
Apr 26   Reading (A) W 1-0
May 3   Chester (H) D 0-0
May 6   Rotherham (A) W 2-0

Total appearances in all competitions 8

BLACKPOOL
1980/81
23rd in the Third Division – Relegated

Aug 23   Huddersfield (A) D 1-1*
Aug 30   Portsmouth (H) L 0-2*
Sep 5   Fulham (A) W 2-1
Sep 13   Hull (H) D 2-2
Sep 16   Sheffield Utd. (A) L 2-4

Football League Cup
Aug 9   (first round first leg) Walsall (A) W 3-2
Sep 3   (second round second leg) Everton (H) D 2-2

Total appearances in all competitions 5 + 2*

CAREER RECORD
Appearances 612 + 5*; Goals Scored 308

Bibliography

Newspapers and Magazines
AFC Bournemouth match programmes and magazines
Back Pass
Blackpool FC match programmes
Bournemouth Daily Echo
Bournemouth Evening Echo
Bournemouth Sports Echo
Bournemouth Times
Charles Buchan's Football Monthly
Daily Express
Daily Mail
Daily Mirror
Exiled
Football League Review
Football Pictorial
Football Supporter
Football Weekly News
Goal
Jimmy Hill's Football Weekly
Manchester United FC match programmes
Marshall Cavendish Book of Football
Match
Mel Machin testimonial brochure
Norwich City FC match programmes
Out Of Court
Portsmouth FC match programmes

Scottish FA international match programmes
Shoot
Soccer Star
Southampton FC match programmes
Striker
The Guardian
The Sun
The Times
West Ham United FC match programmes
York City FC match programmes

Books

AFC Bournemouth – Official History and Championship Souvenir
    Edwards, Leigh and Treleven, John; A.F.C. Bournemouth 1987
All Change At Old Trafford
    O'Farrell, Frank with Welch, Jeff; Jellyfish Print Solutions, 2011
Blackpool – The Complete Record
    Calley, Roy; Derby Books Publishing, 2011
Cherries – First Hundred Years
    Nash, Kevin; Red Post Books, 1999
Football League Yearbook 1972/73
    The Football League Limited, 1972
In That Number
    Holley, Duncan and Chalk, Gary; Hagiology Publishing, 2003
My Manchester United Years
    Charlton, Sir Bobby with Lawton, James; Headline Publishing, 2007
Never Turn The Other Cheek
    Crerand, Paddy; Harper Collins, 2007
Norwich City – the Modern Era
    Hadgraft, Rob; Desert Island Books, 2003
Norwich City – The Seventies
    Couzens-Lake, Edward; Amberley Publishing, 2013
Playing Extra Time
    Ball, Alan with Mossop, James; Sidgwick and Jackson, 2004
Playing For Uncle Sam
    Tossell, David; Mainstream Publishing, 2003

Bibliography

Portsmouth FC 1898–1998
    Jeffes, Peter, Farmery, Colin and Owen, Richard; Bishops
    Printers, 1998
Rothmans Football Yearbooks
    Queen Anne Press, 1970–1981
The Breedon Book Of Football Managers
    Turner, Dennis and White, Alex; Breedon Books, 1993
The Definitive AFC Bournemouth
    Edwards, Leigh and Treleven, John; Soccer Data, 2003
The Diary Of A Season
    McMenemy, Lawrie; Arthur Barker 1979
The Ghost of '66
    Peters, Martin with Hart, Michael; Orion Books, 2006
Tommy Doc
    Tossell, David; Mainstream Publishing, 2013
Tooting Common To The Stretford End
    Stepney, Alex with Saffer, David; Vertical Editions, 2010
West Ham United – The Elite Era
    Helliar, John and Leatherdale, Clive; Desert Island Books, 2005
Where Are They Now
    Pringle, Andy and Fissler, Neil; Two Heads Publishing 1996
Willie On The Wing
    Morgan, Willie with Wadsworth, Simon; Trinity Mirror Sport
    Media, 2013
York City – The Complete Record
    Batters, David; Breedon Books, 2008